New Copies *of* Old Records *from*
HEBRON, CONNECTICUT

1708–1875

ഇരു

Compiled by
Linda MacLachlan

Featuring

Town Death Records, 1796–1860
Not Filmed by Any Library or Indexed by Barbour

~

An 1886 Manuscript by Will J. Warner
Including All the Early Gilead Church Records
and Other Historical Material

~

Births, Marriages and Deaths, 1847–1870:
An Unrecognized Volume of Vital Records
in the Hebron Town Clerk's Office

and

Completing the Barbour Collection for Hebron

HERITAGE BOOKS
2011

HERITAGE BOOKS
AN IMPRINT OF HERITAGE BOOKS, INC.

Books, CDs, and more—Worldwide

For our listing of thousands of titles see our website
at
www.HeritageBooks.com

Published 2011 by
HERITAGE BOOKS, INC.
Publishing Division
100 Railroad Ave. #104
Westminster, Maryland 21157

Copyright © 2011 Linda MacLachlan

Hebron, Conn....Baptisms-marriages-deaths, 1752-1876
Record Group 001, classified manuscripts
State Archives, Connecticut State Library

All rights reserved. No part of this book may be reproduced or transmitted in any form or by any means, electronic or mechanical, including photocopying, recording or by any information storage and retrieval system without written permission from the author, except for the inclusion of brief quotations in a review.

International Standard Book Numbers
Paperbound: 978-0-7884-5339-7
Clothbound: 978-0-7884-8821-4

TABLE OF CONTENTS

INTRODUCTION ix

PART I

A: HEBRON, CONNECTICUT

Note by Connecticut State Library................................. 1

First Settlement of Hebron... 2

Hebron Physicians.. 6

Hebron Captains in the Revolution............................... 7

B: NECROLOGY AND DEATH RECORDS COMPARED

Necrology (largely on even-numbered pages)..................... 9-44

Town Death Records (on odd-numbered pages facing similar entries in the Necrology)..11-45

C: GILEAD CHURCH RECORDS

Baptisms (1752–1831)... 47

Marriages (1752–1876).. 73

Burials (1761–1840).. 85

PART II

INTRODUCTION 99

A: HEBRON VITAL RECORDS: Births (1847–1855)...........107

Hebron Vital Records Marriages (1847–1855)................ 117

Hebron Vital Records Deaths (1847–1855)..................... 125

B: HEBRON MARRIAGE CERTIFICATES (1799–1823)........133

C: ADDITIONS TO BARBOUR'S "BOOK 4"..........................135

PART III

A: COMPLETING THE BARBOUR INDEX: Methodology......137

B: MORE ADDITIONS & CORRECTIONS TO BARBOUR.... 139

INDEX 165

ILLUSTRATIONS

Plate 1: Cover, *Births – Family Records – Book 4 – 1594–1909 – Hebron*: compiler unknown, indexed by Barbour and the Hebron Town Clerk as "Book 4".........................102

Plate 2: Cover of *Births, Marriages and Deaths, Volume Four, 1848-1870.* It includes 1847–1854 Hebron vital records overlooked by the Barbour Index and the Hebron Town Clerk's Vital Statistics Index 103

ACKNOWLEDGEMENTS

It would have been impossible to compile all of the pre-1855 vital records of Hebron, Connecticut without the cooperation and assistance of the Office of the Hebron Town Clerk. On my first visit there, I was given a desk and all the paper I needed to transcribe the records which were not available on microfilm. (Connecticut law, I am told, permits the mechanical replication of old vital records only in the form of expensive certified copies. No public interest is furthered by such restrictions, and genealogists must seek liberalization of this law.)

On my second visit, I found that the Town Clerk's Office wanted an index of its yet unmicrofilmed folio of old death records and we came to an agreement: I would share the transcription I had scribbled on my earlier visit if they would check it against the original and modify my work as necessary to create a single transcription to be used for both my purposes and theirs.

Subsequently, when I was extracting from microfilm, another volume of Hebron records that Barbour missed, I discovered that vital information was concealed on the microfilm because of a "tight binding," The Clerk's Office, in the person of Ann Hughes, very generously agreed to fill in dozens of little blanks on my extraction so that this book would include all of the information in the original record. I hope other researchers will find such outstanding service in other Connecticut towns. Thank you, Ann.

I also must thank Claire Bettag for her advice in presenting the complicated problem of distinguishing two volumes of Hebron records, which Barbour seems to have mistakenly interchanged, one for the other. Thank you, Claire.

Finally I must thank Dorothy Flores for applying her meticulous proof-reading skills to reading, cover-to-cover, a book that was never intended to be read in that way. She patiently went over this boring material again and again so that your search for information would be quick and easy. Thank you, Dorothy. I just wish we could have found the John Warner (b. 1737 in New England, d. 1827 in Maryland) you have been seeking for so long.

Linda MacLachlan
April 15, 2011
ggrandmac@verizon

INTRODUCTION

Do not assume that the Barbour Collection[a] encompasses all early Connecticut vital records. This book illustrates that point by taking one small Connecticut town and finding thousands of its vital statistics that were unreported, incompletely reported, and/or misreported by Barbour.

This book augments the Barbour Collection of Connecticut Town Records for Hebron[b] with transcriptions of two documents; extraction of a third, and analysis of a fourth:

1. **Transcription of unpublished folio.** A 47-page untitled string-bound folio containing death records 1796–1825 and 1853–1860 is generally kept by the Hebron Town Clerk tucked inside a record volume titled *Town Meetings 1791–1826 – Vital Statistics Vol. 3 – Hebron.* Apparently it originally was part of an assortment of early Hebron records, the balance of which was silked and bound as the *First Book of Hebron Town Records.*[c] Its verbatim transcription is a joint endeavor of this compiler and Ann Hughes of the Hebron Town Clerk's Office.[d] This record has never been indexed by the

---

[a] Lucius Barnes Barbour and Lucius A. Barbour, "Barbour Collection of Connecticut Vital Records prior to 1850" (card file, n.d., Connecticut State Library [hereafter "CSL"], Hartford). See also, Family History Library of Salt Lake City (hereinafter "FHL") microfilms (hereafter "films") 2887 through 2966 and 2984).

[b] Lucius Barnes Barbour and Lucius A. Barbour, "Barbour Collection of Connecticut Vital Records prior to 1850," volume 54: Hebron (bound transcript, 1922, CSL, Hartford); FHL film 2972. See also, Dorothy Wear, *The Barbour Collection of Connecticut Town Vital Records: Hartland 1761–1848, Harwinton 1737–1854, Hebron 1708–1854,* vol. 18, (Baltimore: Genealogical Publishing Company [hereafter GPC], 1999); image reprint online at *Ancestry.com.*

[c] Both this volume and the immediately preceding title, may be viewed only in the vault of the Hebron Town Clerk's Office. Neither volume is on microfilm at the Family History Library, presumably because vital records are not bound in either of them.

[d] The Hebron Town Clerk's Office also possesses an photocopy of this

Hebron Town Clerk nor has it been microfilmed or photographed by any known library.

2. **Transcription of manuscript.** A 133-page manuscript completed by Will J. Warner in 1886, and entitled *Baptisms – Marriages – Deaths, 1752–1875* by the Connecticut State Library, is transcribed almost verbatim.[e] The original manuscript and a typed index of the names it contains are in the Connecticut State Archives and accessible through the Connecticut State Library (hereafter "CSL").

3. **Extract.** All vital records in the Town Clerk's Volume Four of Births, Marriages, and Deaths, 1847–54, are extracted in Part II of this work.[f] To them have been added a few other records from two additional volumes in the Town Clerk's Office that Barbour missed. This expands Barbour's collection for Hebron through 1854, as he intended.[g]

Note: This extract is *not* a duplicate of the indexed "Book 4" in Barbour's collection of Hebron Town records.[h] Nor is it a

---

folio which is hand-titled "Deaths 1796–1860." The Connecticut State Library possesses an untitled photocopy of these legal-sized pages, which remains uncataloged. This vital record was first reported by Harlan R. Jessup in "Some Additions and Corrections to Connecticut's Barbour Collection," *Connecticut Ancestry*, 48:47-8 (Aug 2005).

[e] Punctuation is modernized as necessary for readability. See pages iii-iv below.

[f] Hebron Registrar of Vital Statistics, Records of Births, Marriages, Deaths in the Town of Hebron, 1848-1871 (FHL film 1376166, Item 2).

[g] See detailed discussion introducing Part II.

[h] Barbour's "Book 4" is a seventeen-page manuscript (author or compiler unknown) in a slim bound volume, the cover of which is titled *Births – Family Records – Book 4 – 1594–1909 – Hebron*. The original book is in the vault of the Hebron Town Clerk's Office. A photocopy at the Connecticut State Library remains uncataloged there. It is unavailable on microfilm. Many of the family records it contains are not entered in the Hebron Vital Records, perhaps because it is unclear which of the births it reports actually occurred in Hebron. The earliest vital statistic

replica of "The Fourth Book of Births" included in the Hebron Town Clerk's Vital Statistics Index[i] (that "Fourth Book" is actually the same as Barbour's "Book 4", but this extract expands on that material).

4. **Analysis.** The Vital Statistics Index[j] analyzed in Part III of this book makes additions and corrections to Barbour's Collection of Hebron Town Records.

PART I

The Warner manuscript is here presented in three parts:

1. The introductory sections[k] of Warner's manuscript and its final unnumbered page are transcribed as **Section A** of Part I of this book.

2. In **Section B** of Part I, the 1796–1860 Hebron Death Records appear alongside corresponding entries in 1782–1856 Warner's Necrology because the pairs of entries frequently supplement (and occasionally differ from) each other.

3. Warner's careful transcription of the Gilead Church Records is extracted in **Section C** of Part I.[l]

---

it includes is the birth of Robert Carver (said to be the immigrant founder of Hebron's Carver families) in England in 1594.

[i] Hebron Town Clerk, Index to Hebron Births, Marriages, Deaths, 1684–1849 (original in Hebron Town Hall) FHL film 1376165, Item 3. The FHL catalog notes that the "Index also gives references to a vol. 4 of births, and marriages by Justices of the Peace, which are not found in this library." Linda MacLachlan solved the question about Hebron's missing Justices of the Peace marriages in her article, "Marriages by Elihu Marvin, J.P., of Hebron, Connecticut, 1785–1812," *New England Historic Genealogical Register*, 161:175–80 (Jul 2007). Part II of this book resolves the FHL's question about "a vol. 4 of births."

[j] See note i above.

[k] The precise significance of the pedigree and the family grouping reproduced on original pages two and three are unknown.

[l] The Gilead Church Records are also available at the Connecticut State Library and on microfilm through the Family History Library: Gilead

This transcription of Warner is as true to the original as possible except in the following respects:

Periods replace Warner's em dashes to end sentences wherever the sentence structure is clear enough to do so. SMALL CAPITALIZATION is used to highlight family names for the reader's convenience. Headings are in **bold** face. Original page numbers are to the right margin in *italics*. Quotation marks, which Warner over-employs with dates and under superscripts, are eliminated. All ditto marks are translated into [bracketed] text. Additional punctuation is added [in brackets] only as necessary for clarity.

Because Warner never employs Old Style or double dating, his vital record dates are consolidated at the beginning of each entry. They are converted to the genealogical convention of numerical day, followed by three-letter month abbreviations, then four digit years (e.g., 3 Mar 1801). Spacing is as consistent as possible.

Many, if not most, of the vital statistics in Warner's manuscript are not included, or incomplete, in the invaluable Barbour Collection.[m]

PART II

Congregational Church, "Church Records, 1752–1943" (includes baptisms 1752–1878, marriages 1752–1879 and deaths 1761–1883) (originals at CSL) (FHL film 4460, Items 4, 5). The Gilead marriage records have also been transcribed by the Genealogical Records Committee of the Daughters of the American Revolution: Lila James Roney, "Marriage Records in Hebron, Connecticut, 1752–1797" (manuscript 1928) (FHL film 2798) and (New York DAR GRC Report, series 3, vol. 24; 1927).

[m] Lucius Barnes Barbour and Lucius A. Barbour, "Barbour Collection of Connecticut Vital Records prior to 1850," 137 vols. (bound transcripts, 1909–1929, CSL, Hartford). These 137 volumes, including their all-important introductions omitted from the GPC editions, are available on 27 microfilms (FHL films 2967–2983).

The Family History Library catalog entries for Hebron vital records[n] include the Hebron Town Clerk's "Volume Four" on microfilm.[o] It contains births, deaths, and marriages from 1847 through 1854 that were not extracted by Barbour. Because of tight binding on the volume, however, vital information is not completely decipherable on the microfilm. For this publication, the Office of the Hebron Town Clerk graciously provided the important information not evident on the microfilm.

This Hebron Town Clerk's "Volume Four" records many births, marriages, and deaths between 1847 and 1854 (the year Barbour ends his extraction of Hebron records). More important, virtually all the births, marriages, and deaths extracted here contain much vital information not contained in other reports of the same events.[p]

1. **Births.** Birth records through 1854, largely omitted from the Barbour Collection, are all extracted in this book. While some dates of those same events appear in Barbour's "Book 4," the entries are less complete. The information here, taken from the Town Clerk's own Volume Four, generally provide the parents' ages and occupation(s).

2. **Marriages.** Most of the pre-1855 marriages in Volume Four are also in Hebron's Book of Marriages and therefore already in the Barbour index. All are extracted here because the Town Clerk's Volume Four contains valuable additional information, especially the ages and occupations and birth towns and current residence of each bride and groom, and how many times each had been previously married.

---

[n] See introduction to Part II.

[o] Hebron Registrar of Vital Statistics, Records of, Marriages, Deaths in the Town of Hebron, 1848–1871 (FHL film 1376166, Item 5).

[p] Barbour's omission of this volume from his collection of town records is not really unusual. Part II cites such unindexed microfilms from more than forty other Connecticut towns. All towns were required by 1848 to collect the additional information recorded in Hebron. These volumes may therefore provide important new information to genealogists researching the referenced towns.

3. **Deaths.** Most of the 1847–48 death records in Volume Four are also recorded in Volume 3 of the Hebron Records, and therefore are already indexed. All are nevertheless extracted here because the Town Clerk's Volume Four contains the cause of death and the decedent's birth date, birthplace, and occupation.

The Town Clerk's Office also possesses a bound volume of original marriage certificates from which its marriage records likely were extracted.q Marriage certificates with information not in Barbour are extracted in Part II-B.

Part II-C includes a few records extracted from Barbour's "Book 4" that do not appear in the Barbour Index. While "Book 4" is unmistakably derivative in content, it remains the only source for some vital information about Hebron residents.

PART III

The Hebron Town Clerk's Vital Statistics Index provides a convenient means for finding and evaluating hundreds of other additions and corrections to the Barbour Collection of Hebron Town Records. A page-by-page comparison of the Hebron index with the published Barbour Collection reveals:

- Sixty-nine marriages by Justice of the Peace Elihu Marvin between 1785 and 1812 are entered into the Hebron Vital Records for the first time on pages 167 through 172 of this index volume, hidden between the letters "O" and "P."r

- Barbour's indexer skipped a two-page spread of deaths in Book Two.

- A number of other entries in the earliest town records are either missed or miswritten, especially for Hebron's TILLETSON family.

---

q Hebron Town Clerk, Marriage Certificates, 1827–1854, 1799–1819 (FHL film 1376166, Item 6).

r These marriages, first published in the *Register*, (see note i above), are republished here to consolidate all additions and corrections to Hebron's vital records in a single source.

- Much additional information appears in the Vital Statistics Index. For example, cross-references point to vital statistics information in other types of records like land, probate, and church records. In addition, notations tell where some Hebron families came from and/or where they relocated when leaving Hebron.

This methodology may be applied to any Connecticut town that gathered vital records before the Civil War.

PART I
A

HEBRON, CONNECTICUT

This photocopy[1] of a 1866 manuscript housed in the Connecticut State Archives in Hartford, begins with the following typed Introduction by the Connecticut State Library:

> Note:
>   This Photostat copy of Hebron baptisms, marriages and deaths, 1752-1875 was made at the Connecticut State Library from the original manuscript compiled in 1886 by Will J. Warner.
>   The manuscript was loaned for this purpose by Deputy Dairy and Food Commissioner William J. Warner of Hebron, to whom it was returned.
>   The preparation of the Photostat copy was completed in April 1926.
>
>   (s) Geo. S. Godard
> Hartford, Conn.
> April 27, 1926.   State Librarian

HEBRON BAPTISMS – MARRIAGES – DEATHS 1752-1875
Compiled by Will J. Warner

The first unnumbered page is signed Will J. Warner, Gilead, Conn. Sept. 16, 1886

[page 1]

Index
First Settlement of Hebron	Page 4
Necrology	[Page] 14
Hebron Physicians	[Page] 46
Baptisms By E. Lothrop – (1752–1798)	[Page] 48
Marriages [By E. Lothrop – (1752–1798)]	[Page] 87
[Marriages by] N. Gillett – (1800–1825)	[Page] 97
[Marriages by] C. Nichols – (1826–1856)	[Page] 101
[Marriages by] Clerk	[Page] 104
Baptisms By N. Gillett (1799–1825)	[Page] 126
[Baptisms By] C. Nichols (1825– ____)	[Page] 131

---

[1] The present location or existence of Will J. Warner's original manuscript is unknown.

Deaths Record by E. Lothrop (1761–1797)   [Page] 106
[Deaths Record by] N. Gillett (1799–1825)   [Page] 114
[Deaths Record by] C. Nichols (1825–___)   [Page] 120

[page 2][2]

Stephen & Eleanor POST
Abraham & Mary (JORDAN) POST
Stephen & Hannah (HOSMER) POST
Gideon & Mary (CHASE) POST
Jazaniah & Elizabeth (BISSELL) POST
Anna POST. Adonijah BENTON

[page 3]

    Sept. 12, 1824
Anna Cemantha POST.
Caroline Matilda FOX[3]
Abiel Sherman GEER[4]
Charlotte ROOT[5]
POST
Sarah THOMAS   }
Dorothy FREEMAN } colored.
Nathan GILBERT   }

    Polly Caroline
  Jeremiah Hammond
    Samuel Edwin
  ch. of Jeremiah

[page 4]

Copied from the writings of Gov. John S. PETERS of Hebron

First Settlement of Hebron

The first families that settled in Hebron permanently were William SHIPMAN from Saybrook and Timothy PHELPS from Windsor.

They built log houses on the ground that is now occupied by Ira BISSELL and Joel WILLCOX in the autumn of 1705. The following summer SHIPMAN in attempting to repair the roof of his house

---

[2] The significance of the pedigree and the family grouping reproduced on original pages two and three are unexplained by Warner.

[3] Indexed by Connecticut State Library in 1931 under the surname FOX.

[4] Indexed by Connecticut State Library in 1931 under the surname GEER, GEAR.

[5] Indexed by Connecticut State Library in 1931 under the surname ROOT.

fell and broke his leg and died in a few days. He was the first man buried in the yard near Cyrus WARREN's. In the spring of 1706 many families moved into the Town and located themselves in different parts thereof – the names of many of the first settlers are now nearly extinct, (to wit) HIDE – BOND – SHIPMAN – SUTTON – SAWYER – SWEETLAND – MERRIL – OWEN – GAYLORD – PALMER -- DEWEY — and many others. The families and names of many others of the first settlers still remain (to wit) HUTCHINSON – NORTON – POST – BROWN – BARBER -- BARBOUR – PHELPS – CROUCH – TARBOX – JONES – WHITE – MANN – CURTIS – WELLES and others

[page 5]

The first Minister of the Gospel settled in Hebron was John BLISS from Norwich in 1717 – he was dismissed in 1734 – Benjamin POMROY of Suffield was settled in 1735, he died in 1784. Samuel KELLOGG of Hebron was settled in 1788, dismissed in 1793. Amos BASSETT of Derby was settled in 1794, dismissed in 1824. Lyman STRONG of South Hampton was settled in 1825, dismissed in 1830. Hiram P. ARMS of Deerfield was settled in 1830, dismissed in 1832. Moses HARRIS of Maine was settled in 1834, dismissed in 1835. Sylvester SELDEN of Saybrook was settled in 1835, dismissed in 1841. Edgar DOOLITTLE was settled in 1842, dismissed in 1853. Plurality in 1854 – Candidates – Merrick KNIGHT settled in 1854.

The societies of Gilead and Andover were set off in 1747. The first Minister in Gilead was Elijah LOTHROP. He was settled in 1752 and died in 1798. Nathan GILLETT settled in 1799, dismissed in 1824. Charles NICHOLS was settled in 1825.

[page 6]

The first Minister in Andover was Samuel LOCKWOOD, settled in 1749, died in 1791. Royal TYLER was settled in 1749, dismissed in 1817. Augustus COLLINS settled in 1818, dismissed in 1827. Alpha MILLER settled in 1829, dismissed in 1851.

In the Episcopal Society, Rev. John BLISS left the Congregationalists in 1734, and preached for many years in the then new Church built on his own land. There was a plurality of preachers until the year 1760 when Saml PETERS was settled and remained until the year 1774 when the political Revolution made it necessary for him to leave his country. He went to Boston from thence he sailed to London and remained there until the year 1806 when he returned and preached once in the church[. H]e returned to New York – from thence to Washington where he petitioned Congress, to Patent, to himself and Dar^s TITSOM of London, the Carver grant of land situated at the Falls of St. Anthony on the Mississippi. He danced attendance to Congress for many years and at the age of 86 he made a

[page 7]
journey to the Falls to get a title from the Natives. [H]e returned and lived in poverty and obscurity in New York until he was 91 years old, when he reposed in the arms of Death and his bones were brought to Hebron and buried in the new Church yard.

Tollotson BRUNSON was settled in 1794, dismissed in 1799. Evan ROGERS was installed in 1800 and left in 1803. a reformed methodist. Ammi ROGERS and others preached in the Parish until 1821, when the Rev. William JARVIS was settled and remained until 1827: he was succeeded by George C. SHEPARD: he left in 1830. [S]oon after[,] Alpheus GEER of Waterbury preached here and at Middle Haddam for 8 years; afterwards he was stationary until 1844. In 1845 Mr. Solomon G. HITCHCOCK was here stately for 4 years. Mr. FISHER preached 1 year. Mr. WARLAND came from Boston in 1851, is here in 1854.

The first Minister in the Methodist Society was Daniel BURRORS. The second Peter GRIFFING. They have been supplied by a plurality since[,] according with their rules removing their preachers, annually or biannually.

[page 8]
The first Justice of the Peace was Benjamin SKINNER. He lived in Hope Valley, owned a farm and built a grist mill on the ground that Barber's Factory now stands on[. H]e was the progenitor of the late David SKINNER. Since the appointment of Benj. SKINNER there has been a host elevated to the dignified office.

The first Representative to the General Assembly from Hebron was Nathaniel PHELPS in the year 1716, an office at that time that conferred more lasting honors and self gratulations than the office of President of the United States does in the present degenerate age.

The town is about nine miles from North to South and about 4 ½ miles from East to West – It has several good mill priviledges. It has within its limits, one silk thread mill – one paper mill – five grist mills – eleven saw mills – one plaiting mill. The face of the town is uneven and stony. Generally a strong soil, when the stones are removed and the land cultivated

[page 9]
it produces summer crops well − at least it is of an average quality of land in Connecticut.

The inhabitants are chiefly farmers and live on their farms in quantities of land from 50 to 300 acres. Latterly they have improved their land by forming with large stones, walls, making their meadows and arable land feasible. They live comfortably and as harmoniously as other communities. The first settlers were remarkable for a spirit of litigation produced by the conveyance of the land by Uncas Sachem of the Mohigans to Major John MASON − to a company − and to individuals, the deeds were given by the Indian lines, remaining from Watchatiquire to Jeremy's beach, the parties could not agree where they were located. [T]hey became eminent for their tactics in managing their suits and in procuring testimony to support their respective claims, and for their hard scrabbles for those things that perish. [T]his spirit gave rise to a remark of the eccentric Mr. WHITFIELD in a sermon he delivered in the Town. − "you Hebronierns are more fond of the flesh than of the spirit. And of the Earth than of Heaven".

[page 10]
In 1758 during the War between Great Britain and France, the then North American colonies made a noble effort (aided by an army of regulars) to close a war waged with savage ferocity by the combined forces of the French + Indians in taking Lewisburg, a strong fortress + key to the gulf and River St. Lawrence, which was gloriously accomplished by the troops under the command — Gen[l] AMHERST — the glad tidings were wafted − angles wings to every hamlet in the suffering country − gratitude warmed every heart and − lighted up every countenance − warm greetings heated every bosom and enormous pumpkin pies smoked on every board. It was necessary that some demonstration of loyalty should be made by the inhabitants of Hebron to show more clearly the love of King and country that entwined around their hearts. Caps were thrown high and a full chorus from stentorian lungs loudly echoed from the surrounding hills.

But alas! This did not reach the palesade. Its Sanhedrin assembled: After much deliberation a decree went forth. That a cannon should be fired: -- No life destroying instrument of that description had ever broken the silence of this part of the New World – Yankee ingenuity was placed on the rack: a new article was invented and would have been patented forthwith had fashion led the way. – a tremendous oaken log was brought from the forest and without delay transformed into a cannon of the caliber of a hundred and twenty pound. To make all sure and establish the character of this new species of artillery a son of Vulcan placed thereon massive hoops of iron – a three fold cord is not easily broken, in accordance with this truth a cordon of wood hoops were driven over all, so that the infernal machine looked like a mummy dressed for the tomb. – The work was accomplished – the powder horns were brought together and emptied of their contents – The gun was literally crammed and removed to the summit of the highest hill that the thunder thereof might be heard to the ends of the Earth. The torch was lighted, the assembled multitude stood afar off, in breathless anxiety – the awful moment was approaching – the torch was applied to the train, the minim of

mischief crept slowly toward the chamber of sleeping dust, like the serpent to the ear of our mother Eve—

> Let by the brilliant spark from grain to grain
> Runs the quick fire along the kindling train
> On the pained ear drum, bursts the sudden crash
> Starts the red flame and death pursues the flash.

In an instant, hope and fear together with the object of adoration were wafted to terra incognito in a fiery chariot: however the [illegible] there went to uttermost parts of the Earth and was written in the chronicles of George the 3rd who in the plentitude of his goodness provided a substitute made of pure brass that his faithful subjects may ever after sing peons to his victorious arms. This mark of his Majesty's favor was lost in passing the Atlantic Ocean.

As fashion governs the tenants of this Planet, in 1775 the patriotic time had turned the inhabitants again assembled and raised on a high pole, surmounted with the cap of liberty which possessed the talismanic property of turning the hearts of all the people from King to Congress: and they swore that Liberty should have an abiding place in their dwellings forever. – A traveler noticing their fiery heat wrote the following lines and nailed them on the body of the liberty pole –

I am thy God cut from the stump
you sing my praise and fire your pump.

[page 46]

Physicians in Hebron

Doctor Obadiah HORSFORD	From 1706 to 1715
[Doctor] Samuel SHIPMAN Senr	[From] 1715 [to] 1764
[Doctor] Samuel Shipman Junr	[From] 1745 [to] 1762
[Doctor] David SUTTON.	[From] 1760 [to] 1798
[Doctor] ____ STILES	[From] 1770 [to] 1804
[Doctor] Dan ARNOLD.	[From] 1792 [to] 1820
[Doctor] John S. PETERS.	[From] 1797 [to] 1834
[Doctor] Zenas STRONG.	[From] 1795 [to] 1798
[Doctor] David LYMAN.	[From] 1796 [to] 1800
[Doctor] Samuel SIMONS.	[From] 1816 [to] 1821
[Doctor] Gaylord WELLES.	[From] 1818 [to] 1820
[Doctor] Charles DOOSE.	[From] 1834 [to] 1837
[Doctor] James DOW.	[From] 1843 [to] 1845
[Doctor] Orrin C. WHITE.	[From] 1830 [to] ____
[Doctor] Elijah WOODWARD.	[From] 1844 [to] 1855
[Doctor] A.G. CRAIG,	[From] 1854 [to] ____

Andover Society

[Doctor] Joseph PARKER.
[Doctor] John S. PAINE
[Doctor] Adonijah WHITE,

Gilead Society

[Doctor] Reuben SUMNER.
[Doctor] Josiah ROSE. Junr.

[unnumbered page after 132]

[Hebron Captains in the Revolution]

Written By David BARBER Esq and sent the Rev Dr BASSETT of Hebron

Flames of the Captains over the first Military company in Hebron:

Its Capt Obediah HOSFORD – over the whole town (then divided and called the North and south Companies).

Capt Nathaniel PHELPS.	Capt Morris TILLOTSON.
Capt Joseph PHELPS.	Capt Timothy BUELL.
Capt Chas DEWEY.	Capt Samuel FILER.
Capt Alexander PHELPS.	Capt David BARBER.
Capt Obediah HOSFORD.	Capt Stephen BARBER.
Capt Joshua PHELPS.	Capt Royce PHELPS.
Capt John GILBERT.	Capt Hez^h BISSELL.
Cap Elihu POMEROY.	Capt Phineas STRONG.
Capt David BARBER Jr. &	Capt Daniel PHELPS.

    Count them all, they will make nineteen,
    And as generous Captains as ever was seen,
    And not one of them was counted mean.
    All where parade was on the Green.

B

WARNER'S NECROLOGY, 1782–1854
compared with
DEATH RECORDS, 1796–1825 & 1853–1860

Necrology, 1782–1795

[page 14]

1782	2 Dec	Dea. Thos POST	
1783		Mr. Silas OWEN	
1784		Mrs. Lydia PETERS, (w of Col. John PETERS)	
1785		Widow FULLE	
1786		Mrs. YOUNGS	
1787		Pomps wife	
1788		Barnabas PEASE	
1789		Hannah PHELPS	
1790	25 Feb	Martha BROWN, wife of Ezekiel BROWN	
1791		Noah OWEN	
1792		Widow PUFFER	
1793		Fowler MERRILS	
1793		Widow TRUMBULL	Aged 101 yrs
1793		Col. Joel JONES	Aged 72 yrs
1793		James POST	Aged 42 yrs
1793		Benjamin TRUMBULL	Aged 81 yrs
1794		John SAWYER	Aged 84 (85) yrs
1794		Capt Ichabod PHELPS	Aged 85 yrs
1794	Apr	Lieut John GILBERT	Aged 80 yrs
1794		Widw PHELPS, relict of Solomon	Aged 92 yrs
1794		Phoebe SUTTON, dau of J. PETERS[6]	Aged 41 yrs
1794		Timothy BUELL	Aged 83 yrs
1794		Widw NORTON, F. NORTON's Mother	Aged 90 yrs
1784		Dean Thomas BROWN's wife	Aged 53 yrs

[page 15]

1795	Joseph PHELPS	Aged 52 yrs
[1795]	Widw John SAWYER	Aged 92 yrs
[1795]	Dean William BUELL	Aged 89 yrs
[1795]	Amos PERKINS	Aged 78 yrs
[1795]	Waitstill TALCOTT (at sea)	Aged 24 yrs

---

[6] Indexed by Connecticut State Library in 1931 under the surname SUTTON.

Necrology (cont.) 1796–1826

1796 Aug Wid^w ABIGAIL GILBERT, rel^t of J. GILBERT,
                Aged 80 (78) yrs
                Aged 76 yrs [7]
[1796] Sept Jonathan HUTCHINSON   Aged 84 yrs
(21 Feb) 1797 Mrs. Lydia (DAVIS) NORTON, wife of F. NORTON
                Aged 54 51 yrs
[1797]   Abigail BARBOUR, wife of Josiah BARBER, Aged 24 yrs
[1797]   Increase PORTER's wife   Aged 64 yrs
[1797]   Martin POWERS wife   Aged 60 yrs
20 May [1797] Zadock MARTINDALE's wife
16 Jun [1797] Richard DOANE Executed at Hartford
[1797]   Col. Henry CHAMPION – Colchester –
3 Aug [1797] Rev. Elijah LOTHROP
[1797]   Capt. Samuel FINLEY. Glastonbury.
1 Dec [1797] Zadock MARTINDALE
[1797]   William ALLEN's wife
1798   Mrs. FULLER, Roger FULLER's Mother
[1798]   Henry P. SUMNER's wife, Jerusha PERRIN
28 Mar [1798] Ann FOOTE, wife of John FOOTE
8 Apr [1798] Mary, dau of Frances & Lydia (DAVIS) NORTON
26 Mar [1798] Aaron PHELPS' 2nd wife
4 Jun 4 [1798] Solomon HUNTINGTON
                   [page 16]
23 June 1798 Henry DEMING. Wethersfield.
1 Jul [1798] Wid^w HALL, wife of Dea. HALL.
16 Jul [1798] Wid^w GOODRICH
3 Aug [1798] Capt Elijah WELLES of Glastonbury (Suicide)
28 Nov [1798] George O. COOK
25 Jan 1799 Asa WILLEY's Mass. Wife
24 Apr [1799] Joseph MANN.   Aged 86 yrs
29 Jun [1799] Sarah SHIPMAN,   [Aged] 73 yrs
25 Jul [1799] Wife of Ichabod PHELPS. Junr
15 Oct [1799] Mrs. LOTHROP, Relict of Rev. E. LOTHROP
24 [Oct 1799] Reuben PHELPS
6 Nov [1799] Levi BUEL (son of Benj & Sybil BUEL)
31 Dec [1799] Capt William ROWLEY. Aged 53

---

[7] This inexplicable date is on a separate line between two entries with other ages at death.

HEBRON DEATHS: 1796–1823

[first page]

Mrs. Abijail GILBERT	16 Aug 1796
Jonathan HUTCHINSON	17 Sep 1796
John PERRIN	13 Feb 1797
Mrs. NORTON, 21 Feb 1721, 1797, wife to Francis NORTON	
Mrs. Abijah BARBER	10 Mar 1797
I[nc]reas PORTERs wife	15 May 1797
Martin POWERS wife	15 May 1797
Zadock MARTINDALEs wife	20 May 1797

Richard DONE [DOANE] executed at Hartford June 10th 1797 at half past 4 o'clock afternoon __ that there was 30 ??____ and gathered together ___ DONE was executed for the murder [of Daniel M'IVER]

Col CHAMPION	July 23 1797
Rev. Elijah LATHROP	August 3 1797
Capt Samuel FINDLEY of Glastonbury	Aug [1797]
Zadock MARTINDALE	Decr 1st 1797

[second page]

Wm ALLIN wife	23 Dec 1797
Widow FULLER	5 Feb 1798
Henry P SUMNER wife	6 Feb 1798
Miss FOOT, wife to John FOOT	March 28, 1798
Mary NORTON, dau of Mr. Francis NORTON	3 Apr 1798
Miss PHELPS, wife to Aaron PHELPS, 2d wife	16 Apr 1798
Solomon HUNTINGTON	4 Jun 1798
Tom [page torn] ININ of Wethersfield	23 Jan 1798
[page torn] GER	24 Jan 1798
[page torn] ULL	1 July 1798, wife to [Dan'l?] HULL
Widow GOODRICH	16 July 1798
Sampson, Negro wife	2 Augt 1798

[third page]

Capt Elijah WELLS of Glastonbury hung himself

Georg O. COOK	28 Nov 1798
Mrs. WILLEY, wife to Mr. Asa WILLEY	25 Jany 1799
Mr. Joseph MANN	24 Apr 1799, 86 years old.
Miss Sarah SHIPMAN,	29 June 1799
Ms. PHELPS, wife to Mr. Ichabod PHELPS	25 Oct 1799
Mrs. LATHROP, Wife to Revd Elijah LATHROP	15 Oct 1799
Ruben PHELPS	24 Oct 1799
Levi BUEL	6 Nov 1799
Capt. Wm. ROWLEY	31 Dec 1799

Necrology [cont.] 1796–1826

24 Apr 1800	Harmon son of Reuben WELLES
7 May [1800]	Deaⁿ Isaac FORD
31 Aug [1800]	Mrs. HUNTINGTON, relict of Solomon
31 Dec [1800]	Benj ROOT. Marlboro Aged 83 yrs
10 Sep [1800]	Widow (Hannah) TALCOTT
22 [Sep 1800]	Widow Judith CURTIS
14 Nov [1800]	Widow SIMS. Andover
14 Jan 1801	David BARBER Esqʳ
3 Mar [1801]	Obadiah WHITE Aged 88 yrs
18 [Mar 1801]	Polly WASS. (dau of John WASS)
8 [Mar 1801]	Capt. Benj. PHELPS' wife

[page 17]

2 Apr 1801	Rev. Evan ROGER's wife
25 Apr [1801]	Capt. Caleb ROOT's wife
26 Mar 1802	Miss Grace TALCOTT (dau of Capt. Gad TALCOTT)
18 Apr [1802]	Capt. Samuel JONES' wife
12 May [1802]	Henry PETER's wife
16 Jul [1802]	Annis (PETERS) wife of Ezekiel HORTON
2 Nov [1802]	Deaⁿ Thomas BROWN
27 [Nov 1802]	Jude WRIGHT
5 Dec [1802]	Capt. Solomon TARBOX's wife
15 [Dec 1802]	Ellis LUTHER's wife (Sybel POST)
21 [Dec 1802]	Daniel HORSFORD
9 Jan 1803	Mrs. POMEROY, relict of Rev. Dr. POMEROY
3 Mar [1803]	Betsey, dau of F. & Lydia (Davis) NORTON
26 [Mar 1803]	Levi RUSSEL Aged 21 yrs
6 Jun [1803]	David SKINNER's wife
20 [Jun 1803]	Hezekiah FOOT
2 Jul [1803]	Jerusha, wife of J. T. BURNHAM.[8]
17 Aug [1803]	Francis NORTON's 2ⁿᵈ wife. Tabitha (DORMAN)

---

[8] Attached typed note reports: "Entry for death of 'Jerusha, wife of J.T. Burnham,' on July 2, 1803 is incorrect. It was Catherine, mother of J.T. Burnham, who died on that date. Jerusha, his wife, did not die till Apr. 24, 1817. See inscriptions from Old Cemetery. Hebron.)   J.W. Bassett 10/30"

HEBRON DEATHS: 1796–1823 (cont.)

Harman WELLS, son to Reuben WELLS	24 Apr 1800
Deacon Isaac FORD	7 May 1800
Mrs. HUNTINGTON, wife to Solo^n HUNTINGTON	31 Aug 1800
	[fourth page]
Benjamin ROOT	Aug 1800
Widow TALCOTT	10 Sep 1800
Widow CURTICE	22 Sep 1800
Widow SIMS Andover	11 Nov 1800
David BARBER Esqr	11 Jany 1801
[O]badiah WHITE	3 Mar 1801
Polly, wife of [blank]——	Mar 1801
Mrs JONES wife to Gideon JONES	20 Nov 1801
Mrs. PHELPS, wife to Capt Benjn PHELPS	29 Mar 1801
Mrs. ROGERS, wife to the Rev^d Mr. Evan ROGERS	2 Apr 1801. Æ 30
Mrs. ROOT, wife to Capt Caleb ROOT	23 Aug 1801
[side note] Rupell TAYON hung himself	Sept 10 1808
	[fifth page]
Ashael PHELPS	6 Jany 1802
Mr. COOK	Jany 1802
Widow Hannah HUTCHINSON	27 Jan 1802
Miss Grace TALCOTT	26 Mar 1802
Mrs. BILLINGS	27 Mar 1802
Mrs. JONES, wife to CapT Sam^{ll} JONES	18 Apr 1802
Mrs. PETERS, wife to Henry PETERS	12 May 1802
Mrs. Annis HORTON, w. Mr. Ezekiel HORTON of Bolton	16 Jul 1802
Deacon Thos BROWN	2 Nov 1802
Mr. ROGERS	4 Nov 1802
Mr. BENNET, town pauper	Novr 1802
	[sixth page]
Mr. Jude WRIGHT, town pauper	27 Nov 1802
Mrs. TARBOX, w. to Capt Solomon TARBOX	5 Dec 1802
Mrs. LUTHER, w to Mr. Ellis LUTHER	15 Dec 1802
Mr. Daniel HORSFORD	21 Dec 1802
Mrs. POMEROY, w ot the Rev Benj POMEROY	9 Jan 1803
Betsey NORTON	3 Mar 1803
Levi RUSSELL	26 Mar-21 Apr
Mrs. SKINNER, w to David SKINNER	6 June 1803
Mr. Habacolm[?] FOOT	20 June 1803, age 81 y.
	[seventh page]
Mrs. BURNHAM	2 Jul 1803, w2 J. BURNHAM
Mrs. NORTON, 2d w to Mr. Frances NORTON	17 Aug 1803, Æ 42

Necrology [cont.] 1796–1826

12 Oct [1803]	Aaron PHELPS	
3 Dec [1803]	Russel HORTON's wife	
10 [Dec 1803]	Martha ROWLEY	
22 [Dec 1803]	John THOMAS (drowned)	
13 Jul 1804	Major Gen¹ HAMILTON killed in a duel with Aaron BURR	
7 Nov	Elijah KELLOGG Esqʳ	
		[page 18]
29 Jan 1804	Dr. David SUTTON⁹	
18 [Jan 1804]	John SAVORY	Aged 67
9 Nov [1804]	Col. John PETERS	[Aged] 87
1 Jun 1805	Eleazar STRONG Senʳ wife	
4 [Jun 1805]	Miss. Elizabeth FILER	Aged 75
12 [Jun 1805]	Samuel GEER. Crazy	[Aged] 57
23 [Jun 1805]	Miss. Welthy BACKUS	
16 Feb [1805]	Sally, wife of Rev. A. BASSET	
15 Apr [1805]	Jedediah CAULKINS	
6 May [1805]	Gideon HOXEY, shot with a ramrod left in a gun	
Jul 26 [1805]	Talbot OWEN. (D---- -------s)	
11 [Jul 1805]	Reuben SUMNER, Senʳ wife Elizabeth)	
Oct 6 [1805]	Oliver BARBER	
Jan 14 1806	Roger FULLER's wife	
23 [Jan 1806]	Roger HOSFORD	Aged 14
16 Mar [1806]	Hiram ALLEN's wife	
3 Jun [1806]	John MANN	Aged 86
4 [Jun 1806]	John RUSSEL's wife	
3 Jul [1806]	Moses HUTCHINSON, Pauper	Aged 84
22 [Jul 1806]	Capt. Stephen BARBER	
23 [Jul 1806]	James WHITE	About 90 (88)
18 Nov [1806]	Miss. Patty CHAPMAN	60 yrs
7 Feb 1807	Capt. Roger PHELPS	80 [yrs]

---

⁹ Dr. SUTTON's death is entered in Deaths. 1796-1860 on its sixteenth page; herein page 21.

HEBRON DEATHS: 1796–1825 (cont.)

Mr. Aaron PHELPS	12 Oct 1803
Widow Hannah ROOT, town pauper	18 Oct 1803
Mrs. HORTON, w to Mr. Russell NORTON	3 Dec 1803
Walter ROWLEY, Esq.	10 Dec 1803
John THOMAS found dead in John CONES pond	22 Dec 1803
Maj^r Gen HAMILTON was wounded in dewel by Aaron BURR on the 11th & d on the 13th	13 July 1804
Jasper AVERILL	14 Jul 1804
Elijah KELLOGG Esq	7 Nov 1804

[eighth page]

Col^l John PETERS	9 Nov 1804, 97 yrs of age
Mrs. STRONG, w. Mr. Eleazer STRONG	1 Jany 1805
Miss Elizabeth FILER	4 Jany 1805
Mr. Sam^{ll} GEAR	12 Jany 1805
Miss Welthy BACKUS	23 Jany 1805
Mrs. BASSETT, 2nd wife to Revd Amos BASSETT	7 Feby 1805
Miss Polly RUSSELL	16 Feb 1805

[ninth page]

Mr. Jedediah CAULKINS	10 Apr 1805
Mr. Gideon HOXEY who was shot at Columbia, 6 May 1805, in the 27th yr. of his age. The jury brought in accidental death	
Talburt OWEN	26 June 1805
Miss Jerusha DUNHAM	7 July 1805
Mrs. Elizabeth SUMMER, w2 Mr. Ruben SUMMER	11 July 1805
Thos BILL	12 July 1805
Aaron BARBERs child	27 July 1805
Mr. Oliver BARBER	6 Oct 1805
Mrs. FULLER, 2d w Roger FULLER	14 Jany 1806
Roger HORSFORD	23 Jany 1806

[tenth page]

Mrs. ALLIN, wf Mr. Hiram ALLIN	16 Mar 1806
Mr. John MANN	3 Jun 1806
Mrs. RUSSELL, w to Mr. John RUSSELL	4 June 1806
Mr. Wm. ALLIN	12 June 1806
Mr. Moses HUTCHINSON	3 July 1806
Capt Stephen BARBER	22 July 1806
Mr. James WHITE	23 July 1806
Miss Patty CHAPMAN	14 Nov 1806
Capt Roger PHELPS	22 Feby 1807

Necrology, [cont.] 1796–1826

22 [Feb 1807]	Miner HELDRITH	
		[page 19]
28 Mar 1807	Capt. Wm TALCOTT	Aged 65
29 [Mar 1807]	Reuben SUMNER	[Aged] 80
30 Jun [1807]	Frederic PHELPS	[Aged] 60
1 Jul [1807]	Pemberton BROWN, pauper	[Aged] 80
13 [Jul 1807]	Temperance, wife of E. HORTON	
9 Aug [1807]	Rufus COATS. Killed with lightning	Aged 18
6 Jul [1807]	Jemima NORTON ROOT	Aged 40
25 Aug [1807]	Sam¹ GOTT's wife	[Aged] 45
13 Sep [1807]	Daniel GOTT's wife	[Aged] 84
17 [Sep 1807]	Ezekiel BIRGE (cholera)	[Aged] 60
4 Feb 1808	Stephen HORTON	[Aged] 78
2 Mar [1808]	Hannah HORTON (burnt in Bed)	[Aged] 26
15 [Mar 1808]	John CURTIS' wife Sarah)	
8 [Mar 1808]	Joseph W. CASE's wife, A---	[Aged] 62
Jun 4 [1808]	Miss. Betsey BISSEL	
8 [Jun 1808]	Azariah SWEETLAND 2nd	
21 [Jun 1808]	Capt. David TARBOX	84 yrs.
5 Jul [1808]	Ralph JONES (drowned) at M^d Haddam	
Sep 12 [1808]	Capt. Gad TALCOTT's wife Abigail)	
20 [Sep 1808]	Miss. Sarah MANN (dau of A. K. MANN)	
Mar 1809	Horace ROAD	
17 May [1809]	John CONE	aged 34
27 [May 1809]	Sylvanus PHELPS	
Jul 12 [1809]	Manlius MANN	
		[page 20]
4 Aug 4 1809	Mansel BROWN	Aged 18
13 [Aug] 13 [1809]	Roger FULLER's 3rd wife	
7 [Aug] 7 [1809]	Jonathan TRUMBULL Esq. (Gov. of Conn.)	
6 Jul 1810	Deborah PHELPS, wife of Eleazar PHELPS Lenox, Mass.	
12 [Jul 1810]	Miss Polly POST (dau of Joseph & Hannah POST	

HEBRON DEATHS: 1796–1825 (cont.)

Mr. Miner HILDRETH	22 Feby 1807
	[eleventh page]
Capt Wm. TALCOTT	24 Mat 1807, Æ 65
Mr. Reuben SUMNER	2 Mar 1807
Ralph MACK, son to Capt Ralph MACK	1 Mar 1807, Æ 3 yrs. old
Mr. Frederic PHELPS	30 Jun 1807
Mr. Pemberton BROWN	1 Jul 1807
Mrs. Temperance HORTON	13 July 1807
Rufus COATS & child with lightning	9 Aug 1807
Jemima NORTON ROOT,	6 July 1807
Mrs. GOTT, w to Mr. Sam^{ll} GOTT	25 Aug 1807
Mrs. GOTT, wife to Mr. Dan^{ll} GOTT	13 Sep 1807
Mr. David CORWINs son aged 10 yrs.	15 Sep 1807
	[twelfth page]
Mr. David CORWINs son aged 5 yrs.	17 Sep 1807
Mr. Ezekiel BIRGE	19 Sep 1807
Mrs. Stephon HORTON	10 Feby 1808
Miss Hannah HORTON	2 Mar 1808, burnt to death in her bed
Mrs. CUSTER, w to Mr. John CUSTER	Feb 1808
Mrs. CASE, w to Mr. J.W. CASE	8 Mar 1808
Miss Betsey BISSELL	4 Jun 1808
[Mrs?] Azariah SWEETLAND, 2 w.	8 Jun 1808
Capt David TARBOX	21 Jun 1808
Mrs. Ralph JONES, Drowned	3 July 1808
Mrs. TALCOTT, w to Capt Gad TALCOTT	12 Sep 1808
Philo PECKHAM, wife	July 1808
Miss Sarah MANN	20 Sep 1808, dau of Mr. Ab^t MANN
	[thirteenth page]
Mr. Horris ROADE	Mar 1809
Mr. John CONE	17 May 1809
Mr. Sylvanus PHELPS	27 May 1809
Thos BOHAM	1 May 1809
Mr. Manley MANN	12 July 1809
Mr. Munsel BROWN	4 Aug 1809
Mrs. FULLER, 3rd w to Mr. R.F. FULLER	23 Aug 1809
Jonth TRUMBULL Esq Govr	7 Aug 1809
Mrs. Debarough PHELPS, w to Mr. E. PHELPS, Lenox in Burton State ____	6 Jul 1810
Miss Polly POST	12 July 1810

Necrology, [cont.] 1796–1826

11 [Jul 1810]	Benjamin BUEL Esq.	
5 Aug [1810]	Elisha TARBOX's wife	
11 Dec [1810]	Lieut. David TAYLOR. (Bolton)	
27 [Dec 1810]	William HYDE's wife	
31 [Dec 1810]	Anna SEXTON, dau of J. HORTON	
19 Feb 1811	Hannah wife of William PHELPS	
5 Mar [1811]	Hubbel BUEL	
24 May [1811]	John B. WELLES	
28 Jul [1811]	John CURTIS	83 yrs.
28 [Jul 1811]	Benjamin TAYLOR	88 [yrs]
7 Oct [1811]	John Hugh PETERS Esq, 35 yrs. Midd^l Haddam	
15 [Oct 1811]	Thomas POST	aged 80
31 [Oct 1811]	Margeret DAY, relict of Col. Joel JONES	
14 Nov [1811]	Sybil wife of Jethro NORTON	
28 [Nov 1811]	Solomon LATHROP	
20 [Nov 1811]	Thankful BALDWIN (alias TRUMBULL)	
23 [Nov 1811]	William ALLEN's 2nd wife. (Mrs. LENORIS)	
30 [Nov 1811]	Capt. Christopher CROUCH's wife (A. BUELL) Rebecca, dau Samuel	
17 Jan 1812	John FINLEY	

[page 21]

Jan 22 1812	Mrs. Abigail (BARTLETT) BUEL, relict of B. BUEL Esq.	
15 [Jan 1812]	Mrs. Daniel REED	
28 [Jan 1812]	Samuel E. GEER (distracted)	
[1812]	Capt. Solomon NORTON	Aged 96
17 May [1812]	David Whiting TRUMBULL	[Aged] 16
27 [May 1812]	Capt. William TALCOTT's widow (Mary) aged 67	
29 [May 1812]	David NILES	
9 Apr [1812]	Abigail PETERS relict of J. PETERS	74 yrs.
14 [Apr 1812]	Lydia HORTON wife of Rodolphus MANN (died at Balston	
24 May [1812]	Josiah MACK	Aged 90.
26 Jun [1812]	Rev. George COLTON of Bolton	

HEBRON DEATHS: 1796–1825 (cont.)

Daniel WAY, son of Mr. D. S. WAY	12 July 1810
Benjn BUELL Esqr	11 May 1810
Mrs. TARBOX, w to Mr. Elish TARBOX	5 Aug 1810

[fourteenth page]

Lieut David TAYLOR	11 Dec 1810
Mrs. HIDE, w to Mr. Wm HIDE	27 Dec 1810
Mrs. Anna SAXTON, dau of Mr. Joel HOUGHTON	31 Dec 1810
Mrs. Hannah PHELPS 19 July 1811, w to Mr. Wm PHELPS	
Mr. Hubbell BUELL	5 Mar 1811
Mrs. Mary WELLS, w to Edmond WELLS Late of Cambridge	2 Jany 1776
Mr. John B. WELLS	24 May 1811
Mrs. Charity WARREN of Bolton	28 May, 1811, Æ 73
Mr. John CURTICE	28 Jul 1811, Æ 83
Mr. Ben^y TAYLOR	28 July 1811

[fifteenth page]

Mrs. PORTER, w of Mr. Nehemiah [PORTER?]	27 Sep 1811
Mr. John H. PETERS.	7 Oct 1811, Æ 35
Mr. Thos POST	25 Oct 1811
Mrs. Margaret JONES, w to Col^l Joel JONES	31 Oct 1811
Mrs. Sybil NORTON, w to Mr. Jethro NORTON	14 Nov 1811
Mr. Solomon LATHROP	20 Nov 1811
W[idow?] ALLIN, 2d wife to Mr. Wm ALLIN	23 Dec 1811
Mrs Thankfull BALDWIN	Oct 20 1811
Mrs. CROUCH, w to Capt Christopher CROUCH	30 Dec 1811

[2nd entry on eighteenth page]

Mrs. BUELL, w to Benjn BUELL Esqr	22 Jany 1812
Mrs. REED, w to Mr. Daniel REED	15 Jany 1812
Mr. Sam^{ll} GEER	28 Jany 1812
Capt Solomon NORTON	27 Feb 1812, Æ 96
Mrs. ROGERS	16 Mar 1812
David W. TRUMBULL	17 Mar 1812, age 16
Wid^w TALCOTT, w to Capt Wm TALCOTT	27 Mar 1812
Mr. David NILES	29 Mar 1812

[nineteenth page]

Mrs. Abigail PETERS	9 Apr 1812, age 71
Mrs. Lydia MANN, w to Rhodolphus MANN of Bollston,	14 Apr 1812
Capt Josiah MACK	24 May 1812, Æ 90
Rev George COLTON	26 June 1812

Necrology, [cont.] 1796–1826

26 [Jun 1812]	Abraham PALMER.
5 Jul [1812]	Zenas CHAPPEL's wife.
16 [Jul 1812]	Timothy ISHAM. (Bolton)
23 [Jul 1812]	Miss Abigail LUTHER.
25 [Jul 1812]	Capt. Josiah POMROY
2 Aug [1812]	David OWEN.
11 [Aug 1812]	Reuben JONES. (found dead in the road)
20 [Aug 1812]	Jonathan PETERS. Aged 46
17 Sep [1812]	Abigail BUEL, dau Benj. & Abigail (BARTLETT) BUEL hung herself with a skein of yarn in her chamber. 33 yrs. old
14 Oct [1812]	Reuben PORTER.
18 [Oct 1812]	Widow Hannah relict of Capt. Abijah ROWLEY (who died in army)
25 [Oct 1812]	Hon. Roger GRISWOLD. Gov. of Conn.)
16 Jan 1813	Widow OWEN relict of Silas OWEN aged 95
	[page 22]
19 Feb 1813	Deborah wife of David NORTON aged 48
20 [Feb 1813]	Ichabod W. son of David POST (aged) 13)
14 Apr [1813]	David CARVER's wife.
17 [Apr 1813]	David CARVER.
4 May [1813]	Joel POST. Gilead. (aged 69)
9 [May 1813]	Jacob LOOMIS.
12 Jul [1813]	Ichabod PHELPS. ([aged] 74)
14 [Jul 1813]	Ezra BACKUS. [aged] 87
22 [Jul 1813]	John FINLEY 2nd
30 [Jul 1813]	Widow Rhoda FINLEY.
31 [Jul 1813]	Mrs. Deborah WEBSTER, w of Elijah WEBSTER) æ72
14 Aug14 [1813]	Francis NORTON.
17 [Aug 1813]	Elihu MARVIN Esq.
18 [Aug 1813]	Samuel JONES 2nd
15 [Aug 1813]	Clarissa. dau of Anson GILLETT.
16 Sep [1813]	Harvey son of Reuben SUMNER. (aged 16)
19 [Sep 1813]	John H. BUEL Esq.
25 [Sep 1813]	Ebenezer H. JONES.
2 Oct [1813]	Rev. Mr. BIRD.

HEBRON DEATHS: 1796–1825 (cont.)

Mr. Abraham PALMER	26 June 1812
Mrs. CHAPEL, w to Mr. Zenus CHAPEL	5 July 1812
Mr. Timothy ISHAM Bolton	16 July 1812
Miss Abigail LUTHER	25 July 1812
Capt Josiah POMROY	25 July 1812
Mr. David OWEN	2 Aug 1812

[sixteenth page]

Reuben JONES found dead in Road	11 Aug 1812
Mr. Jonathan PETERS	20 Aug 1812, Æ 46
Miss Abigail BUELL committed suicide	17 Sep 1812
Doc^r David SUTTON	29 Jany 1804
Mr. Reuben PORTER	14 Oct 1812
Wid^w Hannah ROWLEE, wife to Capt Abijah ROWLEE	14 Oct 1812
Roger GRISWOLD Esq Govr	25 Oct 1812
Wid^w OWEN	16 Jany 1813, Æ 95, wife to Atty Silas OWEN

[seventeenth page relocated after nineteenth page]
[seventeenth page relocated]

Mrs. Deborah NORTON, w to Mr. Duane NORTON	9 Feb 1813, Æ 48
Ichabod POST, s to David POST	11 Feb 1813
Mrs. CARVER, w to Mr. David CARVER	14 Apr 1813
Mr. David CARVER	17 Apr 1813
Mr. Joel POST	4 May 1813
Mr. Jacob LOOMIS	9 May 1813
Ichabod PHELPS	12 July 1813
Ezra BACKUS	14 July 1813
John FINDLEY, 2nd	22 July 1813
Wid^w Rhoda FINDLEY	30 July 1813

[1st entry on eighteenth page relocated]

Mr. John FINDLEY	17 Juny [sic] 1812

[twentieth page]

Mrs. Deborah WEBSTER	03 July 1813
Mr. Francis NORTON	14 Aug 1813
Elihu MARVIN Esq	17 Aug 1813
Sam^{ll} JONES 2nd	18 Aug 1813
Miss Clarisa GILLET	15 Aug 1813, dau of Capt Anson GILLETT
Harvey SUMNER, son to Mr. Reuben SUMNER	16 Sep 1813
John H. BUELL Esq	19 Sep 1813
Ebenezer T^n JONES	25 Sep 1813
Rev^d Mr. BIRD	21 Oct 1813

Necrology, [cont.] 1796–1826

9 Nov [1813]	David TOWNSEND	
31 Dec [1813]	Widow BLACKMAN	aged 97
17 Feb1814	Ebenezer HORTON	[aged] 81 (80)
20 [Feb 1814]	Solomon SAVORY	
21 [Feb 1814]	Daniel REED, in his one hundreth year	

[page 23]

21 Mar 1814	Dan JOHNSON	
28 [Mar 1814]	Mrs. CURTIS (From Stratford)	
6 Apr [1814]	Richard [No other name written]	
11 [Apr 1814]	Joseph NORTHAM	
11 [Apr 1814]	Anna PORTER	
25 [Apr 1814]	Capt. Samuel JONES	
30 [Apr 1814]	Jesse HAR[R]ISON	
25 Jun [1814]	Abijah MAN	
4 Jul [1814]	Ceasar PETERS	
5 [Jul 1814]	John TAYLOR's wife	
14 [Jul 1814]	Ellis BLISS	
2 Aug [1814]	Hiram BARBER	
6 [Aug 1814]	Widow of Solomon NORTON	aged 90 (92)
3 [Aug 1814]	David CULVER	[aged] 86 (76)
28 [Aug 1814]	Capt. Daniel INGHAM	
28 [Aug 1814]	Maria dau of D. S. WAY	
3 Sep3 [1814]	Phebe dau of Adoniram N. BISSEL	
4 [Sep 1814]	Widow Hannah BROWN	aged 87
28 Oct [1814]	Stephen BARBER's widow	
4 Jan 1815	Jedediah POST. Junr	[aged 64
6 [Jan 1815]	Capt. Asa FELLOWS	
24 [Jan 1815]	Ceasar PETERS' wife <u>Sim</u>	
3 Feb [1815]	Phineas ALLEN	
[3 Feb 1815]	Sarah PHELPS	

[page 24]

6 Feb 1815	Anna BROWN	(aged 30)
28 [Feb 1815]	Edward S. ELLIS' wife. (Mary)	([aged] 32)
18 Mar [1815]	Widow BINGHAM	
[18 Mar 1815]	Anson CLARK	
1 Apr [1815]	Amos HALL	[aged] 79]

HEBRON DEATHS: 1796–1825 (cont.)

David TOWNSEND	9 Nov 1813
Wid^W BLACKMAN	31 Jany 1814 Æ 97
Ebenezer HORTON	12 Feb 1814, Æ 81

[twenty-first page]

Solomon SAVORY	[21?] Feb 1814
Daniel REED	4 Feb 1814, in 100 yr of his age
Dan J[ONSTON?]	21 Mar 1814
Mr _____ CURTIS	28 Mar 1814, from Stratford
Richard TUCK	6 Apr 1814
Joseph NORTHAM	11 Apr 1814
Anna PORTER	11 Apr 1814
Capt Saml JONES	25 Apr 1814
Jesse HARDIN	Apr 1814
Abijah MANN	25 June 1814
Ceaser PETERS	4 July 1814
Mrs. TAYLOR, w to John TAYLOR	5 July 1814

[twenty-second page]

Ellis BLISS	14 July 1814
Hiram BARBER	2 Aug 1814
David CULVER	3 Aug 1814
Wid^W NORTON, w to Capt Sof^l NORTON	6 Aug 1814
Capt Daniel INGHAM	25 May 1801
Mariah WAY, dau of David WAY	28 Aug 1814
Phebe BISSELL, dau of Hiram BISSELL	3 Sep 1814
Widow Hannah BROWN	4 Sep 1814
Widow BARBER, w to Stephen BARBER	28 Oct 1814
Jedediah POST	4 Jany 1815
Capt Asa FELLOWS	6 Jany 1815

[twenty-third page]

Sim, wife to Cesar PETERS	24 Jany 181[5]
Phinias ALLIN	3 Feb 1815
Sarah PHELPS	3 Feb 1815
Anna BROWN	6 Feb 1815
Enoch MANN	15 Feb 1815
Mrs. ROSWELL	18 Feb 1815
Mrs. ELLIS, w to Edward S. ELLIS	28 Feb 1815
Wid^W BINGHAM	18 Mar 1815
Mr Anson CLARK	28 Mar 1815
Mr. Amos HALL	1 Apr 1815

Necrology, [cont.] 1796–1826

14 May [1815]	Mary E. dau of Frances & Thalia (OWEN) (HAYDEN) NORTON	
8 Jun [1815]	Joseph SKINNER's wife.	
31 Aug [1815]	Joseph WHITE Jun[r] wife	
2 Sep [1815]	Polly PORTER	
4 Oct [1815]	Simeon DANIEL's wife. (Bliss)	
12 [Oct 1815]	Charles ARNOLD's wife. (Thomas)	
13 [Oct 1815]	Hannah GEER, wife of Augustus POST	
21 [Oct 1815]	Phineas GILBERT. (colored)	
16 Nov [1815]	Dr. Ichabod WARNER. Bolton, Ct.	
26 [Nov 1815]	Elijah WEBSTER	(aged 81)
27 [Nov 1815]	Thomas WAY	
9 Dec [1815]	Sarah WHITE	
14 [Dec 1815]	Eleazar STRONG	Near 90
30 [Dec 1815]	Deacon FORD's widow	
12 Jan 1816	Capt. Joshua PHELPS' widow	
8 Feb [1816]	Joseph POST's wife, Hannah	(æ 69)
13 Mar [1816]	Abial ROOT	
23 [Mar 1816]	Widow Elenor TILLOTSON	
2 Apr [1816]	Samuel WRIGHT	

[page 25]

3 Apr 1816	Olive ROOT	
15 [Apr 1816]	Godfrey TARBOX's wife	
12 May [1816]	Elijah DUNHAM	(aged 34)
17 [May 1816]	Capt. Elisha BEACH's wife	
15 Jul [1816]	Samuel WRIGHT's wife	
26 Aug [1816]	Col. Ralph POMROY's wife	
31 [Aug 1816]	Israel KELLOGG	
8 Oct [1816]	Almira WELLS daughter, Mary	(æ 2)
14 [Oct 1816]	Jabez BACKUS' wife	
21 [Oct 1816]	Capt. William HIBBARD's wife.	
25 Dec [1816]	Aaron WHITE's wife, Salome (HIBBARD)	
11 Jan 1817	Capt. Simeon DUNHAM	(æ 78)
15 [Jan 1817]	Henry son of A. STRONG	
1 Feb [1817]	Moses KELLOGG's wife	
23 Apr [1817]	Joseph T. BURNHAM's wife	
10 May [1817]	Obedience DUNHAM dau of Capt. Simeon	
17 [May 1817]	Widow Mary LOOMIS	

HEBRON DEATHS: 1796–1825 (cont.)

Mary NORTON	14 May 1815
	[twenty-fourth page]
Mrs. SKINNER, w to Joseph SKINNER	3 Jun 1815
Mrs. WHITE, w to Joseph WHITE Jr.	31 Aug 1815
Polly PORTER	2 Sep 1815
Mrs. DANIELS, w to Simeon DANIELS	4 Oct 1815
Mrs. ARNOLD, w to Charles ARNOLD	12 Oct 1815
Mrs. POST, w to Capt E. POST	13 Oct 1815
Rimus GILBERT, A Black man	-- Oct 1815
Doc^r Ichabod WARNER of Bolton	16 Nov 1815
Elijah WEBSTER	28 Nov 1815
	[twenty-fifth page]
Thos WAY	27 Nov 1815
Sarah WHITE	9 Dec 1815
Eleazer STRONG	14 Dec 1815
Wid^w FORD, w to Deacon FORD	30 Dec 1815
Wid^w PHELPS, w to Capt Joshua PHELPS	12 Jan 1816
Mrs. POST, w to Mr. Joseph POST	3 Feb 1816
Abial ROOT	13 Mar 1816
Wid^w Elenor TILLOTSON	23 Mar 1816
Mr. Sam^{ll} WRIGHT	2 Aug 1816
Miss Olive ROOT	3 April 1816
Mrs. TARBOX, w to Godfrey TARBOX	15 Apr 1816
Mr. Elijah DUNHAM	12 May 1816
	[twenty-sixth page]
Mrs. BEACH, w of Capt Elisha BEACH	17 May 1816
Mrs. WRIGHT, w to Mr. Sam^{ll} WRIGHT	__ July 1816
Mrs. POMROY, w to Col Ralph POMROY	26 Aug 1816
Mr. Isreal KELLOGG	31 Aug 1816
Mary WILLS, dau of Almira WILLS	8 Oct 1816
Mrs. BACKUS, w to Mr. J. BACKUS	14 Oct 1816
Mrs. HIBBARD, w to Capt HIBBARD	21 Oct 1816
Mrs. WHITE, w to Aaron WHITE	25 Dec 1816
Capt Simeon DUNHAM	11 Jul 1817
Henry STRONG	15 July 1817
Mrs. KELLOGG, w to Moses KELLOGG	1 Feb 1817
	[twenty-seventh page]
Mrs. BURNHAM, w to Capt J. BURNHAM	23 Apr 1817
Miss Obedia DUNHAM	16 May 1817

Necrology, [cont.] 1796–1826

20 [May 1817]	Capt. Bazaliel HUTCHINSON's wife	
5 Sep [1817]	Azariah SWEETLAND	
11 [Sep 1817]	Mr. PERKINS (Andover)	
27 [Sep 1817]	Widow BACKUS. (E.B.)	
19 Oct [1817]	Chester HILLS (Eastberry)	
5 Nov [1817]	Mrs. Anna WEBSTER	
14 [Nov 1817]	Elias JONES	

[page 26]

18 Dec 1817	Capt. Hyekiah BISSEL's wife (Phebe (POST)	
8 Feb 1818	Sylvanus PHELPS' wife	
9 [Feb 1818]	Eleazar HUTCHINSON's wife Sally (TALLCOTT)	
2 Apr [1818]	Levi WEST	
[2 Apr 1818]	Joseph SAVORY	
11 [Apr 1818]	Ezekiel HORTON	
21 [Apr 1818]	Hon. Samuel GILBERT	(æ 83)
25 Jun [1818]	Joshua BILL (Columbia)	
30 [Jun 1818]	Ozias GILLETT	
22 Jul [1818]	Widow Anna PHELPS	
15 Oct [1818]	Capt. Daniel BUSHNEL	(æ 72)
14 [Oct 1818]	Daniel GOTT	
20 [Oct 1818]	Capt. Pierce DARROW's wife	
26 [Oct 1818]	John FOOT	(æ 90)
14 Nov [1818]	Bela PORTER	
7 [Nov 1818]	Gustavus WELLS	
13 Dec [1818]	Stephen SKINNER	
26 [Dec 1818]	Lucy LOOMER	(æ 20)
24 Jan 1819	Cynthia KIMBALL (Exeter)	
1 Feb [1819]	E. H, JONES' wife	
16 [Feb 1819]	Harry son of R. COATS	
6 Mar [1819]	Capt. William BUELL (Marlboro)	
9 [Mar 1819]	Hannah, wife of Andrew MANN	
19 [Mar 1819]	Col. Ralph POMROY	
20 Mar 1819	Thomas WAY's widow	aged 90

HEBRON DEATHS: 1796–1825 (cont.)

W^d^w Mary LOOMIS	17 May 1817
Mrs. HUTCHINSON, w to Capt Bezeleel HUTCHINSON	__ May 1817
Mr. Azariah SWE[T]LAND	5 Sep 1817
Mr. PERKINS	11 Sep 1817
Widow BACKUS	27 Sep 1817
Mrs. HILLS, w to Mr. Charles Chester H[ILLS ?] [page torn]	19 Oct 1817
Mrs. Anna WEBSTER, died	5 Nov 181[7]

[twenty-eighth page]

[Mr] Christopher CROUCH Jr.	14 Nov 1817
Elias JONES	14 Nov 1817
Mrs. BISSELL, w of Capt Hezekiah BISSELL	11 Dec 1817
[Mrs] PHELPS, w to Mr. Sylvanus PHELPS	8 [Feb ?] 1818
Mrs. HUTCHINSON, w to E [HUTCHINSON]	9 [Feb] 1818
Mrs HUTCHINSON, w to David HUTCHINSON	8 [March ?] 1818, Æ 33
Levi WEST	2 Apr 1818
Mr. Joseph SAVERY	2 Apr 1818
Ezekiel HORTON	11 Apr 1818
Samuel GILBERT, Esq.	21 Apr 1818, age 84

[twenty-ninth page]

Joshua BILL	25 June 1818
Ozius GILLET	30 June 1818
Wid^w Anna PHELPS	22 July 1818
Capt Dan^{ll} BUSHNELL	10 Oct 1818
Daniel GOTT	11 Oct 1818
Mrs. DARROW	20 Oct 1818
John FOOT	31 Oct 18[18]
Bela PORTER	14 Nov 1818
Gustavus WELLS	7 Nov 1818
Stephon SKINNER	13 Dec 1818
Mrs. Lucy LOOMER	26 Dec 1818
Miss Cynthia KIMBALL	24 Jany 1819

[thirtieth page]

Mrs. JONES, w to L.K. JONES	1 Feb 1819
Mr. Harry COATS, son of Rufus COATS	16 Feb 1819
Capt Wm BUELL of Marlborough	6 Mar 1819
Mrs. MANN, w to A. MANN Esq.	9 Mar 1819
Col Ralph POMROY	19 Mar 1819
Wid^w WAY, w of Mr. Thos WAY	20 Mar 1819, Æ 90

Necrology, [cont.] 1796–1826

20 [Mar 1819]	Ebenezer REED's daughter	[aged] 18
25 [Mar 1819]	Harriet SWEETLAND	[aged] 25
4 Apr [1819]	Ezekiel GILLETT.	[aged] 76
11 [Apr 1819]	Gideon WATROUS (Marlboro)	[aged] 80
6 [Apr 1819]	Anna BISSEL	
24 [Apr 1819]	Anna PHELPS	
17 Jun [1819]	John HUTCHINSON's wife, Molly (POST) ae 57	
29 [Jun 1819]	Levi COLLINS' wife	
16 Aug [1819]	Rufus COATS	
21 Sep [1819]	Roger FULLER	
6 Nov [1819]	Ruth (COX) HUTCHINSON (Widow of Moses, pauper)	
9 [Nov 1819]	Joseph HARRIS' wife, Lucy	
6 Jan 1820	Peggy wife of Lorenzo DOW.	
20 [Jan 1820]	Huldah, dau of Samuel JONES	
[20 Jan 1820]	Eliza BROWN	
20 Feb [1820]	Sarah PORTER	

[page 27]

29 [Feb 1820]	Moses KELLOGG	aged 80
2 Mar [1820]	Amasa HOLDRIDGE	
15 [Mar 1820]	Abel PHELPS' wife	
[15 Mar 1820]	Phebe, relict of J. MANN	aged 90
20 [Mar 1820]	Mrs. BAILEY. Widow)	
28 [Mar 1820]	Mrs. ISHAM	
14 Apr [1820],	Abiatha (PHELPS) POST, relict of Thomas	Aged 90(79)

[page 28]

21 Apr 1820	Mason HORTON	
6 May [1820]	John MERRIL	(ae 81)
22 [May 1820]	Sam¹ TALCOTT's wife Harriot[;] Masse WARNER's daugʳ)	
17 [May 1820]	Mary, wife of Joel MANN, aged 76.(Milton N.Y.)	
10 Jul [1820]	Ira BISSEL's wife	
27 Aug [1820]	Phebe, dau of Levi BISSEL	
18 Oct [1820]	Amelia BLISS	
2 Feb 1821	Roger PHELPS' wife	
5 [Feb 1821]	Dea. Asaph TRUMBUL, aged 83	
19 [Feb 1821]	Cynthia ADAMS	
21 [Feb 1821]	Sam¹ Egbert GILLETT (s. of Rev. Nothan)	

HEBRON DEATHS: 1796–1825 (cont.)

Miss REED, dau of Mr. Eben REED	20 Mar 1819, Æ 18
Miss Harriet SWETLAND	2 Mar [1819]
Ezekiel GILBERT	4 Apr 1818, Æ 76

[thirty-first page]

Gideon WATROUS	6 Apr 1819
Miss Anna BISSELL	6 Apr 1819
Miss Anna PHELPS	24 Apr 1819
Mrs. HUTCHINSON, w to John HUTCHINSON	17 June 1819
Mrs. COLLINS, w to Levi COLLINS	29 June 1819
Mr. Rufus COATES	__ Aug 1819
Mr. Roger FULLER	21 Sep 1819, Æ 72
Wid^W Ruth HUTCHINSON, town pauper	6 Nov 1819
Mrs. HARRIS	9 Nov 1819
Mrs. DOW	5? Jany 1820

[thirty-second page]

Mrs. Hulda JONES	Jany 1820
Miss Eliza BROWN	20 Jany 1820
Miss Sarah PORTER	20 Feb 1820
Mr. Moses KELLOGG	27 Feb 1820
Mr. Ammasa HOLDRIDGE	2 Mar 1820
Mrs. PHELPS, w to Mr. Abil PHELPS	15 Mar 1820
Mrs. Phebe MANN, w to Mr. Joseph MANN	15 Mar 1820
Mrs. BAILEY	20 Mar 1820
Mrs. ISHAM	28 Mar 1820
Wid^W POST	14 Apr 1802, w of Mr. Thomas POST

[thirty-third page]

Mason HORTON	18 Apr 1820 [Æ 33?]
Betty, a Black woman	2 May 1820
Mr. John MERRILL	6 May 1820
Mrs. TOLCOTT, w of Capt Sam^{ll} TOLCOTTE	22 May 1820
Mrs. Marcy MANN, w of Mr. Joel MANN of Milton NY	17 May 1820
Mrs. BISSELL, w to Mr. Ira BISSELL	10 July 1820
Miss Phebe BISSELL	27 Aug 1820
Miss Amelia BLISS	18 Oct 1820
Mrs. PHELPS, w to Mr. Roger PHELPS	2 Feb 1820

[thirty-fourth page]

Capt Aseph TRUMBULL	Feby 5th 1821 in the 83rd year of his age
Mrs. Cynthia ADAMS	Feby 19th 1821
Egburt GILLET	Feby 21st 1821

Necrology, [cont.] 1796–1826

25 [Feb 1821]	Daniel REED's wife	
28 Mar [1821]	Jonathan CHAPPEL	aged 85
19 [Mar 1821]	Godfrey TARBOX	
29 [Mar 1821]	David STRONG	
4 Apr [1821]	Craft GOODRICH's wife. (hung herself)	
22 [Apr 1821]	Thomas SMITH (State pauper)	
14 Jun [1821]	Lydia, relict of J. HORTON	
1 Sep [1821]	Capt. Samuel PETERS `	(æ 63)
3 [Sep 1821]	Hannah, dau of S. WRIGHT	
11 [Sep 1821]	John DAVIS	
6 Oct [1821]	John POST's wife (Sally)	aged 22
30 Nov [1821]	Jonah PORTER	
18 Dec [1821]	Mrs. SUMMERS, relict of Thomas SUMMERS	

[page 29]

24 Dec 1821	John PERKINS' wife	
24 Feb 1822	Aaron BAXTER	(æ 86)
1 Mar [1822]	James HAMILTON	
2 [Mar 1822]	Miss Lydia WILCOX	(æ 49)
19 June [1822]	Thomas WEBSTER's wife	
10 [Jun 1822]	Eunice CRAIN	
14 Aug [1822]	Henry MACK's daughter (Deborah)	æ 22
12 Sep [1822]	Seth COLLINS Esq.	aged 54
6 [Sep 1822]	Mr. DOW	
28 [Sep 1822]	Capt. Hezekiah BISSEL	
9 Oct [1822]	Alvin GILLETT's wife (hung herself)	
[9 Oct 1822]	Clarissa HUTCHINSON, Miss) æ 27 (dau John & Molly (POST) [HUTCHINSON	
12 [Oct 1822]	James BROWN	[æ] 69
19 [Oct 1822]	Caleb ROOT	
26 [Oct 1822]	William LATHAM	
2 Nov [1822]	Aldric CARVER's wife	
21 [Nov 1822]	Samuel HORTON	
23 [Nov] 1822	Nathaniel WOODBRIDGE	
30 [Nov 1822]	Joel JONES Esq.	
12 Dec [1822]	Widow LOOMER	

HEBRON DEATHS: 1796–1825 (cont.)

Mrs REEDE wife to Mr Daniel REED	Feby 25th 1821
Mr Godfree TARBOX	March 19 1821
Mr Jonathan CHAPPEL	March 28 1821
Mr David STRONG	March 29 1821
Mrs GOODRICH wife to Mr Crafts GOODRICH committed suicide April	1821
Mr Thos SMITH	April 22nd 1821

[thirty-fifth page]

Seaser CHAPPEL wife a black woman	May 18th 1821
Widow Lydia HORTON wife of Mr. Joel HORTON	June 14th 1821
Capt Sam PETERS	Sept 1st 1821
Mrs Hannah WRIGHT Daughter of Capt Sam^v WRIGHT	Sept 3 1821
Mr John DAVIS	Sept 11th 1821
Mrs POST wife to Mr John POST	October 6th 1821
Jonah PORTER 2nd	Nov 31 1821

[thirty-sixth page]

Wid^w SUMMERS	18 Dec 1821, w of Mr. Thos SUMMERS
Mrs. PERKINS, w of Mr. John PERKINS	Dec 1821
Mrs. ISHAM	28 Feb 1822
Mr. Aaron BAXTER	24 Feb 182[2]
Mr. James HUNTINGTON	1 Mar 18[22]
Miss Lydia WILCOX	2 Mar 1822
Mrs. WEBSTER, w of Thos WEBSTER	19 Jun 1822
Miss [E]Unice CRAIN	11 June [1822]
Miss MACK, dau of Mr. Henry MACK	Aug 1822

[thirty-seventh page]

Seth COLLINS Esq.	22 Sep 1822
Mr. DOW	6 Sep 1822
Capt Hezekiah BISSELL	28 Sep 1822
Mrs. GILLETT, w to Mr. Alvin GILLETT committed suicide	9 Oct 1822
Miss Clarissa HUTCHINSON	9 Oct 1822
Mr. James BROWN	12 Oct 1822
Capt Caleb ROOT	[blot] Oct 1822
Wm. LATHAM	20 Oct 1822, Farmer[illegible]

[thirty-eighth page]

Mrs. CARVER, w to Aldrich CARVER	2 Nov 1822
Mr. Sam^{ll} HORTON	21 Nov 1822
Mr. Nathaniel L. WOODBRIDGE of Colchester	23 Nov 1822
Joel JONES Esq.	30 Nov 1822
Widow LOOMER	19 Dec 1822

Necrology, [cont.] 1796–1826

16 Jan 1823	Russel Carter WELLES (hung himself)	
5 Mar [1823]	Mrs. PAINE widow of J. PAINE	
[23 Mar 1823]	Joseph WHITE	
12 May [1823]	Elijah BEACH's wife	
		[page 30]
16 May 1823	Elijah HOUSE Esq.	aged 77
10 Jun [1823]	Increase PORTER's wife	[10 Jun 1823]
	Mrs. KINGSBURY	
[10 Jun 1823]	Miss. Polly JONES	
20 [Jun 1823]	Roger FOOTE (Marlboro)	
9 Jul 1823]	Abijah MANN's wife	
22 [Jul 1823]	Daniel S. WAY	aged 55
5 Aug [1823]	Mrs. PALMER	
6 [Aug 1823]	Gaylord PORTER	aged 78
16 [Aug 1823]	Eleazar STRONG's wife Zilpha	(æ 42)
22 [Aug 1823]	Capt. Hezekiah BISSEL Junr	
12 Jul [1823]	Eleazar PHELPS (Lennox Mass.)	
31 Aug [1823]	Mrs. Zilpha TRUMBULL (Widow)	(æ 77)
31 Oct [1823]	Widow Prudence HORTON	Aged 90
26 Dec [1823]	Levi BISSEL's wife	
7 Jan 1824	John SUTTON	Aged 90 yr. 7 mo.
10 Feb [1824]	David W. POST (Capt)	
19 [Feb 1824]	Widow CHAPPEL	
11 Mar [1824]	Betsey, wife of William BROWN	
22 Apr [1824]	Alexander HOUSE (hung himself)	
26 Jun [1824]	Joel POST 2nd (consumption)	
11 Dec [1824]	Joshua ROOT's wife	
22 [Dec 1824]	Depsy (Deborah) NORTON (Fat woman)	
24 [Dec 1824]	Loren ANDREW's wife	
		[page 31]
7 Jun 1825	Abigail. Widow of Roger PHELPS	
30 [Jun 1825]	Hazael GOTT's wife	
9 Feb [1825]	Asahel PORTER	
10 [Feb 1825]	Robert RUSSEL Esq.	
27 [Feb 1825]	John MERRILS' widow, Sarah	æ 91
3 Jul 1826	Thomas WELLES 2nd	aged 66
19 Apr [1826]	Rev. Samuel PETERS, L.L.D	aged 91
25 Jun [1826]	Mrs. David GILLETT	[aged] 27

HEBRON DEATHS: 1796–1825 (cont.)

Rufus C. WELLS committed suicide	16 Jan 1823
Widow PAIN, w to Mr. Joseph PAIN	5 Mar 1822
Deek SAWYER, a Negro	13 Mar 1822
	[thirty-ninth page]
Mr. Joseph WHITE	23 Mar 1823
Capt Elisha BEACH	25 Mar 1823
Mrs. BEACH, w of Mr Elijah BEACH	12 May 1823
Elijah HOUSE Esq.	16 May 1823 Æ 77
Mrs. PORTER, w to Increas PORTER	11 June 1823
Mrs. KINGSBERRY	11 June 1823
Miss Polly JONES	[20?] June 1823
Mr. Roger FOOT	June 1823
Wid^W Abigail PHELPS	7 Jan 1825
Mrs. GOTT, w of Hazeal GOTT	[10?] Jan 1825
	[fortieth page]
Mrs MANN wife to Mr Abijah MANN	July 9 1823
Mr Daniel WAY	July 22 1823 Aged 51
Mr PALMER	Augt 5 1823
Mr Gaylord PORTER	Aug 6th 1823
Mrs STRONG wife to Mr Eleazer STRONG	August 16 1823
Capt Hezekiah BISSELL	Augt 22 1823
Mr Eleazer {ink smudge] wife of Leone___	July 12 1823
	[forty-first page]
Widow TRUMBULL	Augt 31 1823
Widow HORTON	Octr 31st 1823 Æ 91
Mrs BISSELL wife of Mr Levi BISSELL	Dec 26th 1823
Mr John SUTTON	Jany 7th 1824 90 years of last June
Capt David W POST	Feby 10th 1824
Widow CHAPPEL	Feby 19th 1824
Mrs BROWN wif to Wm BROWN Esqr	March 11th 1824
	[forty-second page]
Alexander HOUSE committed suicide	22 Apr 1824
Joel POST	26 Jun 1824
Mrs. ROOT, w of Joshua ROOT	__ Dec 1824
Depsey NORTON	22 Dec 1824
Mrs. ANDROUS, w of Loren ANDROUS	22 Dec 1824
Mr. Asahel PORTER	9 Feb 1825
Robert RUSSELL Esqr	10 Feb 1825
Widow MERRELLS, w of Mr. John MERRELLS	27 Feb 1825

(continued on p. 43)
[NO MORE DEATH RECORDS ENTERED UNTIL 1853]

[Necrology, cont.] 1825–1855

20 Jan 1829	Mary (CONE) ROWLEY.	aged 24
25 Sep [1829]	Mrs. Elizabeth PAGE.	aged 51
12 Mar 1833	Erastus PHELPS.	
23 Jul [1833]	Juliet, dau of R. MANN	
5 Nov [1833]	Joel HORTON	
18 [Nov 1833]	Mrs. Mary CONE.	aged 90
8 May 1835	Mrs. Clarissa WAY	aged 58
24 July [1835]	Lemual PEASE. (N.Y.)	aged 70
16 Dec [1835]	Oliver PEASE ([N.Y.])	[aged] 67
25 Apr 1836	Edmund C. GEER	aged 35 (42)
[25 Apr 1836]	Nathan P. COATS	[aged] 40
26 [Apr 1836]	Martha SHIPMAN	[aged] 76
26 Jun [1836]	Capt. Benjamin PHELPS	[aged] 74
23 Dec [1833]	Annis, relict of H. HORTON	[aged] 70
10 Jan 1837	Mrs. Peter GRIFFIN	[aged] 60

[page 32]

9 Feb 1837	Mabel FORD, wife of Aaron MACK	aged 45
16 Feb [1837]	Alvin GILLETT	[aged] 65
2 Mar [1837]	Elizabeth, relict of J. PHELPS	[aged] 86
26 Mar [1837]	Richard W. HART Esq.(Saybrook)	[aged] 74
2 Apr [1837]	Jemima, wife of W. SUMNER	[aged] 70(74)
3 [Apr 1837]	Ira ROOT's wife	[aged] 42
26 [Apr 1837]	Mrs. Absalom PETERS	[aged] 80
28 Jul [1837]	Candace, wife of E. (Ezekiel) BROWN	[aged] 74
2 Jan 1838	Dea. Jonathan HUTCHINSON	[aged] ~~71~~ 92
5 [Jan 1838]	George HALL's wife (Azubah TRUMBULL) [aged] 75. (70)	
15 [Jan 1838]	Mrs. LEONARD, O F's widow	[aged] 61
20 Mar [1838]	Patience, relict of J. POST	[aged] 84 (87)
30 [Mar 1838]	Mrs. Isaac SKINNER	[aged] 68
14 May [1838]	Mrs. Sylvester GILBERT	[aged] 82
17 [May 1838]	William SUMNER	[aged] 79 (77)
22 [May 1838]	Mrs. Daniel WHITE	[aged] 72
12 Jun [1838]	Increase PORTER	[aged] 81

[Necrology, cont.] 1825–1855

15 Jul [1838]	Anna, wife of Abiel BLISS	[aged] 70
28 [Jul 1838]	John NORTHAM	[aged] 83
6 Aug [1838]	Patience, wife of Joseph MANN	[aged] 70
3 Oct [1838]	Mrs. Phineas POST	[aged] 78
9 Nov [1838]	Stephen BARBER	[aged] 82
[1838]	Henry SUMNER	[aged] 70
13 Jan 1839	Asahel POST	[aged] 45 (57)

[page 33]

10 Mar 1839	Abbe GOTT	aged 18
7 Apr [1839]	Luther FORD's wife, Lucy	[aged] 80,(72)
27 May [1839]	Frederic WHITE	[aged] 24.(46)
4 Sep [1839]	Daniel HUTCHINSON.	[aged] 82. (88)
19 [Sep 1839]	Mrs. Fanny PORTER	[aged] 61
6 Oct [1839]	David NORTON	[aged] 83 (87)
9 Nov [1839]	Mrs. Lydia LYON	[aged] 72
7 Dec [1839]	David NORTHAM	[aged] 51
16 [Dec 1839]	Eleazar PUFFER	[aged] 73
3 Aug [1839]	Ruel BEEBE (Cambridge)	[aged] 82
19 [Aug 1839]	Ira PARMELE ([Cambridge])	[aged] 70
6 Feb 1840	Jonathan NORTHAM (Marboro)	[aged] 80 (84)
29 [Feb 1840]	Gen. Absalom PETERS (N.Y.)	[aged] 86
9 Apr [1840]	Mrs. Selden CURTIS	[aged] 30
20 [Apr 1840]	Mrs. Oliver JONES	[aged] 73
29 [Apr 1840]	Mr. George HALL	[aged] 79 (75)
12 May [1840]	Mrs. Eleazar HUTCHINSON (Ruth)	[aged] 50 (57)
7 Jun [1840]	Mrs. Luther FORD	[aged] 81.(78)
17 [Jun 1840]	Miss. Clarinda PETERS (Ballstone)	[aged] 28
23 Aug [1840]	John TAYLOR	[aged] 70
26 Sep [1840]	Anna POST	[aged] 36
14 [Sep 1840]	Daniel REED	[aged] 60
5 Oct [1840]	David POST	[aged] 86.(88)
15 Jan 1841	Mrs. Waldo WHITE	[aged] 36

[page 34]

19 Feb 1841	Mr. BLACKMER (Elisha)	aged 96

[Necrology, cont.] 1825–1855

22 [Feb 1841]	Joel POST	[aged] 49 (58)
11 Mar [1841]	Asahel KINGSLEY	[aged] 55
18 [May 1841]	Fayette FULLER	[aged] 26
6 May [1841]	Benisle PETERS (Ballston, N.Y.)	[aged] 64
11 Jun [1841]	William LUTHAM	[aged] 50
11 July [1841]	Charles, son of J. PORTER	[aged] 26
2 Aug [1841]	Lucinda PHELPS	[aged] 35
31 [Aug 1841]	Ezekiel A. son of Shipman HORTON	[aged] 25
4 Sep [1841]	Elizabeth, relict of J.S. PETER	[aged] 78
6 [Sep 1841]	David SKINNER	[aged] 84
22 [Sep 1841]	Mrs. George W. TURNER	[aged] 62
23 [Sep 1841]	Jonathan WATROUS	[aged] 79
4 Oct [1841]	Rev. Sylvester SELDEN	[aged] 60
9 Nov. [1841]	Mrs. (Julia BIRGE) Benjamin SPRAGUE	[aged] 87
19 [Nov 1841]	John, son of D. PEASE	[aged] 24
5 [Nov 1841]	Desdemona, relict of L. PEASE	[aged] 71
24 [Nov 1841]	Hiram GOODELL	[aged] 36 (41)
30 [Nov 1841]	Levi A. son of J. ANIBAL	[aged] 10
21 [Nov 1841]	Jethro NORTON	[aged] 81 (86)
29 Dec [1841]	Hannah, relict of D. PETERS	[aged] 81
7 Jan 1842	Franklin, son of A. CROUCH	[aged] 12
15 [Jan 1842]	William PHELPS	[aged] 76
7 Feb [1841	Otis MORSE's wife	[aged] 50
		[page 35]
1 Mar 1842	Albert, son of J. PHELPS	aged 26
28 [Mar 1841]	Caroline GRAVES	[aged] 32
13 Apr [1842]	Eunice ALLEN	[aged] 74
8 May [1842]	John LOOMER	[aged] 70
22 Jun [1841]	Isaac DOANE	[aged] 62
19 Aug [1842]	Mrs. J. LOCKWOOD	[aged] 54
20 Sep [1842]	Mrs. TREAT, mother of Rev. Mr. TREAT	[aged] 70
17 Dec [1842]	Desire TAYLOR	[aged] 72

[Necrology, cont.] 1825–1855

3 Oct [1841]	Champion GILBERT's child. (Henry Champion)	[aged] 3 (4)
4 [Oct 1842]	Widow BINGHAM	[aged] 70
24 [Oct 1842]	Christopher CROUCH Junr	[aged] 65
30 [Dec 1842]	Mrs. Capt. BISSEL (Alice BARBER)	[aged] 93
3 Dec [1842]	Rosamond, wife of Harry B. HORTON.	[aged] 45
26 Jan 1843	Henry JONES	[aged] 55
1 Apr [1843]	Mary Emily GEER	[aged] 19
10 [Apr 1843]	Luther FORD (Jun?)	[aged] 81.(57)
28 May [1843]	Col. Simon HOUSE	[aged] 74
6 Jun [1843]	Reuben SUMNER	[aged] 78
16 [Jun 1843]	Ezekiel HORTON	[aged] 73
5 Jul [1843]	Mrs. Thomas GATES	[aged] 68
29 [Jul 1843]	Joseph MANN	[aged] 83
12 Sep [1843]	Mrs. Job WRISLEY	[aged] 60
24 [Sep 1843]	Julia A. SAUNDERS	[aged] 18
12 Oct [1843]	Sarah HILLS	[aged] 18

[page 36]

15 Nov 1843	Mrs. Henry GILLET	aged 28
20 [Nov 1843]	Leveret WRIGHT	[aged] 18
6 Dec [1843]	Ezekiel BROWN	[aged] 82
19 Apr [1843]	Joseph P. PETERS & Elizabeth SCAIF. br^t from N.Y. buried in Ch. yd.	
8 Dec [1843]	Elizabeth, wife of J. GRAVES	[aged] 55
Feb 10 1844	Amos PHELPS	[aged] 81
16 [Feb 1844]	David CURTIS	[aged] 79
21 Apr [1844]	John PORTER	[aged] 52
13 May [1844]	Mrs. Chester NORTON (Elizabeth A KINGSLEY)	[aged] 25
24 Jun [1844]	Mary DEANE	[aged] 89
25 [Jun 1844]	Austin TUTTLE	[aged] 66
20 Nov. [1844]	Susan C. (PHELPS) BACKUS	[aged] 37
11 Dec [1844]	Adaline POST	[aged] 22

[Necrology, cont.] 1825–1855

7 Jul [1844]	John HUTCHINSON	[aged] 85
4 Aug [1844]	Jabez L. WHITE. M.D.	[aged] 50
5 [Aug 1844]	Bridget LAMB	[aged] 61
16 Sep [1844]	Salmon HORTON	[aged] 36
21 Oct [1844]	Jonathan PAGE	[aged] 73
7 Dec [1844]	Amasa BROWN	[aged 22]
21 [Dec 1844]	Widow Eleazar COLMAN	[aged] 76
22 Feb 1845	Sarah PERRY [of] Manchester	[aged] 27
28 Mar [1845]	Jerusha, relict of J.H. WELLES	[aged] 84
12 May [1845]	Mrs. James BROWN (Deborah TARBOX)	[aged] 84
14 June [1845]	Isaac CRAIN	[aged] 70

[page 37]

22 Aug 1845	Mary P. HORTON (dau of Wm HORTON)	aged 10
4 Sep [1845]	Laura T. HORTON (dau of Wm HORTON)	[aged] 8
8 [Sep 1845]	Amanda FORD	[aged] 20
8 [Sep 1845]	Hiram HORTON	[aged] 86
21 [Sep 1845]	George RATHBUN son of Anthony RATHBUN	[aged] 22
3 Nov [1845]	Chancey ROOT	[aged] 50
19 [Nov 1845]	Mrs. Anson GILLET	[aged] 76
20 [Nov 1845]	Mrs. Col' Samuel GILBERT.(Deborah)	[aged] 92
27 Dec [1845]	Amasa BROWN 2nd	[aged] 48
2 Jan 1846	Hon. Sylvester GILBERT	[aged] 90
20 Mar [1846]	Jeremiah BROWN 2nd	[aged] 41
27 [Mar 1846]	Sarah Theresa GILBERT	[aged] 19
14 Apr [1846]	Thalia (OWEN) HAYDEN NORTON Wid. J. Francis NORTON	[aged] 82 (81)
[14 Apr 1846]	Avery TENANT	[aged] 34
16 [Apr 1846]	Laura NORTHUM	[aged] 40
18 [Apr 1846]	Elisha KELLOGG. Glastonbury	[aged] 74
26 [Apr 1846]	John CHAPPEL	[aged] 81
12 Jun [1846]	Mrs. Daniel PHELPS	[aged] 74

[Necrology, cont.] 1825–1855

5 Jul [1846]	John S. CARVER. son of Joseph CARVER. N.Y.	[aged] 29
12 [Jul 1846]	Joel FOOT, Esq.	[aged] 83
21 [Jul 1846]	Mrs. Nancy, wife of Timothy JONES	[aged] 65
14 Aug [1846]	Mrs. David POST (Martha WARNER)	[aged] 85
22 [Aug 1846]	Joseph ISHAM	[aged] 83
4 Sep [1846]	Mrs. Ulrica Elenora, wife of John SWAN	[aged] 50
7 Sep 1846	George L. GILBERT	aged 26
8 [Sep 1846]	Roger PHELPS	[aged] 84
4 Oct [1846]	Mrs. Elizabeth, wife of Abner HENDEE	[aged] 49
5 [Oct 1846]	Andrew MANN Esq.	[aged] 91
23 [Oct 1846]	John ROOT	[aged] 26
14 Apr 1847	David T. CARVER	[aged] 64
14 Jun [1847]	Mrs. Nelson LOOMIS	[aged] 34
11 Aug [1847]	Mrs. Mary E, wife of Hiram BROWN	[aged] 39
6 Sep [1847]	Samuel ROGERS	[aged] 54
29 Oct [1847]	Mrs. WILCOX	[aged] 93
3/6 Nov [1847]	Mrs. Mary A, wife of William NORTON	[aged] 45 (54)
13 [Nov 1847]	Joseph CULVER	[aged] 79
16 [Nov 1847]	Mrs. Champion GILBERT (Louisa)(ALVORD)	[aged] 30.(38)
13 Jan [1847]	Samuel SIMONDS, M.D. (Bridgeport)	[aged] 55
[1847]	Samuel BLISS	[aged] 70
[1847]	Mrs. Dan JONES	[aged] 60
18 Jan 1848	David GILBERT [3 illeg. words below]	[aged] 49
5 Mar [1848]	Mrs. Mary SUTTON	[aged] 82
[5 Mar 1848]	Widow FREEMAN	[aged] 84
15 Apr [1848]	John Flavel NORTON. son of W^m & Betsey H. NORTON	[aged] 22
29 [Apr 1848]	Widow Sarah ROOT	[aged] 60
17 Jul [1848]	Oliver PHELPS	[aged] 70.(67)
23 [Jul 1848]	Widow CHAPMAN (Prudence)	[aged] 72
31 Aug [1848]	Abigail MERRILL	[aged] 85
1 Sep [1848]	Lucius JONES	[aged] 29
22 [Sep 1848]	Hiram H. MARTINDALE	[aged] 43

[Necrology, cont.] 1825–1855

2 May [1848]	Josiah ROGERS	[aged] 71
18 [May 1848]	Widow Anna LOOMER	[aged] 65
26 [May 1848]	Ezekiel PHELPS	[aged] 76

[page 39]

12 Jun 1847	Thomas WEBSTER	[aged] 83
22 [Jun 1847]	Benjamin FREEMAN	[aged] 68
1 Dec [1847]	William B. GRAVES	[aged] 33
14 Jan 1849	Bishop CURTIS	[aged] 68
15 [Jan 1849]	Adaline GILLETT (Dau David GILLETT)	[aged] 16
19 [Jan 1849]	Daniel WAY 2nd (Gilead)	[aged] 35
1 Feb [1849]	Phineas B. POST	[aged] 37
15 [Feb 1849]	(Mrs. Lydia) Clarissa VIBBARDS (Manchester) [aged] 26. dau of Shipman HORTON	
22 [Feb 1849]	Mrs. Abel BISSEL	[aged] 82
10 Mar [1849]	Mrs. Joseph WHITE	[aged] 94
16 [Mar 1849]	George BUTTON	[aged] 36
27 Apr [1849]	Mrs. Sally WARD, widow of Lewis GILBERT	[aged] 54
14 May [1849]	John C. PHELPS	[aged] 24
19 Jun [1849]	Mrs. Abby A. Widow of Erastus RANDAL	[aged] 23
7 Sep [1849]	Nancy BLISS (Gilead)	[aged] 66
24 [Sep 1849]	Maria BISSEL	[aged] 44
26 Dec [1849]	Mrs. Laura, wife of Elihu WRIGHT	[aged] 58
27 Jan 1850	Mrs. COUZENS	[aged] 87
3 Feb [1850]	[Mrs.] GAY	[aged] 89

[page 40]

5 Apr 1850	Spencer RATHBUN	
13 Jul [1850]	Mrs. Jude PORTER	
15 [Jul 1850]	Mrs. Charles DRINKWATER, Melora (CANDALL)	
17 Aug [1850]	Mrs. Lucinda, wife of Henry TOWNSEND	
26 [Aug 1850]	Mrs. Erastus PHELPS (N. Haven)	
28 Aug [1850]	Mrs. William HARRIS	
23 Oct [1850]	Samuel GILBERT	
14 Nov [1850]	Mrs. Benj. FREEMAN	
26 [Nov 1850]	Mrs. Samuel GILBERT	
30? Nov [1850]	Ozias PHELPS	
20 Dec [1850]	Mary A. BISSEL	
1 Jul [1851]	Alfred B. POST	[aged] 38
[1 Jul 1851]	Mrs. William COOK	[aged] 43

[[Necrology, cont.] 1825–1855

12 Feb 1851	Mrs. WHITTLESEY.	aged 50
13 [Feb 1851]	Jedediah JONES	[aged] 91
11 Mar [1851]	Mrs. Emeline M. BRAGG. (Colchester)	[aged] 21
23 [Mar 1851]	Joseph Waldo WHITE.	[aged] 37
21 Apr [1851]	Israel Augustus BISSEL.	[aged] 48
30 [Jul 1851]	John H.W. WAY, Son of John M. WAY	[aged] 12
13 Aug [1851]	Thomas BROWN.	[aged] 68
19 [Aug 1851]	Miss. Rebecca TAYLOR.	[aged] 89
[1851]	Mrs. Elizabeth Sarah F. GILLET (dau of Thomas BROWN	[aged] 34
[1851]	dau of Thomas BROWN	[aged] 20
26 [Aug 1851]	Julius NICHOLS	[aged] 20
10 Oct [1851]	Miss. Mary BUEL.	[aged] 68

[page 41]

29 Oct 1851	Miss. Lucy PALMER	aged 50
1 Dec [1851]	Miss. Dolly PHELPS	[aged] 69
29 [Dec 1851]	Ruel BROWN	[aged] 67
24 Sep [1851]	Amos POST (Hartford)	[aged] 24
20 May [1851]	Daniel McEntire PETERS	[aged] 34
28 Mar [1851]	Samuel F. JARVIS D.D.L.L.D. (Middⁿ)	[aged] 76
15 Jun 1852	Mrs. William WHITE	[aged] 71
22 [Jun 1852]	Mrs. Henry BANNING	[aged] 36
11 Feb [1852]	Mrs. Arethusa, widow of Dr. ARNOLD	[aged] 89
1 Mar [1852]	Joseph T. BURNHAM	[aged] 79
9 Jun [1852]	Miss. FREEMAN	[aged] 22
8 Jul [1852]	Abner HENDEE	[aged] 73
20 [Jul 1852]	Mrs. Nathan P. COATS	[aged] 62
28 Sep [1852]	William RAMSDALE	[aged] 55
9 Oct [1852]	Mrs. Philena WARNER	[aged] 83
13 [Oct 1852]	Mrs. Joshua ROOT, Junr	[aged] 60
1 Nov [1852]	Daniel PHELPS	[aged] 94
5 Dec [1852]	Mrs. Adoniram BISSELL	[aged] 75
[5 Dec 1852]	Miss. Polly WHITE	[aged] 78
19 [Dec 1852]	Miss Mary Ann BLISS	[aged] __

[Necrology, cont.] 1825-1855

3 Feb 1853	Miss. Maria K. BUEL	[aged] 19
5 [Feb 1853]	George GILLET	[aged] 84
9 [Feb 1853]	Mrs. Neziah BROWN (Clarissa)	[aged] 71
12 [Feb 1853]	Dwight BLISS	[aged] 38

[page 42]

30 Mar 1853	Mrs. WILKA, relict of the Parson	aged 46
3 Apr [1853]	Mrs. Pierce JOHNSON	[aged] 40
5 [Apr 1853]	Joel JOHNSON	[aged] 66
7 [Apr 1853]	William J. ANIBAL	[aged] 37
6 May [1853]	Mrs. Sarah Electa, wife of Henry O. CARVER	
		[aged] 40
3 Jun [1853]	Harry HILLS	[aged] 56
26 [Jun 1853]	Mrs. Ephriam WILCOX.	[aged] 71
16 Jul [1853]	Rhoda SMITH (colored)	[aged] 85
19 Aug [1853]	Mrs. Caroline CONE, widow of Jonathan PETERS	
		[aged] 85
21 [Aug 1853]	Bela POST	[aged] 74
1 Sep [1853]	Uzziel PHELPS	[aged] 78
26 [Sep 1853]	Chauncey STRONG	[aged] 32
7 Oct [1853]	Mary BEACH, dau of Geo. BEACH	[aged] 20
27 [Oct 1853]	George R. BEACH	[aged] 54.
13 Nov [1853]	Mrs. Lavina, wife of Ira BISSEL	[aged] 66
11 Feb [1853]	Mrs. Josiah MACK (Mary)	[aged] 91
2 Jan [1854]	Mary Ann, relict of F. BLISS	[aged] 46
15 Jan 1854	Solomon ROOT	[aged] 58
9 Mar [1854]	Caleb HUBBARD	[aged] 48
17 [Mar 1854]	Dea. Elijah BEACH	[aged] 78
19 [Mar 1854]	Patty PHELPS	[aged] 60
20 [Mar 1854]	Lewd BARBER (colored)	[aged] 73
27 [Mar 1854]	Mrs. Edwin STRONG (Sarah) (colored)	[aged] 46
[27 Mar 1854]	Susan CARR, C. MORGAN's dau^r	[aged] 24

[page 43]

28 May 1854	Miss. Almira, dau of David JOHNSON.	aged 24
3 Jun [1854]	Oscar BARBER (colored)	[aged] 24
5 Jul [1854]	Abigail A.C. GRAVES	[aged] 8
25 [Jul 1854]	Mrs. STAPLES	[aged] 70
27 Jun [1854]	Mrs. Nathan SMITH	[aged] 61

HEBRON DEATHS (cont): 1853-1860

[forty-third page]

Mrs. BLISS, Widow of Flavel BLISS & Daug of Judah PORTER Esq[r.]	2 Jan 1853, Æ 46
Miss Laury BUELL, dau of Mr. Elihu R. BISSELL	3 Feby 1853, Æ 19
George GILLETT Esq.	5 Feb 1853, Æ 42
Mrs. Clarissa BROWN, w of Neziah BROWN, Æ 71	9 Feb [1853]
Mrs. MACK, widw of Mr. Josiah MACK, Æ 91	11 [Feb 1853]
Mr. Dwight BLISS, Æ 34	8 Feb [1853]
Mrs. JOHNSON, w of Pierce JOHNSON	2 Apr [1853]
Mr. Joel JOHNSON, Æ 66	
Mr. William ANIBAL, Æ 34	8 [Apr 1853]
Mrs. WILLCOX, wife of Capt Ep[m] WILLCOX	
MRS. BISSELL, wife of Adam BISSELL	
Mrs. BISSELL, wife of Ira BISSELL	
Deacon Elijah BEACH	
Mr. Caleb HUBBARD	__ Feb 1854
Mrs. Caroline PETERS, w of Jo[n] PETERS	
Mr. Bela POST	
Leude, coloured	
Miss Patty PHELPS	
Mrs. SMITH, wife of Dea[n] SMITH	1854

[forty-fourth page]

Mrs. STRONG, w of Edwin STRONG	1854
Mrs. HALLYE, wife of Elijah HALLYE	
Mrs. ____ STRONG	
Miss Caroline GRAVES, dau of Wm B. GRAVES	
Joseph CARVER Esq.	1854
Mrs. WILLCOX, w of Joel WILLCOX	1854

[Necrology, cont.] 1825-1855

31 [Jun? 1854]	Mrs. Elisha HODGE (Mary L.)	[aged] 41
1 Aug [1854]	Miss Louisa NORTON.	[aged] 49
7 [Aug 1854]	Mary A. WHITE.	[aged] 17
9 Nov [1854]	Mrs. Joel WILCOX (Lucy)	[aged] 37
4 [Nov 1854]	Miss. Jane SCAIF, dau of J. P. PETERS	[aged] 16
[1854]	Joseph CARVER Esq.	[aged] 71
[1854]	Hon. Samuel A. PETERS	[aged] 85
10 Jan 1855	Mrs. Harriet, widow of Trumbull BURNHAM	[aged] 37
2 Feb [1855]	Eleazar POST	[aged] 77
14 [Feb 1855]	Dr. Dan ARNOLD	[aged] 87
5 Mar [1855]	Mrs. Benjamin PHELPS	[aged] 84
19 [Mar 1855]	Elisha LORD	[aged] 55
23 [Mar 1855]	Sally MACK	[aged] 83
7 May [1855]	Samuel BROWN	[aged] 58
1 Jun [1855]	Jabez L. BACKUS	[aged] 78
5 Jul [1855]	Adoniram BISSEL	[aged] 80
10 [Jul 1855]	Cyrus STRONG (son of Geo.)	[aged] 29
12 Aug [1855]	Elihu WRIGHT	[aged] 79
24 [Aug 1855]	Mrs. James WHITE	[aged] 37

[page 44]

5 Oct 1855	Mary L. PORTER (dau. of David PORTER)	[aged] 21
15 Jul [1855]	Aaron BROWN	[aged] 28
18 Jan 1856	Abigail POST	[aged] 71
26 [Jan 1856]	Hazael GOTT	[aged] 89
19 Feb [1856]	William BROWN	[aged] 76
26 [Feb 1856]	Edmond Cyrus MANN, MAN. Cyrus Edwin	[aged] 7
5 Mar [1856]	Davis NORTON	[aged] 73
14 Apr {1856]	Orrin RATHBUN	[aged] 24
5 May [1856]	Samuel TIFT	[aged] 27
13 Jun [1856]	William Alfred POST	[aged] 45
18 [Jun 1856]	Benjamin S. BLISS	[aged] 53
26 [Jun 1856]	Neziah BROWN	[aged] 74
15 Jul [1856]	Henry WHITE	[aged] 28
15 Aug [1855]	Sally, Widow Hiram BARBER	[aged] 82
23 [Aug 1855]	James M. STANTON	

HEBRON DEATHS (cont): 1853-1860

Miss Lucy A. BROWN., dau of Thomas BROWN
Capt Ezekiel A POST
Miss Jane PETERS, d of Doct Joseph PETERS, d in New York
Mr. Ebenezer POST	3 Feb 1855
Dr Dan ARNOLD	14 Feb [1855], Æ 44
Mrs. PHELPS, w of Capt Benj PHELPS, Æ 44	10 Mar [1855]
Mr. Elisha LORD	19 Mar 1855, Æ 56
Miss Sally MACK, Æ --	25 [Mar 1855]
Mrs. HILLS, w of Mr. Jared HILLS, Æ 79	27 [Mar 1855]
Mr. Jared HILLS	30 June 1855
Daughter of Champin GILBERT	__ May [1855]
Miss PORTER, d of David PORTER	__ Oct [1855]
John PETONS wife color	__ Nov [1855]
Mrs. Lucy WELLES, w of F.B. WELLES brought from the State of New York	__ Sep [1856?]
Miss Abigail POST, Æ 72	17 Jan 1856

[forty-fifth page]

Mrs. Sally HORTON, w of Shipman HORTON	14 Jany 1856
Mr. ____ HOWARD, Æ 44	20 [Jany 1856]
Mr. Hazel GOTT, Æ 70	26 [Jan 1856]
William BROWN, Esq., Æ 70	1 Feb^y [1856]
Mrs. Aseneth HOLDRIDGE, w of Robert HOLERIDGE, Æ 49	3 Apr [1856]
Mrs. Deborah GILBERT, w of Col. Samuel GILBERT, Æ 43	20 Nov 1845.

Miss Abby Mosier GILBERT, dau of Peyton R. GILBERT, 7 Apr 1832, Æ 17
Miss Susan Theresa GILBERT, dau of Peyton GILBERT, 26 Mar 1846, Æ 20
Orin RATHBONE, Æ 24	4 Apr 1856

Cyrus MANNs boy, son of the last days of Feb
Miss Elizabeth Jr. POST, dau of Charles POST, Æ 23	25 Feb 1860
Miss Mary F WARLAND, dau of the Rev William WARLAND, Æ 16,	25 Feb [1860]
Eleazer B. STRONG, Æ 83	7 Mar [1860]
Samuel SKINNER, Æ 76	12 Mar [1860]

[forty-sixth page]

Diodate POST, Æ 74	11 Apr 1860
Gen. Andrew WELLS, Æ 77 and 3 days	May 3 1860
Idad WAY Æ 15 years	May 17 1860
Mrs Didate POST hung herself, Æ [sic]	July 4 1860

Mrs Clarinda HORTON wife of Mr H HORTON and daughter of the
    late Gen Andrew WELLS Æ 43 years 7 months 26 days   Oct 29 1860

Section C

GILEAD CHURCH RECORDS

BIRTHS

[page 48]

The Baptisms AD 1752

Baptized by Elijah Lothrop Pastor
Copied from Gilead Church Records.

5 Apr 1752

Margit	Daughter of John PETERS
Elisabeth	Daughter of Joseph WELLS
Abigail	Daughter of Capt. Samuel GILBERT, Jun.
Elijah	Son of Isaac DUNHAM
Solomon	Son of Daniel INGRAHAM
Hannah	Daughter of David NOBLE
John	Son of Thomas BUCK, Jun.
Mary	Daughter of Increase PORTER
Ephriam	Son of Thomas PERRIN, Jun.
Sibil	Daughter of Ebenezer BUCK
Azubah	Daughter of Ichabod PHELPS
Jeremiah	Son of Jude WRIGHT
Sibil	Daughter of Josiah MACK, Jun.
Richard	Son of Richard BAXTER
Deborah	Daughter of Obadiah CULVER
Josiah	Son of Josiah KILBURN
Asahel	Son of Jacob ROOT, Jr.
Eli	Son of Eliphalet YOUNGS

25 Nov 1752

David	Son of Jedediah POST, by Mr. POMEROY
Ester	Daughter of Caleb CHAPPEL
Samuel	Son of Zerubebel ROLLO
John	Son of Obadiah WILCOX

[page 49]

Hannah	Daughter of Joseph WELLS, by Mr. POMEROY
David	Son of Samuel BILL
David	Son of Elisha MACK

1 Apr 1753

Sarah	Born 23 Mar 1753, Daughter of John ELLIS, by Mr. POMEROY
Jonathan	Son of Seth HALL
Joseph	Son of Roger DEWEY

Joshua	Son of Daniel ROOT Jr.
Abigail	Daughter of Daniel POLLY
Patience	Daughter of John ROLLO
Sarah	Daughter of Samuel LUKUS
Simeon	Son of Dea. Ebenezer DEWEY
Hannah	Daughter of John FORD
Hannah	Daughter of Obadiah DUNHAM
Martha	Daughter of John ROW
Zilpah	Daughter of Jonathan HUTCHINSON, b. 17 Sep 1753; d. 11 May 1759
Ruth	Daughter of David NOBLE, Jr.
Susanna	Daughter of Nicholas BOND
Lois	Daughter of Elisha MACK
Daniel	Son of Thomas BUCK
John	Son of John TALLCOTT
Absalom	Son of John PETERS

[page 50]

1 Apr 1754

Samuel	Son of John BLISS
Lucy	Daughter of Obadiah WILCOX
Calvin	Son of Isaac DUNHAM
Abigail	Daughter of Richard BAXTER
Lydia	Daughter of Abner WARTERS
Nathan	Son of Obadiah CULVER
Rosehannah	Daughter of Ebenezer GILBERT
Bathsheba	Daughter of Nathaniel PHELPS
Mary	Daughter of Josiah MACK
Erastus	Son of Daniel INGHAM
Margery	Daughter of Joseph WELLS
Mary	Daughter of Elijah LOTHROP Pastor
Sarah	Daughter of Eliphalet YOUNGS
Esther	Daughter of Obadiah DUNHAM
Stephen	Son of Stephen BOND
Anna	Daughter of Ichabod PHELP[S]s
Elisabeth,	Daughter of Jonathan HUTCHINSON (b. 8 Mar 1725)
John	Son of David NOBLE
Daniel	Son of Edmund WELLS.

1 Apr 1755

Timothy	Son of Dea Ebenezer DEWEY
Abagail	Daughter of Zerubebel ROLLO
David	Son of David NOBLE, Junr.

[page 51]

Sibil	Daughter of Jedediah POST (born 5 May 1755)

Hannah	Daughter of Reuben SUMNER
Maana	Daughter of John ROW
Phebe	Daughter of John FORD
Ezekiel	Son of Jude WRIGHT.
Rachel	Daughter of Samuel BILL
Lydia	Daughter of Roger DEWEY
John	Son of Thomas PERRIN
Walter	Son of John ROLLO
Hannah	Daughter of Daniel POLLY, by Mr. POMEROY.
Sibil	Daughter of Samuel LUKUS
Eunice	Daughter of Thomas BUCK
Molly	Daughter of Jabish ELLIS
Lucy	Daughter of John TALLCOTT
Sylvester	Son of Samuel GILBERT Esqr (b. 26 Oct 1755)
Experience	Daughter of Josiah MACK Jr.
James	Son of James CALKINS
Hannah	Daughter of Elijah LOTHROP, Pastor
Elliner	Daughter of William SHEPARD
Barzellial	Son of Obadiah CULVER
Andrew	Son of John PETERS
Miriam	Daughter of Abner WATERS. By Mr. POMEROY

[page 52]

1 Apr 1756

Naomi	Daughter of Daniel ROOT Jr.
John	Son of John ROOT
Eliezer	Son of Nathaniel PHELPS
Ebenezer	Son of Ebenezer HALL
Hannah	Daughter of Elisha DUNK
Lucy	Daughter of Jacob ROOT, by Mr. POMEROY
Asa	Son of Obadiah WILCOX
John	Son of Richard BAXTER
	Samuel ELLIS Baptised.
	Zilpah the wife of Samuel ELLIS Baptized.
Rebekah	Daughter of Samuel & Zilpah ELLIS
Timothy	Son of Leonard HILL
Anna	Daughter of Nicholas BOND
Abagail	Daughter of Elisha MACK, by Mr. POMEROY.
Anna	Daughter of Obadiah DUNHAM
Eunice	Daughter of Thomas BUCK Jr.
Timothy	Son of Joseph WELLS
Elisabeth	Daughter of Thomas PERRIN
Job	Son of Jonathan HUTCHINSON (b. 20 Mar 1757)
Elisabeth	Daughter of Reuben SUMNER

Sawyer	Son of Jabesh ELLIS.

[page 53]

1 Apr 1757

Huldah	Daughter of Josiah MACK Jr.
Sarah	Daughter of Edmund WELLS
Silence	Daughter of Elijah LOTHROP Pastor
Israel	Son of John SKINNER
Hannah	Daughter of Eldad POST (b. Dec. 13 1756)
Jephthan	Negro Boy of John PETERS
Josiah	Son of Josiah BUSHNEL, by Mr. LORD
Isaiah	Son of John FORD
Hannah	Daughter of John ROLLO, by Mr. POMEROY
Patience	Daughter of Samuel BILL
Sarah	Daughter of Richard BAXTER
Mary	Daughter of John TALCOTT
Ann	Daughter of Daniel POLLY
Samuel	Son of Daniel INGRAHAM
Ezekiel	Son of Gad MERRILS
Israel	Son of William SHEPHERD
Mary)	Twins, Children of John PETERS
Samuel)	
Rhoda	Daughter of James CALKINS
Ezekiel	Son of Jedediah POST (b. 5 Jan 1756; d. 20 Mar 1759)
Samuel Rollo	Son of Roger DEWEY
Melisent	Daughter of Obadiah CULVER
Submit	Daughter of Isaac DUNHAM
Sarah	Daughter of Obadiah WILCOX

[page 54]

John	Son of John STEEL
Theodosia	Daughter of Eliphalet YOUNGS
Huldah	Daughter of James PRAT

1 Apr 1758

Josiah	Son of Josiah MACK Junr.
David	Son of Stephen BOND
Gardiner	Son of Capt. Samuel GILBERT
Abner	Son of Abner WARTERS
Mercy	Daughter of Samuel ELLIS
Hannah	Daughter of Timothy BUELL
Deborah	Daughter of Timothy BUELL
John	Son of Jonathan HUTCHINSON (b. 18 Jan 1759)
Susanna	Daughter of Oleander MACK
Eldad	Son of Eldad POST (b. 20 Dec 1758)

[page 55]

Frederic	Son of John FORD

Rose	Daughter of Jabesh ELLIS
Semerimis	Daughter of Joseph WELLS
Deborah	Daughter of Capt. Ichabod PHELPS

1 Apr 1759

John	Son of Peter POST (b. Mar 28,1758)
Joshua	Son of Oliver BOOTH
Daniel	Son of John TALCOTT
James	Son of James COOX
Enoch	Son of Thomas BUCK
Hannah	Daughter of Elijah LOTHROP, Pastor
Lydia	Daughter of Reuben SUMNER
Tryphena	Daughter of Eliphalet YOUNGS
Elisha	Son of Elisha MACK
Austin	Son of Edmund WELLS
Ebenezer	Son of Azariah BROWN
Ezekiel	Son of Daniel ROOT
Henry	Son of Josiah MACK
Mary	Daughter of William SHEPHERD
Delight	Daughter of Asher MERRILS

[page 56]

Judith	Daughter of John ROLLO, by Mr. NOBLE
James	Son of James PRAT, by Mr. NOBLE
Rachel	Daughter of Samuel BILL
Andrew	Son of John PETERS
Elisabeth	Daughter of Obadiah CULVER
Elisabeth	Daughter of Stephen BOND
Elisabeth	Daughter of Samuel ELLIS
Martha	Daughter of Amos HALL
David	Son of David CULVER
Content	Daughter of Isaac DUNHAM

1 Apr 1760

Twins, Elisabeth and Anna Daughters of Mr. Clament SUMNER

William	Son of Nicholas BOND
Daniel	Son of Daniel POLLY
Rebekah	Daughter of David NOBLE Jun
Mary	Daughter of Peter POST (b. 2 May 1760)
Ralph	Son of John MACK
Rachel	Daughter of Nathaniel PHELPS
Dorothy	Daughter of Jedediah POST (b. 2 Aug 1760)
Elisha	Son of Elisha DUNK
Ambrose	Son of Jonathan BOOTH

[page 57]

Betty	Daughter of Thomas PERRIN

Zerabbabel John Rollo,	Son of Abraham FOX
Aaron	Son of Josiah MACK
Anna	Daughter of the Widow TALCOTT
John	Son of John SKINNER
Phebe	Daughter of John POST (b. 8 Jan 1761)
Phebe	Daughter of John FORD
John	Son of David CULVER
Anna	Daughter of Elijah LOTHROP Pastor

1 Apr 1761

Mary	Daughter of Benjamin SUMNER
Prudence	Daughter of Benjamin SUMNER
Lydia	Daughter of Jabez ELLIS
Olive	Daughter of Abner WATERS
Shaler	Son of Joseph WELLS
Asher	Son of Asher WELLS
Molly	Daughter of Elisha MACK
Katherine	Daughter of Alexander INGHAM
James	Son of James COX
	Sarah SHIPMAN an Adult
Temperance	Daughter of Ebenezer DEWEY
Olive	Daughter of Jesse STRONG
Hosea	Son of Gad MERELLS

[page 58]

Martha	Daughter of Doc[r] Samuel SHIPMAN
Thomas	Son of Thomas WEBSTER
Ellis	Son of Ellis BLISS (b. 5 Apr 1759)
John	Son of Ellis BLISS (b. 7 Apr 1761)
Abagail	Daughter of Jonathan HUTCHINSON (b. 21 Aug 1761)
Bildad	Son of Thomas DAVIS
Huldah	Daughter of Alexander INGHAM
Joseph Phelps	Son of John PETERS
Martha	Daughter of Obadiah WILCOX
Joel	Son of Oleander MACK
William	Son of R[e]uben SUMNER
Elisebeth	Daughter of Jazaniah POST
Katherine	Daughter of John POST (b. 22 Dec 1761. d. 25 Jan 1762)
Sarah	Daughter of Noah PHELPS
Huldah	Daughter of John ELLIS
Mary	Daughter of Obadiah CULVER
David	Son of Jonathan ADAMS
Daniel	Son of Ichabod PHELPS
Jesse	Son of Betty BRIANT

Simeon Marten Son of Elizabeth BETTIS
1 Apr 1762
Dinah	Daughter of Peter POST (b. 6 Apr 1762)
Benjamin	Son of Daniel ROOT

[page 59]

Luther	Son of John FORD
Joseph	Son of Stephen BOND
Benjamin	Son of Joshua TILLOTSON
Armindwell	Daughter of James COX
Mary	Daughter of Medad THORNTON
Abagail	Daughter of Elijah LOTHROP Pastor
Ebenezer	Son of Ebenezer DEWEY
Eunice	Daughter of John MACK
Zurviah	Daughter of Ebenezer BUCK
Hannah	Daughter of Daniel POLLY
Sarah	Daughter of John MERRELLS
Daniel	Son of Thomas DAVIS. By Mr. DUNNING.
John	Son of James NOBLE
Theodosia	Daughter of Eliphalet YOUNGS
Wm Benjamin	Son of Benjamin SUMNER
Samuel	Son of Samuel BILL
Amos	Son of Amos HALL
R[e]uben	Son of Asher MERRELLS
Lydia	Daughter of Gad MERRELLS

1 Apr 1763
Charlotte	Daughter of Thomas PERRIN
Micaiah	Son of Daniel INGHAM
Ruhamah	Daughter of Jabez ELLIS

[page 60]

Israel	Son of Eldad POST (b. 14 Nov 1762)
Roxsalona	Daughter of Nathaniel PHELPS
John	Son of John POST (b. 17 Jan 1762)
Tarza	Daughter of Elexander INGHAM
Hannah	Daughter of Asaph TRUMBULL
Henry	Son of Joseph WELLS
Jeremiah	Son of David CULVER
Hannah	Daughter of Jonathan ADAMS
Warin	Son of Elisha MACK
Salmon	Son of John SKINNER
Persis	Daughter of Thomas BUCK
Mary	Daughter of Joshua TILLOTSON
Daniel	Son of Jonathan HUTCHINSON (b. 26 Sept 1763)
Benjamin	Son of Abner WATERS, by Mr. DUNNING

53

Enos	Son of David NOBLE
Mary	Daughter of Asaph TRUMBULL
John	Son of John ELLIS
Phebe	Daughter of Obadiah WILCOX
Elisabeth	Daughter of Elijah LOTHROP Pastor
William	Son of John PETERS
Melisent	Daughter of Obadiah CULVER
Hannah	Daughter of John MERRILS
Elisha Yeamans, Son of Stephen BOND	

[page 61]

1 Apr 1764

Lydia	Daughter of Gideon POST (b.3 Oct 1763)
Susanna	Daughter of Abel WILCOX
R[e]uben	Son of R[e]uben SUMNER
Allin	Son of Thomas DAVIS
David Hubard	Son of Benjamin SUMNER
Esther	Daughter of Gad MERRILS
Mindwell,	Daughter of Peter POST (b. 15 Jun 1764; d. 3 May 1775)
Deborah	Daughter of Ichabod PHELPS
Melisena	Daughter of James COX
David	Son of James PRAT
Eunice	Daughter of Ebenezer SKINNER
Silve	Daughter of Joel. Negro Servant of Capt. WELLS
Elijah	Son of John POST (b. 14 Nov 1764)
Lydia	Daughter of Samuel GILBERT (b. 27 Sept 1764)
Delight	Daughter of Asher MERRILS
Apollos	Son of Ebenezer DEWEY
Jabez	Son of Jabez ELLIS, by Mr. POMEROY
Susanna	Daughter of John FORD
Henry	Son of David CULVER
Isaac	Son of Simeon DUNHAM
George	Son of Amos HALL
Alexander	Son of Alexander BINGHAM
John Fish	Son of John MACK

[page 62]

1 Apr 1765

Anna	Daughter of Thomas GILBERT
Jane	Daughter of Thomas BUCK
Lucinda	Daughter of Nathaniel PHELPS
Timothy	Son of John SKINNER
Jeremiah	Son of Thomas PERRIN
Mehitable	Daughter of Daniel INGHAM

Mindwell	Daughter of Elisha MACK
Anna	Daughter of Joseph WELLS
John	Son of John MERRILS
Deborah	Daughter of Elijah WEBSTER
Zilpah	Daughter of Asaph TRUMBULL
Rachel	Daughter of Jazaniah POST
Peleg	Son of Jonah PHELPS
Thomas	Son of Daniel POLLEY
Daniel	Son of Eldad POST (b.Nov.18, 1765)
Martha	Daughter of Eliphalet YOUNGS
Oliver	Son of Abner WATERS
Obadiah	Son of Obadiah CULVER
Loisa Octavia	Daughter of Elijah LOTHROP
Lydia	Daughter of Jonathan HUTCHINSON (b. 6 Feb 1766)
Lucina	Daughter of Widow Mary MARKS

[page 63]

1 Apr 1766

Sarah	Daughter of Joshua TILLOTSON
Warin	Son of John ELLIS
Mary	Daughter of Levi POST
Mary	Daughter of Thomas DAVIS
Joseph Otis	Son of Peter POST (b. 12 Nov 1766)
Mary	Daughter of Stephen BOND
James	Son of David CULVER
Sibil	Daughter of R[e]uben SUMNER
John Henry	Son of Benjamin SUMNER
Elisabeth	Daughter of Asher MERRILS
Lydia	Daughter of Ichabod PHELPS
Roman	Son of Joel [____] Negro
Abiah	Daughter of Simeon DUNHAM
Amasa	Son of Jonathan ADAMS
Nathaniel	Son of Nathaniel DAVIS
Zerubabel	Son of Nath¹ DAVIS, by Mr. SUMNER
Josiah	Son of Ezekiel SKINNER
Mehitable	Daughter of Elias JAGGER
Thomas	Son of Alexander INGHAM

[page 64]

1 Apr 1767

Sarah	Daughter of Joel POST (b. 21 Dec 1765)
Abigail	Daughter of John MERRIL, by Mr. DUNNING
Nathaniel	Son of Nathaniel PHELPS
Elijah	Son of Elijah WEBSTER
Lucy	Daughter of Joel POST (b. 25 Apr 1767)

Hannah	Daughter of John MACK
Elizur	Son of John SKINNER
Jordan	Son of Jordan POST (b. 6 Mar 1767)
Charles Whiting, Son of Samuel GOODRICH	
Joseph	Son of Joseph WELLS
Sarah	Daughter of Elisha MACK
Mary	Daughter Jabez ELLIS
Prince Briant	Son of Amos HALL
Anna	Daughter of Jonathan & Eleanor HUTCHINSON (b. 17 Aug 1767)
Mary	Daughter of Thomas PERRIN
Sarah	Daughter of Jonah PHELPS
Obedience	Daughter of Simeon DUNHAM
Azubah	Daughter of Asaph TRUMBULL
Elijah Leonard	Son of Elijah LOTHROP
Mary	Daughter of Eliphalet YOUNGS
Anna	Daughter of Peter POST (b. 21 Jan 1768)
Joseph &)	Twins
Benjamin)	Sons of David CULVER

[page 65]

1 Apr 1768

Oliver	Son of Daniel INGHAM
Molly	Daughter of Jazaniah POST
Russel	Son of Eldad POST (b. 12 Nov 1767)
Hannah	Daughter of Obadiah CULVER
Sarah	Daughter of Elias JAGGER
Gad	Son of Gad MERRILS
Elisabeth	Daughter of John ELLIS
Keziah	Daughter of Thomas DAVIS
Sibel	Daughter of Asher MERRIL
Sarah Poplia	Daughter of Capt. John PETERS
Abigail	Daughter of R[e]uben SUMNER
Lucy	Daughter of Ichabod PHELPS
Gamaliel	Son of Alexander INGHAM

1 Apr 1769

Anna	Daughter of Jazaniah POST
Joseph	Son of Jonathan HUTCHINSON
Elisabeth	Daughter of Joshua TILLOTSON
Isaac	Son of Samuel BROWN
Anna	Daughter of Eliphalet YOUNGS
Moses	Son of Thomas PERRIN
Esther	Daughter of Jonah PHELPS
Mary	Daughter of Jonathan HUTCHINSON (b. 18 Oct 1769)

Ormanda	Daughter of Asher MERRILS
William	Son of William TALLCOTT (& Mary CARTER) (b. 16 Dec 1770) [sic]
Elisabeth	Daughter of John SKINNER
Sibil	Daughter of Eldad POST (b. Nov 18, 1769)
Clarissa	Daughter of Joel POST, by Mr. DUNNING.
Lucynana	Daughter of Elijah LOTHROP
Ezekiel	Son of Elijah WEBSTER
Millesent	Daughter of John MACK
Zia CASE an Adult Baptized	

April 1st 1770

Sarah	Daughter of Asaph TRUMBULL
Mary	Daughter of Obadiah CULVER
Betty	Daughter of Amos HALL
Azubah	Daughter of Zia CASE
Jonathan	Son of John ELLIS

[page 67]

Theodora	Daughter of Alexander INGHAM
Abigail	Daughter of Elias JAGGER
Lovinne	Daughter of John THOMAS
Eunice	Daughter of John THOMAS
Henery	Son of John THOMAS
Lois	Daughter of Elisha MACK
Benjamin	Son of Gad TALLCOTT
Joseph Wells	Son of Elisha WADSWORTH
Ezekiel	Son of Jordan POST (b. Feb.4, 1771)
Elisabeth	Daughter of John ROW
Annar	Daughter of Bateman WELLS
Hiram	Baptised on account of Thomas PERRIN
Thomas	Son of Thomas PERRIN Jnr
Andrew	Son of Thomas PERRIN Jnr
William Porter	Son of Thomas PERRIN Jnr
Martha	Daughter of Thomas PERRIN Jnr
Philoathia	Daughter of Eliphalet YOUNGS

1 Apr 1771

Ruby	Daughter of John MERRILS
Patience	Daughter of Simeon DUNHAM
Anna	Daughter of Gad MERRIL
John Bill	Son of John WELLS
Lucy	Daughter of Azariah BROWN

[page 68]

Mary	Daughter of R[e]uben SUMNER

Zia	Son of Zia CASE
Sarah	Daughter of Bateman WELLS
Samuel Augustus, Son of Sam[ll] GILBERT (b. 25 Jun 1771; d. 27 Oct 1774)	
Mary	Daughter of William TALLCOTT (& Mary CARVER) (b. 28 Aug 1771)
Thomas	Son of Alexander INGHAM
Mary	Daughter of Ichabod PHELPS
William	Son of William ROLLO
Azzan	Son of Joseph WELLS
Esther	Daughter of Stephen POST Jun
Edmond Henery, Son of Edmond WELLS	
Esther	Daughter of John SKINNER
Simeon	Son of Asher MERRILS

1 Apr 1772

Jehiel	Son of Jehiel WILCOX
Rachel	Daughter of Solomon ROOT
Florilla	Daughter of Tom, Negro Servant of Mr. GILBERT
Mariann	Daughter of Benjamin SAWYER
David	Son of Asaph TRUMBULL
Benjamin	Son of Peter POST (b. 24 May 1772; d. 7 Jun 1772)
Abagail	Daughter of Gad TALLCOTT
Lydia	Daughter of Elisha MACK
Ira	Son of Zia CASE

[page 69]

Sarah	Daughter of John MACK
Mindwell	Daughter of Joshua TILOTSON
David	Son of Amos HALL
Elias	Son of Elias JAGGER
Joel	Son of Joel POST (b. 16 Sep 1772; d. 1 Sep 1775)
Jerusha	Daughter of Thomas LOVEMAN
Thankful	Daughter of Elisha WADSWORTH
William	Son of Azariah BROWN
Constantia	Daughter of Eliphalet YOUNGS
Mary	Daughter of Timothy STEVENS
Isaac	Son of Jabez ELLIS
Lydia	Daughter of Jehiel WILCOX
John	Son of William ROLLO
Joel	Son of Elijah WEBSTER

1 Apr 1773

George Oliver	Son of Samuel & Lydia POST GILBERT (b. 15 Mar 1772)
Lydia	Daughter of Elisha MACK

Sarah	Daughter of John ELLIS
Ruth	Daughter of Peter POST (b. 16 May 1773)
John	Son of Edward GRANNIS
Henry Peterson,	Son of R[e]uben SUMNER
Howel	Son of John WELLS
Elisabeth	Daughter of Thomas POST (b. 18 May 1773; d. 23 Nov 1774)

[page 70]

Thomas	Son of Capt. Jedediah POST (b. 6 Sep 1773)
Ezra	Son of Ezra CHAPMAN
Thomas	Son of Thomas POST (b. 3 Apr 1763)
Abitha	Daughter of Thomas POST (b. 15 Mar 1765)
Ichabod	Son of Thomas POST (b. 31 Aug. 1768)
Hannah	Daughter of Thomas POST (b. 29 Mar 1771)
Lydia	Daughter of Thomas POST (b. [29 Mar 1771])
Henry	Son of Jordan POST (b. 3 Dec 1773)
Thankful	Daughter of Bateman WELLS
Oliver	Son of John MERRILS
John Talcott	Son of Simeon DUNHAM
Wait	Son of Gad TALCOTT
Anna	Daughter of Thomas PERRIN Jnr
Solomon	Son of Solomon ROOT

1 Apr 1774

Edward	Son of Daniel ROOT Jnr
Ebenezer	Son of John SKINNER
Ezra	Son of William TALLCOTT (& Mary CARTER) (b. 11 May 1774)
Pain	Son of Malachi LOVELAND
Aaron	Son of Israel LOVELAND
Ichabod Trumbull,	Son of Ichabod PHELPS
Mary Molly	Daughter of Ichabod PHELPS
Prudence	Daughter of John MACK

[page 71]

Sarah	Daughter of Asaph TRUMBULL
John Hall	Son of William ROLLO
Daniel	Son of Daniel ROOT
Martha	Daughter of Zia CASE
Sibil	Daughter of Asher MERREL
Laura Dreima	Daughter of Elijah LOTHROP
Prime	Son of Thomas, Negro Servant of Mr. GILBERT.
Jemima)	Twin Daughters of John FORD
Lucy)	
Mary	Daughter of Jehiel WILCOX

Lydia	Daughter of Amos HALL
Eliphalet	Son of Eliphalet YOUNGS
Sarah	Daughter of Mary BOLTON
Mary	Daughter of Mary BOLTON
Esther	Daughter of Joel POST (b. 25 Jan 1774. d. 17 Mar 1786)
Calvin	Son of Calvin HALL

1 Apr 1775

Roxsa	Daughter of Barret PHELPS
Samuel	Son of Thomas POST
William	Son of George LOVELAND
Levi	Son of Asa BROWN
Elihu Chester	Son of Elihu WELLS

[page 72]

Martha	Daughter of David CURTICE
Elisabeth	Daughter of David CURTICE
Elisabeth	Daughter of John NORTON
Thomas	Baptized on account of Lieut GILBERT
Nathaniel) & Peter)	two Negro Boys of Lieut GILBERT
David	Son of the Widow Judith CURTICE

Abigail Elisabeth Martha, Daughter of the Widow Judith CURTICE

John Ephriam Henry, Son of the Widow Judith CURTICE

Abagail	Daughter of Jonathan & Eleanor HUTCHINSON (b. 17 Aug 1775)

Ezekiel Agustus, Son of Capt Jedediah POST (b. 27 Sep 1775)

Grace	Daughter of Gad TALCOTT
Daniel	Son of Daniel CHAPMAN
Henry Howel	Son of John WELLS
Anna	Daughter of John ELLIS
Abigail	Daughter of R[e]uben SUMNER
Ezekiel	Son of Elijah WEBSTER
Ann	Daughter of Solomon PERRIN
Bennet	Son of William TALCOTT (& Mary CARTER) (b. 24 Mar 1776)
Ephriam	Son of Jordan POST (b. 26 Apr 1776)

1 Apr 1776

Mindwell	Daughter of Peter POST (b. 15 Apr 1776)
Phebe	Daughter of Bateman WELLS

[page 73]

John	Son of John HOUSE
Ebenezer	Son of Jehiel WILCOX
Elisabeth	Daughter of Asa BROWN
Abigail	Daughter of John MACK

Apollos	Son of William ROLLO
Elijah	Son of Solomon ROOT
Lucy	Daughter of John FORD
Esther	Daughter of Asher MERREL
Philomelia	Daughter of Asaph TRUMBULL
Anna	Daughter of Amos HALL
Beula	Daughter of Jabez ELLIS
Rachel	Daughter of Zephiniah DAVIS

1 Apr 1777

Jeremiah)	Twin Son of Thomas POST (b. 16 Mar 1777)
Elisabeth) [Twin]	Daughter of Thomas POST [b. 16 Mar 1777]
Aaron Perrin	Son of Elias JAGGER
Mindwell	Daughter of Daniel ROOT
Benjamin	Son of John NORTON
Mary	Daughter of Daniel WELLS
Sam^{el} Agustus	Son of Samuel GILBERT (b. 10 Sep 1777)
Obedience	Daughter of Simeon DUNHAM
Ichabod	Son of Daniel CHAPMAN
Zepheniah	Son of Zepheniah DAVIS

[page 74]

Mary	Daughter of Walter ROLLO
Elisabeth	Daughter of Joshua ROOT
Benjamin	Son of John MERRIL

1 Apr 1778

Mary	Daughter of R[e]uben SUMNER
Elisabeth	Daughter of Jehiel WILCOX
Benjamin Carter,	Son of Bateman WELLS
William Clark	Son of Eliphalet YOUNGS
Aaron)	Twins of Peter POST
Abagail)	
Joel	Son of Joel POST (b. 28 Jul 1778)
Daniel Lothrop	Son of Daniel WELLS
Eleazer	Son of Jonathan & Eleanor HUTCHINSON
Jerusha	Daughter of Solomon PERRIN
Olive	Daughter of Asher MERRIL
Benjamin	Son of Solomon ROOT
Lucy	Daughter of William ROLLO
James	Son of James BROWN
Joel	Son of Elijah WEBSTER
Jonathan	Son of Asaph TRUMBULL
Phebe	Daughter of Ebenezer SKINNER
Waitstil	Son of Ebenezer SKINNER
Mosely	Son of Gad TALLCOTT

[page 75]

Mary	Daughter of Gardiner GILBERT
David	Son of John ELLIS
Elisabeth	Daughter of Samuel GILBERT (b. July 31. 1779)
George Washington, Son of Jordan POST (b. Aug 26" 1779)	
Joel	Son of Zepheniah DAVIS

1 Apr 1779

Samuel	Son of Daniel BROWN
Henry	Son of Adonijah STRONG
Erastus	Son of Erastus INGHAM
Alfred	Son of John WELLS
David	Son of Amos HALL
Jerusha	Daughter of Simeon DUNHAM
Azubah	Daughter of Jehiel WILCOX
Sarah	Daughter of Joshua WEST
Lucy	Daughter of Daniel CHAPMAN
Sarah	Daughter of William TALLCOTT (& Mary CARTER) (b. 28 Mar 1780)
William	Son of James BROWN
John Noble	Son of Walter ROLLO

[page 76]

Zilpah DAVIS, an Adult person Baptized

Isabella	Daughter of Batemen WELLS
Mary	Daughter of Solomon ROOT
Alice	Daughter of Widow Alice MORLEY
Daniel Bishop	Son of Daniel BROWN
Elisabeth	Daughter of Asaph TRUMBULL
Samuel) William)	Twins, Sons of Erastus INGHAM
Mabel	Daughter of Eliphalet YOUNGs
Anna	Daughter of Ichabod PHELPS

1 Apr 1781

David	Son of John NORTHUM
Don Lewis	Son of Elihu WELLS
Solomon	Son of Solomon PERRIN
Ralph Rodolphus, Son of William ROLLO	
Ezra	Son of Jehiel WILCOX
James	Son of John WELLS
Levi	Son of John ELLIS
Abigail	Daughter of Peter POST
Elijah	Son of Simeon DUNHAM
Israel	Son of Zepheniah DAVIS
Clara	Daughter of Elijah WEBSTER

Sarah	Daughter of Samuel GILBERT (b. 28 Nov 1781. d. 17 Aug 1789)

[page 77]

Clarissa	Daughter of Joel POST
Mary	Daughter of Zacheriah PERRIN
Elisabeth	Daughter of Abijah ROWLEY
Edward Sawyer, Son of Sawyer ELLIS	

1 Apr 1782

Destamena	Daughter of Jordan POST
Hannah	Daughter of Gad TALLCOTT
Ezra	Daughter of Amos HALL
Zilpha	Daughter of Joseph HUTCHINSON
Benjamin	Son of Jabez ELLIS
Neziah	Son of James BROWN
Addi	Son of Ebenezer SKINNER
Abigail	Daughter of Russel WELLS
Ellis LUTHER, an Adult Baptized	
Sibil	Daughter of Ellis LUTHER
Anna	Daughter of Gardiner GILBERT
Asher	Son of Asher MERRIL
Benjamin	Son of Solomon ROOT
Luana	Daughter of Bateman WELLS
Oliver	Son of Jehiel WILCOX
Thomas	Son of Daniel BROWN
Mary	Daughter of Elihu WELLS

[page 78]

1 Apr 1783

Betty	Daughter of Zacheriah PERRIN
Oliver	Son of Zepheniah DAVIS
Josiah Champin, Son of Israel HUTCHINSON (b. 26 Mar 1783)	
Mercy	Daughter of William ROLLO
Asaph	Son of Asaph TRUMBULL
Elijah	Son of John ELLIS
Burnham Fitch, Son of Eliphalet YOUNGS	
Abagail	Daughter of Jedediah POST
William	Son of William TALLCOT (& Mary CARTER) (b. 6 Mar 1784)

1 Apr 1784

Jerusha)	
Mary)	
William)	Children of David CULVER
Abigail)	
Ezra	Son of James BROWN (b. 19 Apr 1784)

John	Son of Ralph MACK
George	Son of John WELLS
Hannah	Daughter of Ellis BLISS (b. 6 Jun 1784)
Payton Randolph, Son of Samuel GILBERT (b. 12 Sep 1784)	
Gardiner	Son of Russel WELLS
Lucinda	Daughter of Job HUTCHINSON
Melisunt	Daughter Jordan POST
Russel	Son of Roger CASE

[page 79]

Elihu	Son of Jehiel WILCOX
John	Son of Daniel TALLCOTT (& Lydia ELLIS TALCOTT)
David Warner	Son of David POST

1 Apr 1785

Mercy	Daughter of Ralph MACK
Mary	Daughter of David NORTON
Aaron	Son of Solomon PERRIN
Martha	Daughter of Asaph TRUMBULL
Israel Ele	Son of Israel HUTCHINSON (b. 16 Aug 1786)
John	Son of Daniel WELLS
Laura	Daughter of Gardner GILBERT
Diodate	Son of David POST
Leonard	Son of Russel WELLS

[page 80]

William	Son of William PETERS
Clarissa	Daughter of Amos HURLBURT
Julia	Daughter of Amos HURLBURT
William	Son of Jethro NORTON
Calvin	Son of Ellis LUTHER
John Henry	Son of Samuel GILBERT (b. Jan 31. 1787)
Permelia	Daughter of Zacheriah PERRIN

1 Apr 1787

Ephriam	Son of Daniel BROWN
Flavel	Son of Ellis BLISS
Chester	Son of James BROWN
Betsey	Daughter of William SUMNER
Laura	Daughter of Bateman WELLS
Justin	Son of Jonathan TOWNSEND
Joshua	Son of Joshua POST
Lydia	Daughter of Daniel TALLCOTT
David Curtice	Son of David CULVER
Samuel	Son of Capt. Gad TALLCOTT
Samuel Agustus, Son of Micaiah INGHAM	
Lydia	Daughter of William PETERS

Russel	Son of Roger CASE
Elisabeth	Daughter of Samuel FIELDING
Esther	Daughter of Amos HURLBURT

[page 81]

Lizander	Son of Shipman WELLS
Elisabeth	Daughter of David NORTON
Clarissa	Daughter of Job HUTCHINSON
Jedediah	Son of David POST (b. 18 Jul 1788)
Oliver	Son of Zepheniah DAVIS
Ruba	Daughter of Bariah PHELPS
Mary	Daughter of Paul PITKIN
Joseph Allen	Son of Joseph ROLLO

April 1st 1789

Hannah	Daughter of Jedediah POST
Salle)	Twin Daughters of Russel WELLS
Sile)	
Ira	Son of David CULVER Jnr
Henry	Son of Daniel BROWN
Asel	Son of Solomon PERRIN
Rhoda	Daughter of Joshua ROOT
Mary	Daughter of William ROLLO
Olive	Daughter of Samuel FIELDING
Sarah	Daughter of Col Samuel GILBERT (b. 25 Dec 1789)
Elijah Russel	Son of Seth KING
Deborah	Daughter of William SUMNER
Laura Lothrop	Daughter of Cha[u]ncey LANGDON

[page 82]

John Bissel	Son of John & Molly HUTCHINSON (b. 14 Jan 1790)
Worthy	Daughter of Zepheniah DAVIS
Benjamin	Son of Asaph TRUMBULL
David	Son of David NORTON
Lydia	Daughter of Jethro NORTON
Daniel Phelps	Son of William PETERS
Hannah	Daughter of Daniel WELLS
Martha	Daughter of Henry MACK
Alleson	Son of David CULVER

1 Apr 1791

Benjamin	Son of Joshua ROOT
Welthia	Daughter of Ralph MACK
Clarissa	Daughter of Samuel FIELDING
Whiting	Son of Bateman WELLS
Elizer Olcot	Son of Elizer TILLOTSON
Sarah	Daughter of Daniel BROWN

Lucy   Daughter of Cha[u]nc[e]y LANGDON
Polly Belinda Daughter of John & Molly HUTCHINSON (b.Oct 1791)
Deborah   Daughter of James BROWN
Sally   Daughter of Joseph & Sybil HUTCHINSON (b. 29 Dec 1791)
Levina   Daughter of Russel WELLS
Aaron   Son of Henry MACK
Sophia   Daughter of Jedediah POST   (b. 26 Feb 1792)

[page 83]

William Agustus, Son of William SUMNER
David Trumbull, Son of Shipman WELLS
Asahel   Son of David CULVER
Elijah   Son of David & Martha POST   (b. 31 Jul 1792)
Laura   Daughter of Daniel & Mary HUTCHINSON
Turner   Son of Elizaer TILLOTSON
Anna   Daughter of David NORTON

1 Apr 1793
Aaron ALLEN   Grandson of William ALLEN
Sally   Daughter of Samuel FIELDING
Pruda   Daughter of Hannah WELLS
Simeon   Son of Simeon DUNHAM
Patta   Daughter of David TRUMBULL
Nabba Marie   Daughter of Samuel GILBERT   (b. 29 Aug 1793)
Josiah   Son of Henry MACK
Samuel   Son of Oliver BINGHAM
Betsey,   Daughter of John & Molly HUTCHINSON (b. 6 Oct 1793)
William   Son of Azariah BEACH
Lucy   Daughter of Azariah BEACH
No name given   Daughter of Roger PHELPS
Ira   Son of Joshua ROOT
          Capt. Solomon NORTON Baptized in 79th year of his age.
Randolph   Son of Russel WELLS

[page 84]

Augustus   Son of Capt William ROLLO
John Henry   Son of David POST   (b. 14 Jul 1794)
Samuel   Son of Samuel FIELDING
Obediance   Daughter of Jacob RUSSELL
Ezra   Son of Daniel & Mary HUTCHINSON
Abigail   Daughter of David CULVER
Lydia   Daughter of Ralph MACK
Rebekah   Daughter of Paul PITKIN
Mary   Daughter of John MERRILS Jnr
William Augustus, Son of Anna BURGE

Laura	Daughter of William SUMNER
Elijah Lyma	Son of Elijah WEBSTER Jnr
Augustus	Son of Elijah WEBSTER Jnr

1 Apr 1795
Content BIRGE, Baptized an Adult Person
Anna BIRGE, Baptized an Adult Person
Samuel Augustus, Son of David BROWN
David Bishop   Son of David CURTICE
Samuel Smith   Son of David NORTON
Clarissa, Daughter of John & Molly HUTCHINSON (b. 20 Jul 1795)
Phathena   Daughter of Shipman WELLS
Hannah   Daughter of Samuel FIELDING
Seluta   Daughter of Seth KING

[page 85]

William Dart   Son of Thomas STEVENS
Chester   Son of Jonathan HALL
Horace   Son of Mordica ELLIS
Solomon   Son of Joshua POST

1 Apr 1796
Jonathan)
Hannah)   Children of Jonathan HALL
Abigail   )
William)
Betsey   Daughter of Oliver INGHAM
Aner   Daughter of Russel WELLS
Isaac Ansel   Son of Isaac DUNHAM
Salla   Daughter of James BROWN
Ebenezer Rockwell, Son of Asa BROWN
Chester Hall   Son of Henry MACK
Leonard Elijah Son of Elijah L. LOTHROP
Sarah   Daughter of Elijah WEBSTER Jnr.
Charles Champion, Son of CoL Samuel GILBERT (b. 14 Apr 1797)

Entries by Samuel GILBERT, Church Clerk 25 Jan 1798
Horace   Son of David CURTICE
Susanna   Daughter of David NORTON
Catharine   Daughter of Samuel FIELDING

[page 86]

Sally   Daughter of Reuben SUMNER
Jerusha   Daughter of Henry P. SUMNER by the Rev. Mr.
                   CONE (b. 22 Apr 1798)
Augustus   Son of John & Polly HUTCHINSON by the Rev.
                   Aaron HUTCHINSON of Vermont [b.] July

William	Son of John ROLLO by Mr. WEST
Ichabod	Son of David POST by Mr. CONE (b. 4 Mar 1798)

7 Jul 1799

John   Son of Anna HALL by Mr. TYLER
Edmund CORNWELL, July 28th -dedicated by Samuel and Hannah GEAR
Phila   Daughter of Ralph MACK
Lucy Luther)
Gilbert   )   Children of Luther and Lucy FORD
Cyrus   Son of Isaac DUNHAM
Daniel   Son of Oliver INGRAHAM
Hannah Lencey, Daughter of Ezekiel A. POST by the Rev. Mr. CONE of Colchester   (3 Oct 1798)

Continued on Page 126

[page 126]

Baptisms by Nathan Gillet, Pastor

13 Nov 1799

Betsey POST, An Adult Daughter of Joseph POST
Deborah   Daughter of Henry MACK
Jerusha   Daughter of Joshua ROOT
Ira   Son of John & Molly HUTCHINSON (b. 1 Mar 1800)
Joseph POST, an Adult Baptized
Hiram   Son of R[e]uben SUMNER
Mary Elizabeth Daughter of Leonard E. LATHROP
Welthy   Daughter of David CURTICE
Solomon   Son of David NORTON   (b. 27 May 1800)
Sarah Bingham, Daughter of John CONE   (b. 27 Sep 1788)
Hervy   Son of James BROWN
Henry Tudor   Son of Henry P. SUMNER
George Oliver   Son of William SUMNER
Hannah Emely, Daughter of John CONE
Sophia   Daughter of Isaac DUNHAM
William   Son of John & Molly HUTCHINSON (b. 24 Jan 1802)
Mariah   Daughter of Samuel FIELDING
Matilda   Daughter of Henry P. SUMNER
Ichabod Trumbul, Son of David NORTON (30 Mar 1802)
Laura Lenesa   Daughter of Leonard E. LOTHROP
Esther   Daughter of John CONE.
Cynthia Mariah, Daughter of William SUMNER
Israel Austin   Son of Zepheniah DAVIS Jnr.
Lydia Emeline Daughter of Nathan GILLET

[page 127]

Ralph Gilbert   Son of Ralph MACK

Lucy	Daughter of Samuel FIELDING
William Orsimus	Son of Henry SUMNER
Anna	Daughter of John & Molly HUTCHINSON (b. 8 Nov 1894)
Nathan Edwin	Son of Nathan GILLET
Hannah Louisa	Daughter of David NORTON
Clarinda Gypson	Daughter of Oliver HILLS
Silence Laurinda	Daughter of Leonard E. LOTHROP
Fanny Post	Daughter of John CONE
Benjamin Thomas	Son of William SUMNER
Philander	Son of Samuel FIELDING
Hervy	Son of Isaac DUNHAM
William Champion	Son of Ralph MACK
~~William~~ Eleazer CARTER, Son of Eleazer & Sally HUTCHINSON	
Thomas Leverett	Son of Thomas BROWN
Thomas Blish	Son of William TALLCOTT
Samuel Egbert	Son of Nathan GILLET
Harvy	Son of John & Molly HUTCHINSON (b. 23 Mar 1857)
Almira	Daughter of David NORTON
Jerusha	Daughter of John CONE
Wait	Son of William TALLCOTT
Joel	a black boy of Col. Samuel GILBERT
Ezekiel Ely)	Sons of Ezekiel WEBSTER (b. 17 Jan 1806)
John Luman)	(b. 30 Jan 1807)
Florilla	Daughter of William SUMNER

[page 128]

William	Son of Samuel FIELDING
Mercy Maria	Daughter of Edward S. ELLIS
Laura	Daughter of Ezekiel WEBSTER, b. [sic]
William Hubbard	Son of William TALLCOTT
Ezekiel A)	Children of Ezekiel A. POST
Jedediah G.)	b. 1 Dec 1808
Hersa)	Children of Elijah DUNHAM
Elijah Hart)	
Almanda Miranda	Daughter of Nathan GILLET
Dorothy	Daughter of Ezekiel WEBSTER
Simeon Harlow	Son of Elijah DUNHAM
Abby Lauretta	Daughter of Edward S. ELLIS
Betsey Grant)	
Sylvester Grant)	Children given up in Baptism by Luther FORD & his Wife, Maryann GRANT)

January 1812

Ralph Jones	Son of Nathan GILLET
Lucy Ann	Daughter of Thomas BROWN

Luta Ann	Daughter of Samuel SIMONS
Chester Hiram	Son of Elijah DUNHAM
Luna Louisa)	Children of Tallcott HORSFORD
Harriot Emeline)	
Samuel	Son of Ezekiel A. POST
John Post)	Children of Luther FORD Jnr
Hannah Emily)	

May 1813

Lurana Olmstead	Daughter of Oliver WILCOX
Mary Ann	Daughter of R[e]uben SUMNER
Edwin Randolph)	
Josiah Champion)	Children of Payton R. GILBERT
Melissa Ann)	
Gustavus Hammond	Son of Oliver WILCOX

May 1814

Mary Elvira	Daughter of Edward S. ELLIS
William Chapin	Son of Ezekiel WEBSTER
Theodosia Harriot	Daughter of Elijah DUNHAM
Deborah	Daughter of Ezekiel A. POST
William Henry	Son of Ralph R. ROLLO

1815

Lucy Ann)	
Sibil Emeline)	Children of Ralph R. ROLLO
Ralph Rodolphus)	

Jan 1815

Phila Martha ADAMS
Thomas & Julius PERRIN

Clarissa Mariah	Daughter of Oliver WILCOX
Abby Mariah	Daughter of Payton R. GILBERT
William Henry	Son of R[e]uben SUMNER

1816

Martha Mariah	Daughter of Joel WEBSTER
Lucinda	Daughter of Ralph R. ROLLO
Humphrey Blodget	Son of Elijah DUNHAM

Austin Shipman HORTON, an Adult

1817

Harvy MARVIN, an Adult

Mary Luesia	Daughter of Joel WEBSTER
Charles Augustus	Son of Payton R. GILBERT
Mary Ann	Daughter of R[e]uben SUMNER
Sarah Louisa	Daughter of Thomas BROWN

Israel Champion	Son of Israel E. HUTCHINSON (b. 9 Dec 1815)	
Harriot Mariah	Daughter of Ezekiel A. POST	

1818

Dudley	Son of Ezekiel WEBSTER	
Silas Alfred)		
Joel Albert)	Twin Sons of Nathan GILLET	

1819

Samuel Augustus	Son of Ralph R. ROLLO	
Henrietta Manervy	Daughter of Ezekiel A. POST	
Ralph Porter	Son of Payton R. GILBERT	
Samuel Leonard)		
Abby Juliet)	Children of Samuel C. HORTON	
Ellis Luther)		
Jedediah Luther	Son of Luther FORD Jnr	
Mary Ann	Daughter of George TRYON	

1821

William Egbert	Son of Ralph R. ROLLO
Harriot Marilla	Daughter of Ezekiel A. POST

1822

Celia Almira	Daughter of Ezekiel WEBSTER
Samuel Epaphroditus	Son of Payton R. GILBERT
George Oliver	Son of Oliver WILCOX

Florenda, Mary Ann, Adeline Amelia, Caroline Adelia, Abby Louisa [daughters of Eleazer B. STRONG]

Emely, William Henry, Humphrey Hutchinson, & Harriot Newell, Children of Eleazer B. STRONG

[page 131]

Baptisms by Charles NICHOLS

Oct 1825

Flavius Augustus	Son of Ezekiel A. POST	
Hannah Minerva)	b. 28 Mar 1819	
Edmund Sylvester)		
Harriet Jerusha)	[4] Children of Edmund C. GEAR	
Mary Emily)		
Sally Sumner [10]	orphan child of John H. POST.	28 May
Elisha Manly	Son of Elisha LORD	11 Jun
Lucy Amanda	Daughter of Luther FORD Jr.	18 [Jun]
David Edwin	Son of David HUTCHINSON	2 Jul
Jerusha Jane	Daughter of Ely MACK	
Sally Clarissa	Daughter of Selden MINER	30 [Jul]

---

[10] Indexed by Connecticut State Library in 1931 under the surname SUMNER

Lyman	Son of Sarah THOMAS, a woman of colour	10 Aug
Sally Theresia	Daughter of P. R. GILBERT	8 Oct
Emeline Cornelia	Daughter of O. WILCOX	22 Apr
Henry Wait Warner)		
Harriet Hester)	Children of Sam¹ TALCOTT	21 Nov
Anna Elizabeth	Daughter of Willm HUTCHINSON	8 Jun
Julia	Daughter of Charles NICHOLS	4 Jul
Ezekiel Lavius	Son of Ezekiel A. POST	6 [Jul]
Sylvester Georg	Son of Elisha LORD	4 Aug
Josiah Augustus	Son of Ely A. MACK	14 Sep
David Hall	Son of Aaron MACK	8 Feb
Joel Carlos	Son of Ezekiel WEBSTER	July
Hannah Eliza	Daughter of David HUTCHINSON	2 Oct

[page 132]

1830

Frances Elizabeth)	Children of E C. GEAR	16 May
Charles Gilbert)		
Joseph Durfey	Son of Joseph LATHAM	[16 May]
George Manton	Son of Oliver WILCOX	22 [May]

1831

John Giles	Son of Aaron MACK	[May]
John Cone	Son of widow (of David) Sarah (Cone) HUTCHINSON	12 Jun
Julius	Son of Charles NICHOLS	15 Jul
Henry Cushman	Son of Eleazer B. STRONG	17 [Jul]
David Whiting)		
Mary Minerva)	[2] Children of Jonathan TRUMBULL	[17 Jul]

[The following are 6] Children of John B. HUTCHINSON [17 Jul]

Mary Lauretta	b. 23 Sep 1819
Harriet Belinda	b. 21 Jan 1821
Clarissa Velina	b. 21 Mar 1823
John Calvin	b. 29 Mar 1825
George Champion	b. 22 Apr 1827
Amelia Rhoda	b. 28 Nov 1829
Elizabeth Frances	adopted child of James WHITE
Erastus Henry	Son of Erastus NEWELL

Julia (b. 3 Jun 1831) Daughter of Thomas L. BROWN [bap] Sept 3

MARRIAGES

[page 87]

Married by Elijah Lothrop Pastor

Date	Groom	Bride	Surname
11 Jun 1752	Peter	SWETLAND & Ann	BOND
[11 Jun 1752]	Abner	WATERS & Lydia	ROOT
6 Dec [1752]	Obadiah	DUNHAM & Hannah	PINNEO
22 [Dec 1752]	John	TALLCOTT & Abiah	PHELPS
25 Oct 1753	Marten	TOWNZEN & Rhoda	INGHAM
7 Sep [1753]	Samuel	ABENS & Mary	INGHAM
26 Sep 1754	James	CALKINS & Mary	MANN, MAN
2 Oct [1754]	Thomas	PERRIN & Eliseth	WILLIAMS
14 Nov [1754]	Jabez	ELLIS & Mary	SAWYER
[14 Nov 1754]	Ebenezer	HALL & Mary	WADSWORTH
26 Dec [1754]	Ebenezer	HORTON & Temperance	SHIPMAN
16 Jan 1755	Abijah	ROWLE & Hannah	CURTICE
13 Mar 1755	Simeon	PORTER & Sarah	KILBURN
Oct 16 [1755]	W^m	SHEPHERD & Rachel	HUTCHINSON
1 Jan 1756	Moses HUTCHINSON Jr. & Ruth		COOX
15 [Jan 1756]	Eliphalet	HOUSE & Lucretia	HOWELL
22 [Jan 1756]	John	SKINNER & Elizath	MERRIL
29 [Jan 1756]	Amasa	TOWNZEN & Phebe	INGHAM
11 Mar [1756]	Jonathan	ADAMS & Hannah	YEAMON
22 Apr [1756]	John	MACK & Eunice	FISH
9 May [1756]	Ebenezer	SUMNER & Persis	PEASE
15 Jul [1756]	Gad	MERRIL & Mary	SKINNER
Mar 1757	Elijah	HORTON & Sarah	COOX
May [1757]	Amos	HALL & Martha	WILCOX

[page 88]

Date	Groom	Bride	Surname
Oct 1757	James	COOX & Ann	POLLY
Nov [1757]	Ephriam	YOUNGS & Elisabeth	CURTICE
Feb 1758	Zadek	MARTINDALE & Sibil	SHIPMAN
Jan 1759	Asher	MERRILS & Delight	SAWYER
Apr [1759]	Gideon	WATERS & Lydia	POLLEY
May [1759]	Alexander I	NGHAM & Catherine	NOBLE
[1759]	Jonathan	BOOTH & Tarzo	NOBLE
Jul [1759]	Nicholas	BOND & Thankfull	FOOT
Jan 1760	Capt Benoni TRUMBULL & Phebe		POST
29 May [1760]	Samuel	GILBERT Jnr. & Lydia	POST
29 [May 1760]	Jazaniah	POST & Elizabeth	BISSEL
Jul [1760]	Benjamin	SWETLAND & Phebe	WILCOX
[1760]	Ebenezer	DEWEY & Temperance	HOLDRIGE
Nov [1760]	Joshua	TILLOTSON & Elisabeth	BROOKER
Dec [1760]	Benjamin	TRUMBULL & Martha	PHELPS

Date	Given Name	Surname & Spouse	Mother
4 [Dec 1760]	Asaph	TRUMBULL & Zilpah	PHELPS
11 Dec [1760]	John	ELLIS & Elisabeth	SAWYER
Jan 1761	Ichabod	PHELPS & Martha	TRUMBULL
Jun [1761]	Thomas	SUMNER & Rebeker	DOWNER
Jul [1761]	George	LOVELAND & Anna	MALLEY
Sept [1761]	John	MERREL & Sarah	CULVER
Oct [1761]	David	BROWN & Lydia	SWETLAND
Nov [1761]	Dea Ebenezer	DEWEY & Christian	PHELPS
[Nov 1761]	John	PETERS Jnr. & Ann	BARNETT

[page 89]

Date	Given Name	Surname & Spouse	Mother
1761	Benjamin	BALDWIN & Lydia	PETERS
Jan 1762	Joseph	TAYLOR & Elisabeth	SUMNER
[1762]	Abel	WILCOX & Susanna	HALL
Mar [1762]	Amos	HALL & Betty	BRIANT
17 Jun [1762]	Thomas	POST & Abitha	PHELPS
Oct [1762]	Elijah	OWEN & Deborah	HOLDRIGE
16 Dec [1762]	Elijah	WEBSTER & Deborah	POST
Apr 1763	Nathaniel	DAVIS & Rachel	ROLLO
[1763]	Capt. Benoni	TRUMBULL & Marget	WARNER
May [1763]	Jonathan	WEBSTER & Elisabeth	WILCOX
Sep [1763]	Ebenezer	SKINNER & Eunice	CULVER
Jan 1764	Henry	WHITE & Sarah	DEWEY
[1764]	Philip	JUDD & Mary	PETERS
[1764]	James	ROW & Esther	MACK
9 Feb [1764]	Joel	POST & Sarah	BUSHNEL
Mar [1764]	John	FOOT & Ann	THOMPSON
Sep [1764]	Simeon	WEBSTER & Rebekah	BROWN
Nov [1764]	Jonah	PHELPS & Sarah	MACK
[1764]	Ebenezer	ROOT & Deborah	BUCK
[1764]	John	THOMAS & Lovina	BROWN
Apr 1765	Eliphalet	YOUNGS & Martha	BURNHAM
July [1765]	David	CURTICE & Judith	WRIGHT
Nov [1765]	Elias	JAGGER & Mahetable	ROOT

[page 90]

Date	Given Name	Surname & Spouse	Mother
Jan 1766	Asabel	PHELPS & Jerusha	PERRIN
May [1766]	Isaac	RILEY & Hannah	YOUNGS
Aug [1766]	Jedediah	WARD & Esther	POST
11 Sep [1766]	Jonathan	HUTCHINSON & Elonor	POST
Dec [1766]	Timothy	STEVENS & Mary	WAYERS
Feb 1767	Ebenezer	KILBORN & Sarah	BILL
Apr [1767]	Jesse	MUNSON & Miriam	ROWLEY
May [1767]	Peter	ROBINSON & Sarah	BUCK
May [1767]	Elias	JAGGER & Sarah	PERRIN

Jul [1767]	Josiah	MACK & Elisabeth	ROWLEY
Nov [1767]	Solomon	LOTHROP & Elisabeth	ROLLO
Mar 1768	Samuel	BROWN & Prudence	SAWYER
Nov [1768]	John	BISSEL & Susannah	YOUNGS
Nov [1768]	Nathaniel	DARBE & Temperance	BOND
Jun 1769	John	ROW. Jnr. & Elisabeth	BILL
Sep [1769]	Zia	CASE & Azubah	PHELPS
Oct [1769]	Charles	LOOMIS & Lucy	FORD
Nov [1769]	Benjamin	SAWYER & Sarah	DEWEY
Jan [1769]	Phineas	GROVER & Ruth	NICHOLS
Feb [1769]	Samuel	COVEL & Anna	MACK
Feb [1769]	Edmund	WELLS & Welthia	GOODRICH
Apr [1769]	William	ROLLO & Lucy	HALL
[Apr 1769]	John	TOON & Chloe	TOWNSEND
19 Dec [1769]	James	POST & Thankful	WELLS

[page 91]

Apr 1771	Jehiel	WILCOX & Lydia	MACK
Jun [1771]	Thomas	LOVELAND & Jerusha	LOVELAND
Jan 1772	Ebenezer	WRIGHT & Jerusha	DUNHAM
May [1772]	Jacob	RUSSELL & Esther	DUNHAM
Jun [1772]	Enos	BLOSSOM & Mary	ELLIS
Oct [1772]	John	HUBBARD & Thankful	ROWLEE
Nov [1772]	Edward	GRANNIS & Hannah	WELLS
Dec [1772]	David	TAYLOR & Rosehannah	GILBERT
Mar 1773	Ebenezer	BILL & Rachel	ROOT
Jun [1773]	Julius	COLLINS & Deborah	CULVER
[Jun 1773]	Solomon	PERRIN & Ann	CELLOGG
Aug [1773]	Thomas	JUDD & Mary	ROLLO
Feb 1774	David	PERRY & Kezia	ROOT
Mar [1774]	Adam	[___,] Negro & Chloe	COOK
Apr [1774]	David	MACK & Mary TALCOTT, dau of John	
May [1774]	Asa	BROWN & Elisabeth	DUNHAM
Sep [1774]	Joshua	PAGE & Margery	WELLS
Oct [1774]	Thomas	CHAMPLIN & Jemima	LOVELAND
[Oct 1774]	William	WRIGHT & Comfort	POST
[Oct 1774]	Abner	MORLEY & Alice	TOWNSEND
Nov [1774]	Joseph	DAVIS & Dorithy	BROWN
[Nov 1774]	Nathaniel	DAVIS & Sibil	MACK
[Nov 1774]	Elihu	WELLS & Hannah	HUTCHINSON
Jan 1775	Daniel	CHAPMAN & Lucy	TALLCOTT

[page 92]

Mar 1775	Nehemiah	PORTER & Abigail	STRONG
Oct [1775]	Daniel	WARNER & Hannah	SUMNER

Oct [1775]	Eleazer	WILCOX & Mary	MACK
Jan 1776	Larance	RAWLIN & Thankful	HUTCHINSON
Jan [1776]	Jabez	INGRAHAM & Naomi	ROOT
Feb [1776]	Daniel	WELLS & Hannah	LOTHROP
Aug [1776]	Dea. Thomas	POST & Elisabeth	CULVER
Sep [1776]	Weltor	ROLLO & Mary	WELLS
Nov [1776]	Daniel	BROWN & Anna	PHELPS
Jan [1776]	John	FINLEY Jur & Phebe	FORD
Jan 1777	David	WRIGHT & Patience	BILL
Feb [1777]	Moses	GOODRICH & Mary	FORD
Jun [1777]	Adonijah	WHITE & Hannah	KINGSBURY
Jul [1777]	Joseph	MARTAIN & Eleanor	SHEPARD
4 Dec [1777]	James	BROWN & Deborah	TARBOX
Jun 1778	Gardner	GILBERT & Anna	LATHROP
[Jun 1778]	Alexander	WHITE & Azubah	TOWNSEND
[Jun 1778]	Oliver	COOK & Elisabeth	SUMNER
Oct [1778]	Joseph	PETERS & Sarah	WELLS
[Oct 1778]	Samuel	HORTON & Hannah	MORRIS
[Oct 1778]	Erastus	INGHAM & Elisabeth	HUTCHINSON
Jan 1779	Elijah	FOX & Sabra	NETTLETON
Feb [1779]	Ebenezer	CARRIER & Prudence	WELLS
Mar [1779]	Ruel	BEBE [BEEBE] & Mercy	PETERS

[page 93]

Apr 1779	Joseph	HUTCHINSON & Sibil	MACK
Jul [1779]	Elihu	MARVIN & Azubah	CASE
Sep [1779]	Russel	WELLS & Sarah	CARTER
Jan 1780	Simeon	BLISS & Anna	CASE
Mar [1780]	Daniel	COLBURN & Roxelanie	PHELPS
May [1780]	John	NORTHUM & Elisabeth	WHITE
Jul [1780]	Thomas	ROWLEE & Eunice	COOPER
Aug [1780]	Col. Thomas	BROWN & Mary	LOTHROP
Sep [1780]	Eleazer	PHELPS & Hannah	HORTON
5 Oct [1780]	Ellis	LUTHER & Sibil	POST
[1780]	Abijah	ROWLEE & Elisabeth	CULVER
19 Oct [1780]	John	POST & Mary	PRAT
[1780]	Abial	BLISS & Anna	BROWN
Dec [1780]	Zebulun	ISHUM & Rese	ELLIS
Jan 1781	Zacheriah	PERRIN & Mary	TALCOTT,
dau of Sam[l] of Bolton			
Feb [1781]	Joseph	CLARK & Submit	DUNHAM
Mar [1781]	James	MCCULLOC & Hannah	ROLLO
Jun [1781]	Peter	RIPLEY & Lova	NORTON
Oct [1781]	Seth	KING & Silence	LOTHROP

Date	Name	Parents	Surname
Nov [1781]	John	STRONG & Lydia	SUMNER
Jan 1782	Joseph	TILDEN & Elisabeth	BROWN
Feb 1782	John	CULVER & Dinah	POST
Jul 1782	Ezekiel	DANIELS & Elisabeth	PERRIN
Sep 1782	Henry	COVEL & Sarah	GOODRICH

[page 94]

Date	Name	Parents	Surname
1782	Samuel	PETERS & Hannah	TRUMBULL
Oct [1782]	Thomas	WELLS & Clarissa	PETERS
Nov [1782]	Ezekiel	BROWN & Martha	HORTON
[1782]	Eleazer	PHELPS & Deborah	MANN
26 Dec [1782]	Samuel	ABENS & Dorothy	POST
6 Feb 1783	Ralph	MACK & Lydia	GILBERT
May [1783]	Job	HUTCHINSON & Experience	MACK
Jul [1783]	Nehemiah	ROSELL & Mahetable	ALLEN
Oct [1783]	Samuel	MARKS & Content	DUNHAM
8 Jan 1784	Daniel	TALLCOTT & Lydia	ELLIS
Feb [1784]	Thadeus	PARKER & Lydia	HORTON
3 Jun [1784]	William	SUMNER & Jemima	TARBOX
Oct [1784]	Ebenezer	BUCK & Anna	TALCOTT
[1784]	Paul	PITKIN & Abagail	LOTHROP
Nov [1784]	Eliakim	JONES & Rebekah	WEBSTER
Dec [1784]	Daniel	TAYLOR & Ruhamah	ELLIS
3 Feb 1785	David	NORTON & Deborah	PHELPS
May [1785]	Reuben	WELLS & Mary	TRUMBULL
[1785]	Silas	PERRY & Thankful	NORTON
[1785]	William	DART & Charlotte	PERRIN
Sep[1785]	William	PETERS & Lydia	PHELPS
Dec [1785]	Jethro	NORTON & Sibil	SUMNER
Feb 16 1786	Micaiah	INGHAM & Eunice	MACK

[page 95]

Date	Name	Parents	Surname
Apr 1786	Shipman	WELLS & Zilpah	TRUMBULL
[1786]	Spencer	WOOD & Persis	BUCK
14 May [1786]	Capt Ichabod	PHELPS & Mrs Hannah	POST
[--- -- 1786]	Christopher	CROUCH & Lydia	HUTCHINSON[11]
[1786]	John	TAYLOR & Elisabeth	WELLS
Dec [1786]	Henry	MACK & Mahetable	HALL
Jan 1787	Asa	HOW & Eunice	BUCK
Feb [1787]	John	WATERS & Mindwell	JONES
[1787]	Roger	PHELPS & Anna	JONES
Sep [1787]	Nathaniel	TOWNSEND & Mary	BASSET

---

[11] This church record, and no other, is missing in the Warner manuscript, but included (in this location) in the Gilead Church Records.and in the Post transcription at the DAR. See note 1 above at p. iv.

Nov [1787]	Samuel	KELLOGG & Elizabeth Septame	LOTHROP
Jan 1788	Joseph	ROLLO & Barbarry	ALLEN
[1788]	Daniel	MERREL & Huldah	ELLIS
[1788]	David	BUCK & Abagail	PALMERTER
Feb [1788]	John	MANN & Lydia	DUTTON
Dec [1788]	Levi	LOOMIS & Louisa	LOTHROP
7 Apr 1789	Chauncey	LANGDON & Lucynana	LOTHROP
29 Sep [1789]	Joseph	WELLS & Abiaih	DUNHAM
Dec [1789]	Jabez	ELLIS Jur & Hanna	MACK
Mar 1790	Daniel	HITCHCOCK & Sarah	ALLEN
[Mar 1790]	Jerre	BURDON & Sliva MORGAN, Negroes	
Oct [1790]	George	HALL & Azubah	TRUMBULL
[Oct 1790]	Jacob	SKINNER & Phebe	PALMETER
Mar 1791	Daniel	HUTCHINSON & Mary	ELLIS
19 May 1791	Ichabod M.	WARNER & Mary	TALCOTT

[page 96]

Nov 1791	David	TILLOTSON & Sarah	WELLS
Feb 1792	Col. Abial	PEASE & Mary	LOOMIS
Jul [1792]	Roswel	HUBBARD & Martha	JORDAN
Aug [1792]	David	TRUMBULL & Thankful	WELLS
Sep [1792]	Simeon	DUNHAM & Betty	HALL
Feb 1793	Thomas	STEVENS & Lucy	PERRIN
Aug [1793]	Charles	KELLOGG & Lydia	HOSFORD
Oct [1793]	Samuel	SCOTT & Melicent	MACK
Jan 1794	Charles	COLLINS & Abelene	CURTICE
Feb 1794	Samuel	PIPER & Lucy	DANIELS
May 1794	Oliver	HUNTINGTON & Abigail	TALCOTT
[May 1794]	Elijah L.	LATHROP & Betty	HUBBARD
Jun 1794	Harvy	MORRISON & Prudence	DUNHAM
2 Nov [1794]	Reuben	SUMNER & Anna	PERRIN
Dec [1794]	Israel	THOMPSON & Sarah	FOOT
[1794]	Alvin	GRISWOLD & Anna	WASS
Jan 1795	John	FINLEY & Anna	MORGAN
Feb [1795]	Mordica	ELLIS & Mary	HUTCHINSON
Nov [1795]	Amos	DEAN & Marsilvah	INGHAM
Dec [1795]	John	FINLEY & Rhoda	MORRIS
[1795]	John	ROLLO & Philomelia	TRUMBULL
Aug 1796	Samuel	FIELDING & Lydia	HILDRETH
[1796]	Richard	CROCKER & Lucinda	KELLEY
19 Sep [1796]	Edward	ROOT & Thankful SHADOCK (SHATTUCK)	

[page 97]

11 Oct 1796	Henry	SUMNER & Jerusha	PERRIN
Nov [1796]	Daniel	LOOMER & Anna	HUTCHINSON

[1796]	Nehemiah	SEELEY & Mabel	HORTON
Dec [1796]	Jonah	ROOT, Jr. & Sally	ROOT
Jan 1797	John	ISHAM 3rd & Betsey (Elizabeth)	GILBERT

Marriages by Nathan GILLETT, Pastor

Jan 1800	Hezekiah	WICKUM & Elisebeth	BUELL
Feb [1800]	_____	ATHERTON & Sally	PHELPS
Mar [1800]	Appollus	ROLLO & Betsey	WASS
Apr [1800]	David	FINLEY & Polly	HORSFORD
Nov [1800]	William	BUELL & Delight	FINLEY
27 Dec [1800]	Samuel A.	GILBERT & Nabby	WELLS
Jan 1801	Samuel	POST & Lucy	ROLLO
Aug [1801]	Levi	BISHOP & Lucy	ROOT
Nov [1801]	Zepheniah	DAVIS & Betsey	WILCOX
	Elijah	HOLCOM & Betsey	POST
Mar 1802	John	FINLEY & Florinda	RISLEY
Apr [1802]	James	WARREN & Esther	CONE
Aug [1802]	Jeremiah	PERRIN & Hannah	WRIGHT
Oct [1802]	William	BROWN & Betsey (Elizabeth)	TRUMBULL
Apr 1803	Thomas	BROWN & Lucy	FORD
Aug [1803]	Samuel E.	GEAR & Polly	WELLS

[page 98]

Sept 1803	Edward S.	ELLIS & Mercy	ROLLO
19 Oct [1803]	Eleazer	HUTCHINSON & Sally	TAL[L]COTT
Nov [1803]	David	BROWN & Temperance	PETTICE
Dec [1803]	Joel	DAVIS & Azubah	WILCOX
[Dec 1803]	Ellis	LUTHER & Sarah	MERRILS
Apr 1804	Eliphas	HUNT & Anna	PHELPS
Sep [1804]	Kirtland	WARNER & Sally	TRUMBULL
Oct [1804]	Ruben	WEST & Nancy	HORTON
[undated]	Orry	NICHOLS & Hannah	FINLEY
[undated]	Eleazer	STRONG & Zilpha	HUTCHINSON
Dec [1804]	Benjamin	BENJAMIN & Betsey	DIX
Jan 1805	Abiah	SUTLIFF & Clarrissa	WEBSTER
Feb 1806	Benjamin	POWERS & Eliza	AMOS
Apr [1806]	Thomas	BISHOP & Lydia	CRAFT
Sept [1806]	Henry H.	WELLS & Sila	WELLS
Oct [1806]	Samuel C.	HORTON & Sibil	LUTHER
Apr 1807	Roswell	WEST & Betsey	SUMNER
Jun [1807]	Trumbull	WELL & Hannah	MARTINDALE
Aug [1807]	Charles	LOOMIS & Anna	HALL
Feb 1808	John	CARRIER & Jemima	SUMNER
5 May [1808]	John H.	GILBERT & Polly	ROOT
Oct [1808]	Neziah	BROWN & Clarissa	POST

[1808]	Elisha	ROOT & Deborah	SUMNER
27 Oct [1808]	Luther	FORD Jnr. & Hannah	POST

[page 99]

Aug 1809	Eleazer	POST & Sena	BROCKWAY
Sep [1809]	James	WELLS & Nancy	CORKINS
Oct [1809]	Ezra	HALL & Phila	FORD
Nov [1809]	Amos	DEAN & Lavina	BROCKWAY
May 1811	George W.	TURNER & Catharine	ADAMS
Sep [1811]	David	HUTCHINSON & Martha	HORSFORD
Jan 1812	Joseph	BRADLEY & Harriot	WELLS
4 Mar [1812]	Israel E.	HUTCHINSON & Mary	WARNER
[1812]	Elam	MORE & Lydia	WELLS
[1812]	Dudley	WRIGHT & Eliza	AMBROS
Apr [1812]	John D.	SWETLAND & Betsey	NORTON
Jun [1812]	David	STRONG & Clarissa	BISSELL
Oct [1812]	Nathaniel	BACKUS & Hannah	BISSELL
16 Dec [1812]	Calvin	LUTHER & Polly B.	HUTCHINSON
[1812]	Nehemiah	PORTER & Hannah	GEAR
Feb 1813	Anson	CULVER & Isabella	HORTON
Mar [1813]	Simeon	DANIELS & Abigail	BLISS
[1813]	Walter	HIBARD & Lucinda	JONES
[1813]	Chester	BROWN & Luta	HORTON
Jun [1813]	Elijah	STRONG & Lucy	FINLEY
Dec [1813]	Warren	WARNER & Weltha	POST
Mar [1813]	David	NORTON Jur. & Martha	WELL
Apr [1813]	Solomon	BECKWITH & Emma	WAY

[page 100]

12 Jul 1815	Samuel	JONES & Abby Maria	GILBERT
19 Aug [1815]	Samuel	SKINNER & Mary	NORTON
Nov [1815]	Obadiah K.	SMITH & Hannah	WELLS
Mar 1816	Ezekiel A.	POST & Abigail	ABBY
Apr [1816]	Simeon	DANIELS & Elizabeth	LEONARD
Jun [1816]	Asahel	PERRIN & Betsey	HAMMOND
Aug [1816]	David	NORTON & Mahitable	INGHAM
Jan 1817	Josiah	SHATTUCK & Pethena	WELLS
[1817]	Gilbert	SHATTUCK & Hannah L.	POST
[1817]	Salmon	HOUSE & Unice	GRAY
Apr [1817]	David	PORTER & Jerusha	SUMNER
May [1817]	Zenas	CHAPEL & Nancy	NORTON
Jun [1817]	James	WHITE & Lucina	HORTON
[1817]	John	SPRAGUE & Sally	SHEPHERD
Aug [1817]	Joseph	WEBSTER & Sally	GRAY
Jan 1818	Henry	REED & Laura	SUMNER

Date	First Name	Surname & Spouse	Officiant/Other
Mar [1818]	Arunah	POST & Jerusha	DANIELS
Apr [1818]	Jonathan	SHIRTLIFF & Abigail	WEBSTER
Sep [1818]	Eliphalet	GILLETT & Betsey	HUTCHINSON
Oct [1818]	Thomas	TWINING & Rachel	JONES
28 [Oct 1818]	John B.	HUTCHINSON & Mrs. Lauretta (Jewett)	HUTCHINSON
2 Jun [1818]	John H.	POST & Sally	SUMNER
Jan 1820	Moses K.	BURNHAM & Susannah	NORTON
[1820]	Abel S.	BISSELL & Laura	TRUMBULL

[page 101]

Date	First Name	Surname & Spouse	Officiant/Other
Feb 1820	Russell	BIDWELL & Mary	WILCOX
Apr [1820]	Elijah	STRONG & Lu	No name given
Mar 1821	Elijah	WARNER & Abigail	BUELL
May [1821]	Marvin	BIRGE & Sally	HUTCHINSON
Oct [1821]	Augustus	ROLLO & Martha	HORTON
Nov [1821]	Ichabod	WATROUS & Phebe	FREMAN
May 1822	David	HUTCHINSON & Sarah	CONE
Sep 1823	Ela A.	MACK & Esther	CONE
Feb 1824	John	SWAN & Ulrica E.	PHELPS

Marriages by Charles NICHOLS, Pastor

Date	First Name	Surname & Spouse	Officiant/Other
19 Jan 1826	William	BROWN & Anna	HORTON
12 Nov [1826]	Joshua	ROOT & Betsey	JACKSON
7 Mar 1827	William	HUTCHINSON & Polly C?	POST
4 Apr [1827]	Charles	NICHOLS & Mrs. Louisa (West)	POST
3 Jan 1828	Dan¹	HODGE & Wealthy	CURTICE
25 Jun [1828]	Joshua W.	EATON & Anna	HUTCHINSON
24 Dec [1828]	George	WILLIAMS & Jerusha	CONE
13 May 1829	Joseph Otis	POST & Electa M.	LUCAS
10 Jun [1829]	Chauncey L.	ROOT & Cynthia M.	SUMNER
1830	Hiram	GOODELL & Martha P.	BROWN
7 Jun [1830]	Frederick	WELLES & Maria	COLEMAN
14 Nov 1831	Harvey	DUNHAM & Abby J.	HORTON
27 [Nov 1831]	Ezekiel A.	POST & Clarissa	BROWN
28 [Nov 1831]	Nathan	PERSONS & Julia M.	POST
19 Dec [1831]	Francis	WEST & Florenda	WRISLEY

[page 102]

Date	First Name	Surname & Spouse	Officiant/Other
26 Dec 1831	Elliot	PALMER & Florilla	SUMNER
Mar 18 1832	Charles	CARD & Mercy	PERRY
19 [Mar 1832]	Joel C.	LATHAM & Caroline A.	STRONG
29 [Mar 1832]	Nelson A.	HARDIN & Jerusha	LEE
6 May [1832]	Henry L.	ELY & Mary A.	STRONG
27 Feb 1833	Levi	SPENCER & Martha	MACK

Date	Groom	Surnames	Bride	Bride Surname
7 Apr [1833]	John L.	WEBSTER &	Mary M.	CHAPEL
[7 Apr 1833]	Lucuis	WOOD &	Laura	WEBSTER
Nov [1833]	John P.	BLISS &	Florenda	STRONG
13 May 1834	Willm A.	LEE &	Delia C.	BRITTON
2 Sep [1834]	Asahel H.	BROOKS &	Sally	BROWN
2 Nov [1834]	Champion S.	TURNER &	Matilda C.	FOX
19 May 1835	Hiram H.	MARTINDALE &	Martha M.	WEBSTER
21 [May 1835]	John Meigs	HALL &	Melissa A.	GILBERT
24 Jun [1835]	Horace	BABCOCK &	Rhoda	ROOT
3 Sep [1835]	Roswell G.	PINNEY &	Abby L.	STRONG
26 Oct [1835]	David T.	BROWN &	Alvira	NORTON
16 Dec [1835]	Leonard	DOAN &	Mary M.	SUMNER
27 Jun 1836	Joseph C.	NICHOLS &	Adeline A.	STRONG
13 Sep [1836]	John M.	WAY &	Elizebeth Jerusha	WELLES
21 [Sep 1836]	John W.	BUELL &	Mary Ann	POST
27 Nov [1836]	Henry	TAYLOR &	Esther	LEE
1837	Edwin W.	STRONG &	Sarah	STAPLES
26 Apr [1837]	Stephen W.	BIDWELL &	Henrietta M.	POST

[page 103]

Date	Groom	Surnames	Bride	Bride Surname
10 Dec 1837	Ben	BENJAMIN &	Harriet	WATSON
24 Dec 1837	David W.	TICKNOR &	Hannah M.	GEAR
21 Aug 1838	Christopher A.	WOODBRIDGE &	Mary A.	SUMNER
10 Dec [1838]	Augustine	KNEELAND &	Hannah E.	FORD
6 Feb 1839	Isaac	HALING &	Deborah	BROWN
6 Mar [1839]	Anson	CHAPPEL &	Harriet N.	HUTCHINSON
17 [Mar 1839]	Russel	BROWN &	Joanna	BLISH
22 Apr [1839]	Hubbil	GOSS &	Nancy	LOCKWOOD
1 Oct [1839]	William	ADAMS &	Jerusha	STRONG
21 Nov [1839]	John	LEWIS &	Cynthia Ann	BROWN
15 Apr 1840	Gera G.	KEENEY of Manchester &	Harriet M.	POST
19 May 1841	Daniel	WAY &	Harriet B.	HUTCHINSON
26 Aug 1841	Eleazer E.	STRONG &	Lucy	WARNER
5 Sep 1841	Samuel S.	HYDE &	Harriet N.	STRONG
[5 Sep 1841]	James H.	THOMPSON &	Fanny	BILL
19 Sep 1841]	Benjamin	CARPENTER &	Betsey	WEST
22 Sep 1841]	J. A.	GILLETTE &	Sarah L.	BROWN
6 Oct [1841]	Eben	WITTER &	Mehetable	JEWETT
29 Dec. [1841]	Solomon	NORTON &	Matilda	WEBSTER
14 Sep 1842	Ralph P.	GILBERT &	Mary L.	HUTCHINSON
30 Aug 1843	Andrew	PRENTICE &	Clarissa V.	HUTCHINSON
9 Oct [1843]	Spencer	SMITH &	Mary	MACK
29 [Oct 1843]	Nathan	GILLETT &	Abigail E.	BUELL
27 May 1844	David C.	BRAY &	Amelia R.	WEBSTER

Date	Groom		Bride	Bride Surname
24 Feb [1843]	Ralph M.	CARPENTER &	Sarah J.	ROOT

[page 104]

9 Mar 1848	Nelson	KEENY &	Nancy L.	SUMNER
6 Sep [1848]	Josiah C.	GILBERT &	Sarah S.	POST
31 Dec [1848]	Sherwood	WHEELER &	Sarah	PARISH
6 Jun 1849	George Hinman	LORD &	Anna Elizabeth	HUTCHINSON
1 Jul [1849]	Simeon F.	WATROUS &	Julia E.	DINGLEY
22 May 1850	George C.	HUTCHINSON &	Mary T.	LOOMIS
21 Nov [1850]	Wm N.	GOSLEE &	Sarah A.	ROLLO
12 May 1851	James M.	HURLBURT &	Mary Jane	JOHNSON
3 Jun [1851]	Abel P.	POST &	Sarah A.	ROLLO
14 Sep 1853	William T.	WARNER &	Olive M.	HUTCHINSON
8 Jun 1854	S. Leander	OTIS &	Maria L.	WEST
12 Oct [1854]	Elisha	HODGE &	Delia A.	BIDWELL
15 Apr 1855	J. M.	McKINNEY &	Phebe A.	WATROUS
[15 Apr 1855]	___ ___	_____ &	Frances	CASE

[Clerk?]

12 Sep 1860	Jewett E.	HUTCHINSON &	Louisa D.	ROOT
1863	Charles N.	BROWN &	Elizabeth	TICKNOR
12 Mar [1863]	Joseph	TREAT &	Marion J.	PORTER
24 Dec [1863]	Gilbert B.	JAYCOX &	Jane L.	HYDE
27 May 1865	Clarence D.	STRICKLAND &	Clara	WEST
4 Jul [1865]	Dwight	SCRIPTURE &	Harriet	WEST
19 Oct [1865]	Henry	SPRAGUE &	Augusta	DICKINSON
1 Nov [1865]	Charles W.	HYDE &	Esther	HAYWARD
29 [Nov 1865]	Henry	HANMER &	Clara E.	WAY
7 Dec [1865]	Charles	JOHNSON &	Ellen	TICKNOR
14 [Dec 1865]	Edward	JOHNSON &	Jane	HANNA
17 Jan 1866	Daniel W.	BROWN &	Emma	ELLIS
1 [Jan 1866]	John	COOLEY &	Jane	WELLES
Apr [1866]	Leverett	PETERS &	_____	_____
[1866]	Samuel	ROOT &	Hattie	CHURCH

[page 105]

12 Sep 1866	Charles D.	WAY &	Kate	CHESEBRO
20 Dec 1866	George E.	WELLS &	Emeline L.	ROOT
11 May 1867	Charles W.	HYDE &	Fannie M.	GATES
28 Nov. 1866	James A.	WAY &	Anna	GRIDLEY
17 June 1868	David	HALL &	Eliza	TRACY
23 [Jun 1868]	Henry C.	RYDER &	Georgia	TALCOTT
15 Jul 1869	Chester M.	HILLS &	Josephine M.	HUTCHINSON
26 Oct 1869	Daniel	GRISWOLD &	Carrie	PINNEY
31 Aug 1870	Wm A.	COLLINS &	Florilla S.	ROOT
12 Oct [1870]	Olin	CLARK &	_____	ELDRIDGE

15 Dec. [1870]	Albert	BINGHAM &	Eunice	TAYLOR
25 Apr 1871	Henry	POST &	Mrs. Melissa (HUXFORD)	ROOT
13 May [1871]	Julius J.	STRICKLAND &	Florence	BOLLES
14 [May 1871]	George	FLINT &	Jennette	HYDE
12 Sep [1871]	Albert P.	BURT &	Sarah H.	PRENTICE
4 Oct [1871]	Samuel	TALCOTT &	Rosa	TALCOTT
7 Nov [1871]	Wm M.	CALDWELL &	Elizabeth	LOCKWOOD
30 [Nov 1871]	George Solomon	NORTON &	Abby M.	STRICKLAND
17 Jan 1872]	William	TAYLOR &	Elizabeth	LEE
3 Apr [1872]	Thomas L.	BROWN &	Eunice	WHITE
16 May [1872]	John H.	BUELL &	Abby	ELLIS
17 Apr [1872]	M. L.	GATES &	Mary A.	HYDE
30 May [1872]	Alfred W.	HUTCHINSON &	Huldah	HOLBROOK
15 Aug [1872]	Harlow	TRACY &	Lizzie	DUNHAM
27 Apr 1875	Calvin A.*	PRENTICE &	Rosa D.	STRICKLAND*
12 Nov [1875]	Ele*	HUTCHINSON &	Ida B.	*STRICKLAND*
30 Aug 1876	John R. *	GILBERT* &	Mary C.	*DAVIS*

BURIALS

[page 106]

The number of Deaths to Persons Buried in this Burying Place from Feby 1st 1749 to April 1761 are 78 Persons. Nicholas BOND was the last, who Died April 10th 1761. A child of Deacon John ELLIS was the first who Died Feby 1st 1749. [12]

[Death Record by E. LOTHROP]
An account of the deaths from April 1761.

21 Apr 1761	the Widow Anna BOND	in old age
May [1761]	a child of Ebenezer BUCK	Still Born
[1761]	Henry CURTICE & Elihu PHELPS	in one Day
[1761]	John WARNER	an old Man
[1761]	Martha wife of Dea Ebenezer DEWEY	
[1761]	Elisha son of Elisha DUNK	
[1761]	Isaac OWEN	
5 Jun [1761]	a child of Jonathan ADAMS	
6 Jun [1761]	Martha (-----) wife of Amos HALL	
[6 Jun 1761]	the widow INGHAM	in old age
8 Jun 1761	Ebenezer WILCOX	much lamented
16 Jun 1761	Elizabeth wife of Ebenezer WILCOX	
17 Jun 1761	Ephriam YOUNGS	
26 Jun 1761	Melisent Daughter of Obadiah CULVER	
[26 Jun 1761]	James Son of James COX	
6 Aug [1761]	Peleg Son of Noah PHELPS	
Jan 1762	Katherine Daughter of John POST	
19 Sep [1762]	Phebe (POST) wife of Capt Benoni TRUMBULL	
30 [Sep 1762]	a child of Abel WILCOX	Still Born
30 Mar 1763	Henry Son of Edmund WELLS	

[page 107]

21 Apr 1763	Daniel ROOT	in the 79th year of his age
19 Jun 1763	Ephriam YOUNGS with the Consumption	
Jul [1763]	Joseph Son of Stephen BOND	
18 Nov [1763]	~~Mary~~ (Martha Phelps) Wife of Benjamin TRUMBULL	
Jany 1764	an infant child of Mary JUDD	
24 Oct [1764]	Abigail Wife of Samuel GILBERT Esq.	
18 Aug 1765	Elisha DUNK	much lamented
27 Mar 1766	Edward SAWYER	in the 79th year of his age

---

[12] The first half of Warner's burial entries include the word "Died" between the date and the name. The word is omitted in all entries for consistency.

[1766]	Lucinda Marvil Daughter of Widow Mary MARKS	
3 Oct [1766]	Katharine Wife of John POST	
Dec [1766]	Mehitable (ROOT) Wife of Elias JAGGER	
Jany 1767	Samuel ROWLEE	in 80 year of his age
Feb [1767]	Hannah Daughter of Daniel POLLY	
Apr [1767]	the Wife of the aged Josiah MACK	
Jun 1768	Abigail Daughter of Jedediah POST	
Aug [1768]	Esther MERRELLS	an aged Widow
Sep [1768]	the aged Widow TILLOTSON	
Oct [1768]	Sibil infant child of Asher MERRELLS	
Jul 1769	Anna infant child of Jazaniah POST	
Aug [1769]	Thomas child of Alexander INGHAM	
Oct [1769]	Moses [child of] Thomas PERRIN	
Oct [1769]	John Son of John MACK	
6 Oct [1769]	Mathew FORD	in old age
Nov [1769]	Josiah MACK	in a good old age
Nov [1769]	Abigail Wife of Ellis BLISS	

[page 108]

Dec 1769	Lois Daughter of Elisha MACK	
16 Feb 1770	Widow Mary FORD	
17 May [1770]	[Widow] SHALER	in old age
18 May [1770]	Mary (Thompson) POST, Wife of Peter POST	
Jul [1770]	Capt Benoni TRUMBULL	
24 Dec [1770]	The aged Widow WELLS	
22 Mar 1771	Joseph DAVIS	in old age
30 Sep [1771]	John TALLCOTT	in the prime of life
Oct [1771]	the aged Mary MAJER	
14 Jan 1772	Widow Hannah RISLEY	
30 [Jan 1772]	Deborah (CURTICE) Wife of Capt Jedediah POST	
Apr 1772	a Negro child of Mr. GILBERT	
7 Jun 1772	Benjamin infant child of Peter POST	
8 Jun 1772	Jonathan BUSHNEL	
31 Jul [1772]	Sarah Daughter of Asaph TRUMBULL	
Sep [1772]	an infant child of Joel POST	
16 Mar 1773	Ephriam PERRIN	in the prime of life
22 [Mar 1773]	John infant child of Wm ROLLO	
[22 Mar 1773]	Lydia child of Elisha MACK	
31 [Mar 1773]	Widow Esther DUNK	
1 Apr [1773]	Mahitable Wife of Capt INGHAM	
Jun [1773]	John POST	
Aug 1774	Jane Daughter of Thomas BUCK	
29 Oct [1774]	Samuel A[u]gustus Son of Samuel GILBERT Esqr	
Nov [1774]	Prince Negro Boy of [Samuel GILBERT Esqr]	

[page 109]

Nov 1774	~~Lydia~~ (Elizabeth?) Daughter of Thomas POST
[Nov 1774]	Lucy infant child of John FORD Jnr
[Nov 1774]	Buly Daughter of Nathaniel PHELPS
11 Jan 1775	John HALL in the 28th year of his age
8 Feb [1775]	Lydia (POST) Wife of Samuel GILBERT Esqr
26 Feb [1775]	Stephen POST in old age. (80 yrs of age)
[Feb 1775]	Ichabod Trumbull Son of Ichabod PHELPS
Mar 1775	a child of Daniel ROOT Jnr
[Mar 1775]	[a child of] Peter POST
[Mar 1775]	[a child of] Simeon WRIGHT
[Mar 1775]	Calvin Noble a child of Calvin DUNHAM
[Mar 1775]	a child of Elias JAGGER
Apr [1775]	Mindwell Daughter of Elisha MACK
May [1775]	Martha [Daughter of Elisha MACK]
[May 1775]	Mindwell [Daughter of] Peter POST
[May 1775]	Lois [Daughter of] Elisha MACK
[May 1775]	Abigail [Daughter of] Ruben SUMNER
Jul [1775]	a child of David CURTICE
Aug[1775]	Martha a child of David CURTICE
[Aug 1775]	David CURTICE
[Aug 1775]	Mary Daughter of Ruben SUMNER
[Aug 1775]	Elizabeth [Daughter of] Widow CURTICE
[Aug 1775]	Elizabeth (WILLIAMS) Wife of Thomas PERRIN
Sep 1775	Joel Son of Joel POST
[Sep 1775]	Joel [Son of] Elijah WEBSTER

[page 110]

Sep [1775]	an infant child of Simeon WRIGHT
[Sep 1775]	Thomas an adopted child of Lieut. GILBERT
[Sep 1775]	Ezekiel Son of Elijah WEBSTER
Oct [1775]	Daniel PHELPS in his youth
[Oct 1775]	a child of Joel POST
[Oct 1775]	Dinah (Brown) the Wife of Dea. Thomas POST
[Oct 1775]	Howel Son of John H. WELLS
Nov [1775]	David Son of Amos HALL
[Nov 1775]	an infant child of David CULVER
Jan 1776	Mary Wife of Capt WELLS
[Jan 1776]	an infant child of John SKINNER
May [1776]	Obedience [child of] Simeon DUNHAM
Jul [1776]	Widow Martha TILLOTSON old age
[Jul 1776]	an infant child of Zia CASE
Aug [1776]	Twins infant children of Simeon DUNHAM
[Aug 1776]	a Negro [infant] child of Capt PHELPS

Sep [1776]	an infant [child of] Samuel GILBERT Esqr	
[Sep 1776]	William Son of William TALLCOTT	
[Sep 1776]	Martha & Molly, Twins of Zia CASE	
Oct [1776]	Ezra Son of William TALLCOTT	
[Oct 1776]	Elizabeth TALLCOTT Niece of William TALLCOTT	
Jan 1777	Joseph Son of Nathaniel DAVIS	
25 Mar [1777]	John N. ROLLO of the small pox much lamented	
Apr [1777]	Zia Son of Zia CASE	
May [1777]	Zia CASE	

[page 111]

May 1777	Bennet Son of William TALLCOTT	
Aug [1777]	Benjamin TARBOX	
Oct [1777]	a child of Ichabod PHELPS Jnr	
[1777]	Ezekiel WRIGHT	with small pox
[1777]	Lydia BAKER	
23 Nov [1777]	Elizabeth child of Thomas POST	
Apr 1778	Benjamin infant child of John MERREL	
Jul [1778]	The Widow BOLTON	
Oct [1778]	Lieut. John MACK	
Dec [1778]	a child of Peter POST	
Jan 1779	Martha Daughter of Amos HALL	
Apr [1779]	Mindwell BUSHNEL	in prime of life
Sep [1779]	Samuel infant child of Daniel BROWN	
Oct [1779]	the aged Ebenezer SKINNER	
Mar 1780	Dr Josiah ROSE	
[Mar] 1781	the Wife of John FORD	
Jun [1781]	a child of Daniel COLBURN	
Sep [1781]	Mr. John FORD	
Oct [1781]	Sarah ROOT	
Nov [1781]	Daniel ROOT	
Apr 1782	Rose the Wife of Dea ELLIS	in old age
Sep [1782]	Mercy MACK	in the flower of life
Dec [1782]	Dea Thomas POST	in old age
9 Jul 1783	Sarah (BUSHNELL) Wife of Joel POST	
Nov [1783]	an infant of Jonathan TOWNSEND	

[page 112]

Nov 1783	an infant of James POST	
[Nov 1783]	the Widow MACK	in old age
[Nov 1783	Daniel INGHAM Jnr	
Feb 1784	Lydia Wife of Col. John PETERS	
Feb 1784	an infant child of Ezekiel DANIELS	
Mar [1784]	[an infant child of] Eliphalet YOUNGS	
[Mar 1784]	Martha (BURNHAM) Wife of [Eliphalet YOUNGS]	

Apr [1784]	Edmund Son of Ellis LUTHER	
Dec [1784]	Widow BUSHNEL	in old age
Feb 1785	Elisabeth ROLLO	in the Bloom of youth
Apr [1785]	Alfred Son of Jonathan TOWNSEND	
Aug [1785]	Deborah (Mrs. TARBOX) Wife of Capt POST	
Sep [1785]	Hannah Daughter of Lieut Gad TALLCOTt	
Oct [1785]	Eliphalet YOUNGS	
Dec [1785]	Widow BINGHAM	in old age
Jan 1786	Widow YOUNGS	
3 Feb [1786]	Martha Trumbull Wife of Capt PHELPS	
Mar [1786]	a child of Amos HURLBURT	
[Mar 1786]	a Son of Daniel LOOMER	
[Mar 1786]	a Daughter of [Daniel LOOMER]	
[Mar 1786]	Esther Daughter of Joel POST	
[Mar 1786]	Capt Jedediah POST	
[Mar 1786]	Benjamin Son of Dea Jabez ELLIS	
[Mar 1786]	Oliver [Son of] Zepheniah DAVIS	
Apr [1786]	an infant child of Dr Joseph PETERS	

[page 113]

Oct 1786	an infant of Spencer WOOD	
Mar 1788	Rhoda Daughter of Joshua ROOT	
May [1788]	a child of Nehemiah ROSWELL	
3 Feb 1789	Mary Wife of Capt Josiah MACK	
Jul [1789]	the aged Thomas PERRIN	
Sep [1789]	Philis Wife of Sampson WILSON Negro Man	
Dec [1789]	Laura LOTHROP	much lamented
[Dec 1789]	Mehetable Wife of Jordan POST	
Aug [1789] [sic]	Sarah Daughter of Samuel GILBERT Esqr	
[Aug] 1790	Elizabeth Wife of Col John PETERS	
[Aug 1790]	Jonathan CURTICE	
Nov [1790]	Lucy (HALL) Wife of William ROLLO	
Mar 1791	a child of Zecheriah ROLLO	
Jun [1791]	[a child of] Nehemiah ROSWELL	
Mar 1792	Elijah POST	in the prime of Life
Oct [1792]	Dea[con] John ELLIS	in the 88th year of his age
Jan 1793	Fowler MERRIL	in the prime of life
[Jan 1793]	James POST	Middle aged
Jun [1793]	Patty Daughter of Capt TRUMBULL	
Oct [1793]	Deborah [Daughter of] James BROWN	
Nov [1793]	Phebe (FORD) Wife of John FINLEY	
1 Jan 1794	Mr. John SAWYER	in the 86th year of his age
8 [Jan 1794]	Capt Ichabod PHELPS	in the 86th year of his age
[Jan 1794]	an infant child Henry LAWRENCE	

[Jan 1794]	Lieut John GILBERT in the 80th year of his age
	[page 114]
Feb 1794	Insign Benjamin TRUMBULL brought from Bolton
Apr [1794]	Josiah Son of Samuel PIPER killed by the fall of a Tree
Jul [1794]	Mary Wife of Capt WELLS in the 50th year of his age
Dec [1794]	Abigail infant child of David CULVER
30 Jan 1795	Widow SAWYER in the 93rd year of her age
Feb [1795]	an infant child of Leonard E. LOTHROP
Mar [1795]	Wm Augustus Son of Anna BURGE
May [1795]	Sarah Wife of Benjamin ARCHER
Jun [1795]	an infant child of Henry MACK
Dec [1795]	the Wife of Samuel FIELDING aged 33 yrs
June 1796	Israel Son of Zepheniah DAVIS aged 15 yrs
Feb [1796]	Ezra [Son of] Jehiel WILCOX [aged] 15 [yrs]
Feb [1796]	Philomelia Daughter of Jonathan TOWNSEND
Mar [1796]	Chester Son of Jonathan HALL
Apr [1796]	Anna (MORGAN) Wife of John FINLEY
May [1796]	Dea[con] Seth HALL in the 88th year of his age
Aug [1796]	Abigail the aged Widow of John GILBERT in [her} 79th year
26 Sep [1796]	Jonathan HUTCHINSON in 77th year of his age
Oct [1796]	Chester Hall infant child of Henry MACK
Jan 1797	Isaac Dunham in 86th year of his age
Feb [1797]	John PERRIN*
Apr [1797]	an infant child of John Bill WELLS
3 Aug [1797]	Rev Elijah LOTHROP Aged 72 y. 8 m. & 15 Days
15 Oct 1799	Madam Silence LOTHROP Aged 68 y. 5 m. & 18 d.
31 Dec [1799]	Capt William ROLLO Aged 53
	[page 115]
Jul 1800	Benjamin ROOT*
10 Sep [1800]	the Widow Hannah TALLCOTT*
[10 Sep 1800]	[the Widow] Judith CURTICE*
Dec [1800]	Sampson WILSON a Black Man
Feb 1801	Augustus Son of John & Molly HUTCHINSON
Mar [1801]	Polly Daughter of John WASS*
May [1801]	Capt. Daniel INGHAM Aged 78
Nov [1801]	the Widow Jerusha DUNHAM
Jan 1802	[the Widow] Abigail HUTCHINSON*
Mar [1802]	Grace Daughter of Capt Gad TALLCOTT*
Nov [1802]	Mr Jude WRIGHT in old age
Dec [1802]	Mrs Sybel (POST) LUTHER Wife of Ellis LUTHER*

[Dec] 1803	Walter ROLLO Esq from Cambridge N.Y.	
	John THOMAS*	
Jan 1804	Doctor David SUTTON	
23 Jun [1804]	Abiah DUNHAM Wife of Capt Simeon DUNHAM	
Nov [1804]	Colo John PETERS	Aged 87 years
Jan 1805	Samuel GEAR	58th year of his age
Feb [1805]	Jerusha DUNHAM	Aged 26^t years
Jul [1805]	Elizabeth SUMNER Wife of Ruben SUMNER	
[1805]	a Black woman of Mr. ELLIS's	
Aug 1806	an infant child of Eleazer & Sally HUTCHINSON	
21 Aug 1806	William R. Son of Edward S. ELLIS	
Sep [1806]	Martha CHAPMAN	Aged 26
28 Mar 1807	Capt William TALCOTT	Aged 65

[Page 116]

Apr 1807	Ralph Son of Ralph MACK	aged 3 yr
[1807]	Ruben SUMNER	Aged 80 years
Feb 1808	Stephen HORTON	[Aged] 78 [years]
[1808]	Sarah CURTICE Wife of John CURTICE	
Mar [1808]	Hannah HORTON	Aged 26
[1808]	A. CASE Wife of Joseph W. CASE	Aged 62
Apr [1808]	Joel a black Boy of Col S. GILBERT	
[1808]	Matilda Daughter of Henry P. SUMNER	
Jul [1808]	Robe PEEKUM a Negro Woman	
12 Sep [1808]	Abigail (ROOT) Wife of Capt Gad TALCOTT*	
Feb 1809	an infant of Capt Jonathan TRUMBULL	
17 May [1809]	John CONE	Aged 43 years
Aug [1809]	Manson BROWN	in the 19th year of his life
Mar 1810	Samuel FIELDING	
15 Jul [1810]	Polly Daughter of Joseph POST (& Hannah)	
[1810]	Daniel Son of Daniel S. WAY*	
Sep [1810]	the Wife of Thomas WELLS	
11 Feb 1811	Norman O. son of Eleazer B. STRONG	
May [1811]	John B. WELLS	
Jul [1811]	John CURTICE	Aged 83 years
13 Oct [1811]	Thomas POST	[Aged] 80 [years]
Nov [1811]	an infant of Eleazer B. STRONG	
Jan 1812	Samuel E. GEAR*	
Feb [1812]	Susan a Negro woman	
8 Feb [1812]	Capt ~~Samuel~~ Solomon NORTON	Aged 96

[page 117]

Mar 1812	Whiting TRUMBULL	Aged 16
27 [Mar 1812]	Mary TALCOTT (Wid of William)	[Aged] 67(66)
Apr [1812]	Abigail PETERS	[Aged] 74

May [1812]	an infant child of Richard COLEMAN	
24 May [1812]	Capt Josiah MACK	Aged 90
Aug [1812]	Jonathan PETERS*	
Sep [1812]	an infant child of Capt Ezekiel A. POST	
Oct [1812]	the Widow Hannah ROWLEY*	
Feb 1813	Deborah (PHELPS) the Wife of David NORTON	
[1813]	Ichabod Son of David POST	Aged 13
May [1813]	Joel POST in the 70th year of his age	
Jul [1813]	Ichabod PHELPS	Aged 74 years
[1813]	Deborah (Post) Wife of Elijah WEBSTER	Aged 72
Sep [1813]	Harvey Son of Ruben SUMNER	[Aged] 16
[1813]	Mary Ann Daughter of Ruben SUMNER [Aged] 16 mos	
Dec [1813]	Benjamin TALLCOTT	Aged 42
Feb 1814	Ebenezer NORTON	[Aged] 80
[1814]	Whiting Son of Capt Jonathan TRUMBULL. 13 mo	
Jun [1814]	an infant child of Eleazer & Sally HUTCHINSON	
Aug [1814]	David CULVER	Aged 76
[1814]	the Widow ____ Solomon NORTON	[Aged] 92
[1814]	a child of Daniel S. WAY*	
Sep [1814]	the Widow BROWN*	
[1814]	an infant child Ezekiel A. POST	
Oct [1814]	William Henry Son of Ralph R. ROLLO Aged 6 mo	

[page 118]

1814	Zilpha A. Daughter of Ruben WELLS	aged 5 yrs
Dec [1814]	a child of John LOOMER	
4 Jan 1815	Jedediah POST	Aged 64 years
Feb [1815]	Ann BROWN	[Aged] 30 [yrs]
[1815]	the Widow ROSWEL*	
28 [Feb 1815]	Mercy (ROLLO) wife of capt Edward S. ELLIS	
		Aged 32 years
Apr [1815]	Amos HALL in the 81st year of his age	
Jul [1815]	Widow WELLS	
Oct [1815]	Mrs. DANIELS Wife of Simeon DANIELS	
[1815]	Hannah (GEER) Wife of Ezekiel A. POST	
[1815]	Primus a Black Man	
Nov [1815]	Elijah WEBSTER	Aged 81 years
[1815]	Mr WAY	
3 Feb 1816	Hannah Wife of Joseph POST	aged 69
13 May [1816]	Elijah DUNHAM	
Sep [1816]	Willard Son of Cyrus ALLEN	aged 4 yrs
Oct [1816]	Mary Daughter of Almira WELLS	[Aged] 2 [yrs]
*11 Jan 1817	Capt Simeon DUNHAM	[Aged] 78 [years]
10 May [1817]	Obedience Daughter of Capt Simeon DUNHAM	

Oct [1817]	An infant child of George TRYON	
Nov [1817]	Christopher CROUCH*	
9 Feb 1818	Sally (TALLCOTT) Wife of Eleazer HUTCHINSON*	
Mar [1818]	Martha (HORSFORD) Wife of David HUTCHINSON*	
21 Apr [1818]	Colo Samuel GILBERT	aged 83 years
Jul [1818]	George Son of Joel POST	

[page 119]

Oct 1818	Capt. Daniel BUSHNEL	aged 72 years
[1818]	Mr. John FOOT	[aged] 90 [years]
Dec [1818]	William son of George TRYON	[aged] 3 [yrs]
[1818]	Lucy LOOMER	[aged] 20 [years]
Jan 1819	Widow Annice PETERS	[aged] 78 [years]
[1819]	Miss. Cynthia KIMBALL*	
Mar [1819]	the Widow of Thomas WAY*	
Apr [1819]	Gideon WATERS*	
[1819]	an infant child of Charles [____,] Negro	
[1819]	Lucy Wife of Joseph HARRIS*	
Jun [1819]	Molly (POST) Wife of John HUTCHINSON Aged 57 yrs*	
[1819]	Harriot Mariah Daughter of Ezekiel A. POST	
Oct [1819]	a child of Asahel POST	
Nov [1819]	Widow Ruth of Moses HUTCHINSON Aged 93 yrs	
Jan 1820	a child of John LOOMER	
[1820]	Eliza BROWN	
Mar [1820]	the Widow BALEY*	
14 Apr [1820]	Abitha the Widow of Thomas POST	
May [1820]	John MERRILS	
[1820]	Harriot WARNER Wife of Capt Samuel TALLCOTT*	
Feb 1821	Dea[con] Asaph TRUMBULL	aged 82 years
[1821]	Cynthia ADAMS	
25 [Feb 1821]	Samuel Egbert Son of Rev Nathan GILLET*	
Sep [1821]	Capt Samuel PETERS	Aged 63 years
[1821]	John DOW	[Aged] 48 [years]

[page 120]

Oct 1821	Sally SUMNER the wife of John H. POST	
		aged 25 years
Feb 1822	Aaron BAXSTER	[aged] 86 [years]
Mar [1822]	Miss Lydia WILCOX	[aged] 49 [years]
Aug [1822]	Miss Deborah MACK	[aged] 22 [years]
Oct [1822]	Miss Clarissa HUTCHINSON	
	(dau of John & Molly)	[aged] 27
[1822]	James BROWN	[aged] 69 [years]
Nov [1822]	Samuel HORTON	
Feb 1823	a child of Asahel POST [aged] 20 mos	

Mar [1823]	[a child of] Charles RICHARDS	
17 Aug [1823]	Zilpha HUTCHINSON Wife of Eleazer B. STRONG	[aged] 42 years
[1823]	the Widow Zilpha TRUMBULL	[aged] 77 [yrs]
Feb 1824	Capt David W. POST	
Mar [1824]	Betsey (TRUMBULL) Wife of Wm BROWN Esqr	
Jun [1824]	a child of Henry HINKLEY	
Jul [1824]	Zacheriah ROLLO	
Aug [1824]	Joel POST	
21 Nov [1824]	George Oliver son of Capt Oliver WILCOX	
Dec [1824]	Miss Deborah NORTON	
Feb 1825	Widow Sarah (CULVER) MERRILS	Aged 91 yrs
Mar [1825]	Welthy Lauretta Daughter of Asahel POST	
May [1825]	Widow (of Joel) Lucy POST	Aged 79 yrs
17 Oct [1825]	John Henry POST	[Aged] 31
26 Jan 1826	Anna HORTON	[Aged] 80
3 Mar [1826]	Lydia BUSHNELL	[Aged] 82
7 Mar [1826]	John H. WELLS	[Aged] 82

[page 121]

23 Mar 1826	Jethro colored	aged 78 yrs
4 Apr 1826	Lavina THOMAS	[aged] 79 [yrs]
6 Apr [1826]	Susannah TALCOTT	[aged] 69 [yrs]
6 Jun [1826]	Elizabeth DANIELS	[aged] 70 [yrs]
3 Jul [1826]	Thomas WELLS	[aged] 66 [yrs]
29 Sep [1826]	Cyrus DUNHAM	[aged] 27 [yrs]
1 Oct [1826]	Mary DEAN	[aged] 83 [yrs]
19 Dec [1826]	Child of Danl LOOMER	[aged] 3 [yrs]
16 Jan 1827	Josiah MACK	[aged] 70 [yrs]
24 Feb [1827]	Child of Charles (colored)[13]	[aged] 4 mos
25 Mar [1827]	Benjamin (colored)	[aged] 2 days
26 Mar [1827]	Betsey WEBSTER	[aged] 79 yrs
9 May [1827]	George WELLES (died near Boston)	[aged] 42 [yrs]
7 July [1827]	Charles RICHARDS (colored)	[aged] 3 [yrs]
15 Sep [1827]	Nathan (colored)	rising of 60 [yrs]
20 Nov [1827]	Isaac DUNHAM	aged 62 [yrs]
22 [Nov 1827]	Hannah CONE (wid of John CONE)	[aged] 49 [yrs]
3 Dec[1827]	Hester TALCOTT (wife of Saml TALCOTT)	[aged] 38 [yrs]
3 Feb 1828	Joseph HUTCHINSON	[aged] 79 [yrs]

---

[13] For unspecified reasons, the index to Warner's manuscript created by the Connecticut State Library in 1931, assigns this entry the surname RICHARDS, RICHARD.

20 May [1828]	Joseph POST	[aged] 81 [yrs]
25 Aug [1828]	Ceasar CHAPPELL (colored)	[aged] 69 [yrs]
2 Sep [1828]	Eunice Dunis HINCKLEY	[aged] 28 [yrs]
6 Jan 1829	Betsey HALL	[aged] 89 [yrs]
31 Jan [1829]	Ezekiel DANIELS	[aged] 76 [yrs]
18 Mar [1829]	Lavina CURTISS.	Past middle life

[page 122]

13 Sept 1829	Sarah ROLLO	aged 80 yrs
19 Nov [1829]	Lydia HALL	[aged] 54 [yrs]
7 May 1830	Jonathan TOWNSEND	[aged] 79 [yrs]
12 Jun [1830]	An infant child of Mr. COLEMAN	
21 Jun [1830]	Betsey a person of color	in the middle of life
21 [Jun 1830]	Elisha Manly LORD	[aged] 4 [yrs]
9 Jul [1830]	Deborah MACK	[aged] 92 [yrs]
[Jul 1830]	Mrs CULVER	
9 Aug [1830]	Julia NICHOLS	[aged] 2½ [yrs]
28 [Aug 1830]	Infant child of Dudley HODGE	
4 Sept [1830]	Edward ELLIS	[aged] 49 [yrs]
[4 Sept 1830]	Sawyer ELLIS	[aged] 73 [yrs]
9 Sept [1830]	Abigail ELLIS	[aged] 69 [yrs]
25 Sept [1830]	Sarah JONES	[aged] 55 [yrs]
29 Sept [1830]	Nathan BLISS	[aged] 80 [yrs]
3 [Oct 1830]	Gad TALCOTT	[aged] 85 [yrs]
6 [Oct 1830]	Abby Lauretta ELLIS	[aged] 20 [yrs]
12 [Oct 1830]	Edmund R. BRAINERD	[aged] 8 mos
13 [Oct 1830]	Abiel BLISS	[aged] 78 yrs
30 [Oct 1830]	Mercy Maria ELLIS	[aged] 22 [yrs]
14 Nov [1830]	Sybil HUTCHINSON wf of Joseph	[aged 78 [yrs]
4 Dec [1830]	Gustavus GOODELL	[aged] 26 [yrs]
28 Jan [1831]	David HUTCHINSON	[aged] 47 [yrs]
16 Aug [1831]	Joshua ROOT	[aged] 78 [yrs]
20 Oct [1831]	Clarissa HAMILTON	[aged] 63 [yrs]
1 Dec [1831]	Mrs. WILSON	

[page 123]

28 Dec 1831	Widow GREEN	Aged 79 yrs
25 Feb 1832	George Alfred WELLES	[Aged] 21 [yrs]
7 Apr [1832]	Abby Maria GILBERT	[Aged] 17 [yrs]
20 [Apr 1832]	James CULVER	[Aged] 66 [yrs]
29 May [1832]	Jehiel WILCOX	[Aged] 84 [yrs]
1 Jun [1832]	Daniel BROWN	[Aged] 85 [yrs]
20 Jun [1832]	Harry POWERS (colored) about	[aged] 30 [yrs]
[1832]	a colored child of Charles SHEPHERD	[aged] 4 [yrs]
Jul [1832]	Edmund HORTON killed instantly at a raising	

		[aged] 65 [yrs]
26 Aug [1832]	Eleanor Wife of Dea Jonathan HUTCHINSON	[aged] 88 [yrs]
15 Feb 1833	Henry MACK	
Mar [1833]	Mrs. THOMPSON	
29 Aug [1833]	Mehetable (HALL) widow of Henry MACK	
3 Nov [1833]	John MACK Son of Aaron MACK	aged 2 ½ yrs
9 Jun 1834	Eleazar HUTCHINSON	[aged] 55 [yrs]
4 Oct [1834]	Levi POST Son of Arunah POST	[aged] 16 [yrs]
27 Oct [1834]	Lucy Vandelia GOODALE	[aged] 15 mo
10 Nov [1834]	Ezekiel Ela WEBSTER son of Ezekiel	[aged] 29 yrs
6 Dec. [1834]	Mary (DIBBLE) wife of Israel HUTCHINSON	[aged] 79 [yrs]
26 Dec [1834]	Jeremiah BROWN	in advanced life
Jan 1835	Ichabod WARNER	[aged] 36 [yrs]
[1835]	Semantha HORTON	in youth
[1835]	Mrs. WATROUS	in old age
12 Apr [1835]	Mahitabel INGHAM Wife of David NORTON	[aged] 70 [yrs]
6 May [1835]	James WELLES	[aged] 54 [yrs]

[page 124]

21 May 1835	Elizabeth ROOT	Aged 76 yrs
11 Feb 1836	~~Polly~~ Mary DUNHAM	[Aged] 64 [yrs]
15 Mar [1835]	Child of Horace CURTICE	[Aged] 2 [yrs]
28 [Mar 1835]	John POST	[Aged] 30 [yrs]
24 Apr [1835]	Mrs --- NORTHAM wife of Dea NORTHAM Marlborough	(in old age)
25 Apr [1835]	Edmund C. GEAR. Much lamented	[Aged] 42 [yrs]
19 Aug [1835]	Grace RICHARD	[Aged] 46 [yrs]
22 Aug [1835]	Child of David PORTER	[Aged] 9 [yrs]
21 Sep [1835]	William Henry STRONG, He hung himself being partially damaged.	[Aged 20 [yrs]
20 Oct[1835]	Infant child of Josiah WATROUS	
1 Dec [1835]	John Henry MACK Son of Aaron	[Aged] 1 ½ [yrs]
23 [Dec 1835]	Wife of Hiram HORTON	[Aged] 72 [yrs]
28 [Dec 1835]	Child of Chauncey L. ROOT	[Aged] 2 [yrs]
7 Feb 1837	Mabel MACK	[Aged] 44 [yrs]
10 [Feb 1837]	Infant child of Mr. HARVEY	
12 [Feb 1837]	Child of Charles MORGAN. Colored.	
7 Mar [1837]	Infant child of Horace CURTISS	
1 Apr [1837]	Jemima (TARBOX) wife of William SUMNER	aged 74 yrs
Jul [1837]	Wife of Wm WILSON.	Advanced in life.

28 [Jul 1837]	Wife of Ezekiel BROWN.	in old age (73 yrs)
10 Aug [1837]	Anna (PHELPS) BROWN relict of Dan[l] BROWN	[Aged] 82 [yrs]
11 Dec [1837]	Widow Hannah PORTER	[Aged] 79 [yrs]
1 Jan 1838	Dea Jonathan HUTCHINSON	[Aged] 92 [yrs]
4 [Jan 1838]	Azubah HALL	[Aged] 70 [yrs]
18 [Jan 1838]	Henry SUMNER	

[page 125]

Jan 20 1838	Infant Child of Mr. DOANE	aged 2 yrs
28 Mar 1838	Patience POST (Relict of Jedediah)	[Aged] 87 [yrs]
17 May 1838	William SUMNER	[Aged] 77 [yrs]
June 1838	Child of Mr. SAUNDERS	[Aged] 4 [yrs]
15 Jul 1838	Mrs. BLISS (wife of Abial)	advanced in life
[1838]	Child of Ephraim COLEMAN	
Oct [1838]	Henry LEE found dead in the street.	[Aged] 64 [yrs]
13 Jan 1839	Asahel POST	[Aged] 57 [yrs]
4 Feb [1839]	Mrs. BURDIT	[Aged] 27
7 Apr [1839]	Lucy wife of Luther FORD	[Aged] 72 [yrs]
25 May [1839]	Frederick WHITE	[Aged] 46 [yrs]
24 May [1839]	Infant child of John SUMNER	
5 Sept [1839]	Israel HUTCHINSON	[Aged] 88[yrs]
6 Oct [1839]	David NORTON	[Aged] 87
3 Feb 1840	Dea Jonathan NORTHAM of the Ch in Marlborough	[Aged] 84 [yrs]
28 Apr [1840]	George HALL	[Aged] 75 [yrs]
29 [Apr 1840]	Ruth HUTCHINSON (Eleazar's 2nd wife) died in Bolton	[Aged] 57 [yrs]
8 Jun [1840]	Luther FORD	[Aged] 78 [yrs]
28 Sep [1840]	Arunah POST	[Aged] 51 [yrs]
4 Oct [1840]	David POST	[Aged] 88[yrs]
15 Jan 1841	Abalena (TICKNOR) HIGGINS wife of Henry HIGGINS	Aged] 24 [yrs]
21 Feb* [1840]	Joel* ROOT*	[Aged] 58 [yrs]
20 Nov* [1840]	John* POST* * *	[Aged] 79 [yrs]
24 Nov [1840]	Hiram GOODALE	[Aged] 41 [yrs]
21 Dec [1840]	Jethro NORTON	[Aged] 86 [yrs]
29 Dec [1840]	Hannah PETERS	[Aged] 80 [yrs]

PART II

BIRTH, MARRIAGES & DEATHS 1847-1855
And Other Vital Records Not in Barbour

We have uncovered one previously unindexed folio of pre-1855 vital records in the Office of the Hebron Town Clerk. Could there be others? How can that question be definitively answered? Such an inquiry must begin by studying Barbour's own description of his extraction:[14]

> This volume contains a list alphabetically arranged of all the vital records of the town of Hebron from its incorporation to about 1854. This list was taken from a set of cards based on a copy of the Hebron Vital Records made in 1921 by Mrs. Anne C. Gilbert, of Hebron, Conn. The entire record for this town prior to 1854, is contained in five volumes. References to the fifth volume are indicated by the letter "M" added to the page numbers,
> but the volume has been referred to as "Volume 4".
> The Gilbert copy, now in the possession of the Connecticut State Library, has been compared with the original, but this alphabetical list has not and doubtless errors exist. It is hoped that as errors or omissions are found notes will be entered in this volume and on the cards which are included in the General Index of Connecticut Vital Records also in the possession of the Connecticut State Library.
>
> Hartford, Conn., December, 1922.

The Family History Library has tried to microfilm all of Hebron's vital records. The next step, therefore, should be to compare Barbour's catalog of early Hebron vital records with the Family History Library Catalog on the same subject.[15]

---

[14] Barbour and Barbour, "Barbour Collection of Connecticut Vital Records prior to 1850," volume 54: Hebron (bound transcript, 1922, CSL, Hartford); FHL film no. 2972. This important introduction is inexplicably omitted in Dorothy Wear, *The Barbour Collection of Connecticut Town Vital Records: Hartland 1761–1848, Harwinton 1737–1854, Hebron 1708–1854*, vol. 18, (Baltimore: GPC, 1999).

[15] See http://FamilySearch.org/library/FHLC/frameset_fhlc.asp.

Two relevant Family History Library microfilms (1376165 and 1376166) contain ten items from the Town Clerk's records and the Registrar of Vital Statistics:

1. *Births, Marriages, Deaths, Vol. One, 1684–1801.*[16]

2. *Births, Marriages, Deaths, Vol. Two, 1750–1792.*[17]

3. *Births, Marriages, Deaths, Vol. Three, 1770–1849.*[18]

4. *Hebron Marriages (1820–1854).*[19]

5. *Vital Statistics Index, 1684–1854.*[20]

6. *Births, Marriages, Deaths, Vol. Four, 1848–1911* [sic].[21]

7. *Births, Marriages, Deaths, Vol. Five, 1871–1890.*[22]

8. *Births, Marriages, Deaths, Vol. Six, 1891–1911.*[23]

9. *Marriage certificates, 1799–1819 & 1827–1854.*[24]

10. *An alphabetized recopy of vol. 1 of the Vital Records.*[25]

---

[16] Hebron Town Clerk, Records of Births, Marriages, and Deaths, 1684-1849 (original in Town Hall) vol. 1 (FHL film 1376165, Item 2).

[17] Hebron Town Clerk, Records of Births, Marriages, and Deaths, 1684-1849 (original in Town Hall) vol. 2 (FHL film 1376165, Item 4).

[18] Hebron Town Clerk, Records of Births, Marriages, and Deaths, 1684-1849 (original in Town Hall) vol. 3 (FHL film 1376166, Item 1).

[19] Hebron Registrar of Vital Statistics, Record of Marriages, 1820-1854 (FHL film 1376166, Item 3).

[20] Hebron Town Clerk, [Index to] Births, Marriages, Deaths in v. 1-3 [sic], (original in Hebron Town Hall) (FHL film 1376165, Item 3). The catalog notes: "Index also gives references to a vol. 4 of births ... not found in this library."

[21] Hebron Registrar of Vital Statistics, Records of Births, Marriages, Deaths in the Town of Hebron, 1848-1870 vol. 4 (FHL film 1376166, Item 2).

[22] Hebron Registrar of Vital Statistics, Records of Births, Marriages, Deaths in the Town of Hebron, 1848-1911 (FHL film 1376166, Item 4).

[23] Hebron Registrar of Vital Statistics, Records of Births, Marriages, Deaths in the Town of Hebron, 1848-1911 (FHL film 1376166, Item 5).

[24] Hebron Town Clerk, Marriage certificates, 1827-1854, 1814-1819 [sic] (FHL film 1376166, Item 6) (includes a typescript listing the names of the groom and bride and the marriage date for most certificates).

Neither Barbour's statement nor the FHL microfilmed vital records reference the previously unpublished 47-page folio of death records transcribed with Warner's Necrology in Part I above[26]. The first three volumes of Hebron records and the Book of Marriages referenced by Barbour are clearly identifiable in the Family History Library catalog. Barbour's "Book 4," however, is not.

The contents of the volume that the Hebron Town Clerk call *Births, Deaths, Marriages, Volume Four, 1848–1870* and the Family History Library misdates as 1848–1911, are not what Barbour identifies as "Book 4." Nevertheless, the information in Barbour's "Book 4" *does* appear indexed into Hebron's Vital Statistics Index, 1684–1854 as the "Fourth Book of Births."

The information that both Barbour and the Hebron Town Clerk index as "Book 4" is from a slim volume (author or compiler unknown) in the Town Clerk's Office titled *Births – Family Records – Book 4 – 1594–1909 – Hebron*. This seventeen-page book presents the births of Hebron residents, family-by-family, listing first a couple and then their (perhaps only surviving) children, without stating where the births occurred. The earliest birth listed in the book is of the immigrant ancestors of Hebron's Carver family in England in 1594. Some 1922-24 entries in this bound manuscript are signed by "Anne Gilbert, Asst. Registrar," probably the same Anne Gilbert whom Barbour credits with the compilation of his collection of Hebron vital records in 1922.

The Hebron Town Clerk's Office considers the information in this book reliable. Nevertheless, it remains a derivative work by an unknown compiler. Barbour therefore implicitly misrepresents it as the equivalent of the original vital records in the first three volumes of Hebron's Birth, Marriage, and Death registers. Family History Library has no microfilm of this "Book 4", but a complete though uncataloged photocopy is available for examination at the Connecticut State Library.

The Family History Library catalog describes the Hebron's Vital Statistics Index as the index to only volumes one through three of its vital records. In addition it warns that the "Index also gives reference to a vol. 4 of births ... which [is] not found in this

---

[25] Hebron Town Clerk, First Book of Records, Births, Marriages and Deaths, Town of Hebron (FHL film1376165, Item 1).

[26] See text at note d above.

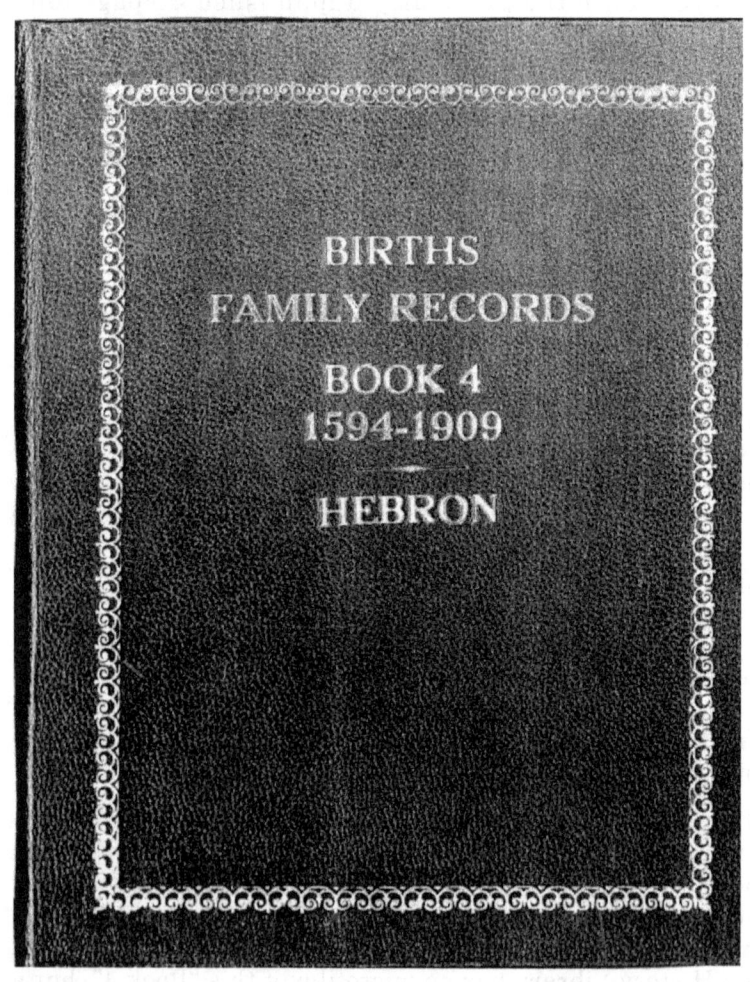

Plate 1: Cover of *Births – Family Records – Book 4 – 1594-1909 – Hebron*: The, unmicrofilmed derivative source (author or compiler unknown) indexed by Barbour and the Hebron Town Clerk as "Book 4."

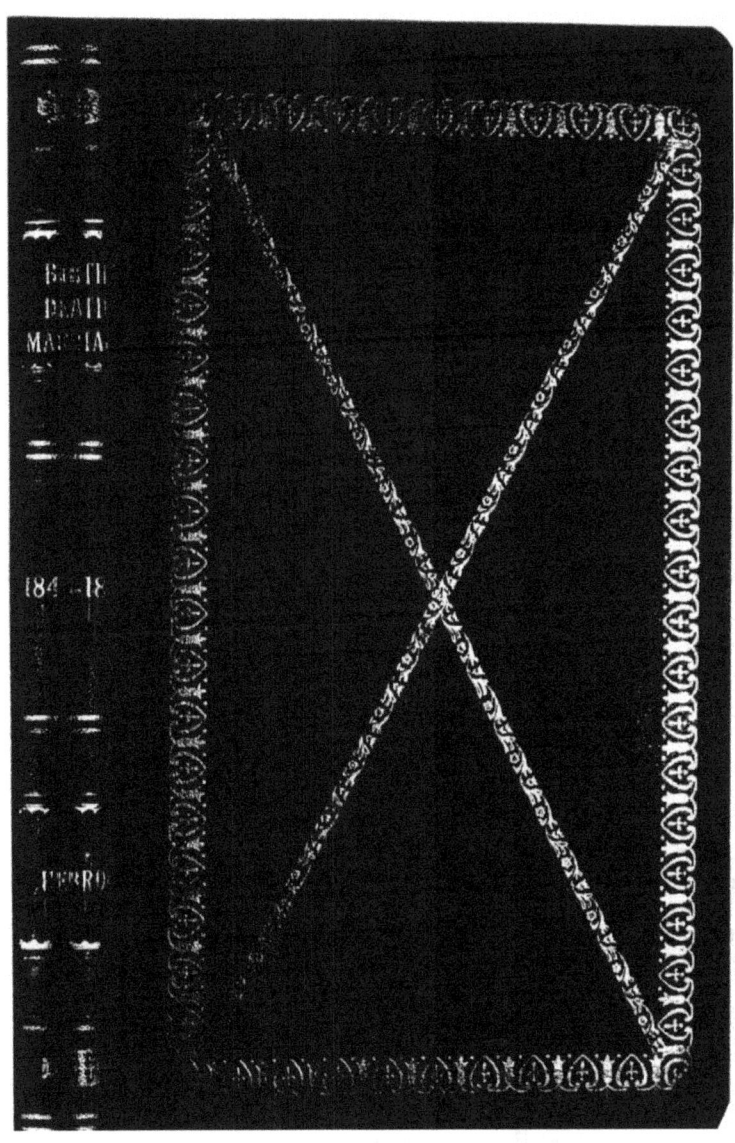

Plate 2: Cover of *Births, Marriages and Deaths, Volume Four, 1848-1870*: It includes 1847–1854 Hebron vital records overlooked by the Barbour Index and the Hebron Town Clerk's Vital Statistics Index

library.[27] Hebron Town Clerk's *Birth, Marriages and Deaths, Volume Four, 1848–1911* was probably not indexed by the clerk because it was yet incomplete at the time completed volumes of Hebron vital records were indexed. These records from 1847 forward may have been missed by Barbour because they were omitted from the town clerk's index of early vital records.

Hebron is far from the only Connecticut town whose post-1847 vital records were missed by Barbour. Connecticut town vital records volumes that include the years following 1847 were frequently omitted from the Barbour Collection of Connecticut Vital Records, even though it generally purports to include town vital records through at least 1850. Comparisons of Barbour's sources in other Connecticut town collections with corresponding FHL microfilms show that he overlooked such vital records books in at least thirty-eight Connecticut towns.[28]

---

[27] See note i, above.

[28] See, e.g., **Bethlehem**, Records of Births, Marriages & Deaths, 1847–1948, (FHL film 1522005, Items 4-5); **Bridgeport**, Records of Births in the Town of Bridgeport, 1847–1854 (FHL film 1428299, Items 1–2); **Bristol**, Records of Births, Marriages & Deaths, vol. 4, 1847–1871, (FHL film 1316018); **Canaan**, Births, Marriages & Deaths, 1847–1948) (FHL film 1503196, Items 2-3); Cheshire, Town Records vol. 4 1845–1884 (FHL film 1412760); **Colebrook**, Births, Marriages & Deaths, 1846–1852 (FHL film 1503206, Item 4); **Columbia**, "Records of Births, Marriages & Deaths, 1847–1947 (FHL film 1376168, Items 2-3); **Danbury**, Births in the Town of Danbury, 1847–1910 (FHL film 1435526); **Darien**, Records of Births, Marriages & Deaths, vols. 1-3, 1847–1909 (FHL film 1434227, Item 3-5); **Durham**, "Records of Births, Marriages & Deaths, 1847–1916, (FHL film 1398795, Item 2); Fairfield, Reports of Births, Marriages & Deaths in the School Districts, 1847–1850 (FHL film 1434093, Item 2); **Farmington**, Record of Births, Marriages & Deaths in the Town of Farmington, v. 1 1847–1868 (FHL film 1315115); **Greenwich**, Births, Marriages & Deaths v. 1-2 (p.1-191) 1847–1892 [FHL film 1434365]; **Groton**, Births, Marriages & Deaths, vol. 4, 1848–1875 [FHL film 1306249, Item 3]; Killingworth, Records of Births, Marriages & Deaths, 1847–1908, FHL Film 1378453, Item 2; **Marlborough**, Records of Births, Marriages, and Deaths, 1852-1940, FHL film 1318178, Items 2]; **Middletown**, Records of Births, Marriages & Deaths, Vol. 6 Births 1852–1868 (FHL Film 1513708, Item 5), Vol. 7 Marriages 1852–1855 (FHL Film 1513709, Items 3), & Vol. 8 Deaths 1852–1878 (FHL Film 1513709, Items 4);. **Milford**, Records of Births, Marriages & Deaths, v. 7-8 1847–1849 & 1852–1867 (FHL film 1428120); **New Hartford**, Records of Births, Marriages & deaths, 1852–1921 [FHL Film 1318241, Item 4]; **North Branford**, "Records of Births,

Such overlooked records also exist in at least three other Connecticut towns that Barbour never indexed at all.[29] Unique to Barbour's treatment of Hebron, however, is that he extracted a derivative source — instead of an available original source— without so advising those who rely upon his work.

The contents of all post-1847 vital records volumes noted above are organized by school district and contain extraordinary detail. Despite Barbour's neglect, Connecticut researchers should utilize all these films to ensure comprehensive research.

No survey has been taken to determine how many Connecticut towns retain marriage certificates that are presumably the basis

---

Marriages & Deaths, 1847–1908" (FHL film 1420924, Item 3); **Norwalk**, Records of Births, Marriages & Deaths, 1848–1909, [FHL Film 1434202]; **Rocky Hill**, Births, Marriages & Deaths v. 1 1847–1868 (FHL film 1316153, Items 2-3); **Roxbury**, Report of Births, Deaths & Marriages, 1847–1851, (FHL film 1522004); **Salisbury**, Records of Births, Deaths & Marriages, 1847–1905, [FHL Film 1509740, Items 6-7];. **Simsbury**, "Records of Births, Marriages & Deaths, v. 1-2, 1847–1908" (FHL film 1314487, Items 2-3); **Southbury**, "Records of Births, Marriages & Deaths, 1848–1905" (FHL film 1420657, Items 3-5); **Southington**, "Records of Births, Marriages & Deaths, 1847–1900" (FHL film 1316016, Items 3-4); **Stamford**, "Records of Births, Marriages & Deaths, 1847–1906" (FHL film 1434311); **Stonington**, Records of Births, Marriages & Deaths 1847–1869 [FHL Film 1309873, Items 2-4]; **Tolland**, Records of Births, Marriages & Deaths, 1848–1926 (FHL film 376026, Item 4); **Washington**, "Records of Births, Marriages & Deaths in the Town of Washington, 1852–1913" (FHL film 1517000, Items 3-4); **Waterbury**, Record of Births, Marriages & Deaths, 1852–1858, (FHL film 1412840, Items 3-4); **Watertown**, Births, Marriages & Deaths, v. 1, 1847–1902 (FHL film 1521444); **Weston**, "Records of Births, Marriages & Deaths in Weston, 1847–1867" (FHL film 1435804, Item 1); **Westport**, Births, Marriages & Deaths, 1852–1903 [FHL film 1480168, Items 2-5]; **Willington**, Births, Marriages & Deaths, 1847–1912 (FHL film 1376043, Items 3-5); **Winchester**, Births, Marriages & Deaths, 1847–1903 (FHL film 1503204); **Wolcott**, "Records of Births, Marriages & Deaths, 1847–1949" (FHL film 1412960, Item 2).

[29] See Linda MacLachlan and Jan Taylor, "**Trumbull**, Connecticut: A Town Barbour Missed," *The Connecticut Nutmegger*, 41:136-147 (September 2008); Linda MacLachlan and Jan Taylor, "**Seymour**, Connecticut: Another Town Barbour Missed," *The Connecticut Nutmegger*, 41:148-152 (September 2008); Linda MacLachlan, '**New Britain**, Connecticut Vital Records, 1848–1865," *The Connecticut Nutmegger,* 43:290 *et seq.* (March, June and September, 2011).

for the marriage entries in the vital records books. Such records are important, because they—rather than town Books of Marriages—constitute the original sources of marriage information. Any discrepancy between contents of the "official record" and the marriage certificate, must take into account that the certificate is the original source and must therefore be given more weight. The certificates also invariably contain the name of the person who solemnized the marriage.

Barbour accurately extracted most of these original Hebron marriage records. A dozen of these marriage certificates, however, were either never entered in the Hebron marriage records or entered incorrectly. Extracts of those twelve marriage records appear in Part B, below, along with the parental permission slip for the marriage of one presumably under-aged bride. [30]

For these reasons all 1847–55 vital records in Hebron's *Birth, Marriages and Deaths, Volume Four, 1848-1911* appear extracted in Section A below. Section B transcribes selected marriage certificates from *Marriage certificates, 1799–1819 and 1827–54*. Section C includes a few additional vital statistics from the derivative source, author unknown, titled *Births – Family Records – Book 4 – 1594–1909 – Hebron*.

---

[30] See note 35, below.

Section A
BIRTH, MARRIAGES & DEATHS 1848-1854[31]
BIRTHS

<u>Hebron Society First School District</u>

11 Feb 1848	[child of] Lyman BARBER, age 39, black, farmer	4:1B
10 Oct [1848]	John Butler, [son of] David S. NORTHOM, age 26, farmer of Hebron	4:1B
12 Nov [1848]	George Dexter, [son of] David BROWN, age 40, stone mason	4:1B

<u>Hebron Society Second School District</u>

6 Sep 1848	Harriet A. LATHAM, [dau of] Acer A. (age 40, farmer) & Abby (age 34) LATHAM	4:1B

<u>Hebron Society Third School District</u>

1 Nov 1847	Josephine E. PORTER, [dau of] Royal (farmer) & Fanny PORTER	4:1B

<u>Hebron Society Fourth School District</u>

24 Jun 1848	____ WILCOX, [child of] George (age 42, farmer) & Frances H. (age 31) WILCOX	4:1B
12 Jun 1848	David T. CARVER, [son of] Flavel A. (age 37) farmer) & Mary E. (age 24) CARVER	4:1B
27 Feb 1868	Ralph R. BISSELL, [son of] Ralph S. (age 27, farmer) & Caroline W. (age 28) BISSELL	4:1B
5 Aug 1848	Hezekiah Asa BISSELL, [son of] Hezekiah (age 31, farmer) & Mary J. (age 23) BISSELL	4:1B
4 May 1848	Frederic C. BISSELL, [son of] Frederic P. (age 26, farmer) & Almira (age 21) BISSELL	4:1B

<u>Hebron Society Fifth School District</u>

26 Nov 1847	infant of James WHITE, Hebron farmer	4:1B

<u>Hebron Society Sixth School District</u>

16 Aug 1847	L Jenette BANNING, [dau of] Eliphalet (age 36, paper maker) & Louisa (age 30) BANNING	4:1B

<u>Hebron Society Seventh School District</u>

23 Jan 1848	Alphonso B. STARR, [son of] James M. (age	

---

[31] Hebron Registrar of Vital Statistics, Records of Births, Marriages, Deaths in the Town of Hebron, 1848-1911 (FHL film 1376166 Item 2) (Barbour's 4), This volume contains separately paginated sections for birth, marriages and deaths. A reference to 4:1B, for example means that the entry is in Volume Four on page one of Births.

	39, joiner) & Betsey (age 38) STARR	4:1B
13 Apr 1848	William M. JOHNSON, male, David (age 40, joiner) & Piercy (age 38) JOHNSON	4:1B
29 Dec 1847	not named, [child of] William PORTER 2nd (age 38, butcher) & Lovinda C. PORTER (age 38)	4:1B
8 May 1848	Not named, [infant of] Enoch G. (age 28, mason) & Jemma E. (age 26) WALES of Hebron	4:1B

Gilead Society, Center District

28 Nov 1867	James B. PERKINS, [son of] Sherlock W (age 35, mechanic) & Ann M. (age 25) of Hebron	4:2B
28 Sep 1847	John H. POST, [son of] Bissel E. (age 30, farmer) & Eliza (age 28) POST of Hebron	4:2B

Gilead Society, East District

13 Oct 1848	Jane CHAPPEL, [dau of] Anson (age 38, farmer, & Harriet N. (age 32) CHAPPEL of Hebron	4:2B

Gilead Society, West District

2 May [1848]	Ezra DICKINSON, [son of] Seth B. (age 33, farmer) & Mary (age 32) DICKINSON of Hebron	4:2B
21 Oct [1848]	[child of] Thompson (age 35, Farmer) & Melissa (age 33) STRICKLAND of Hebron	4:2B
18 Dec [1848]	[child of] Benjamin T (age 42, farmer) & Mary E (age 38) (BUELL) SUMNER of Hebron	4:2B

Hebron Society
First School District per Royal R. THOMPSON

15 Aug 1848	Charles C. PHELPS, [son of] Augustus (age 51, carpenter) & Almira (age 37) PHELPS	4:3B
20 Dec 1846	Charles C. MANN, [son of] Cyrus (age 52, farmer) & Elizabeth C. (age 33) MANN	4:3B
11 Jan 1849	Henry N. DOOLITTLE, [son of] Edgar J. (age 38, Minister) & Jane E. (age 28) DOOLITTLE	4:3B
14 [Jan] 1849	Lucy A. BACKUS, dau of] Ezra L. (age 40, farmer) & Jane A.(age 36) BACKUS	4:3B
27 Apr 1849	[dau of] Dwight (age 35, carpenter) & Marcy (age 34) BLISS	4:3B
20 May 1849	[dau of] John (age 49, farmer) & Nancy (age 43) SWAN	4:3B
28 May 1849	Sarah M. RANDALL dau of Erastus R. (age 25, tailor & Abby A. (age 23) RANDALL	4:3B
[28 May 1849]	Abby S. RANDALL [dau of Erastus R. (age 25, tailor & Abby A. (age 23) RANDALL	4:3B

Second School District per David NILES & Timothy F. JONES

27 Feb 1849	[dau of] David (age 27, farmer) & Mary R. (age 23) KELLOGG	4:3B

Third School District per George W. PORTER

20 Jun 1849	[dau of Griswold (age 36, farmer) & Eliza (age 30) BURNHAM	4:3B

Fourth District per Joel WILLCOX

29 Jul 1849	[child of] Judson (age 31, farmer & joiner) & Jerusha (age 29) STRONG	4:3B

Fifth District per David PHELPS

20 Jun 1849	[son of] Ephriam H. & Mary THOMPSON	4:3B
31 Jan 1849	James STAUNTON, {son of} Albert L. (age 33, paper maker) & Lurania (age 24) STAUNTON	4:3B
7 MAR 1849	Ralph H. MINER, [son of] Joseph C. (age 35, tanner) & Adeline (age 32) MINER	4:3B

Gilead Society

First District, per John P. FORD

28 Jul 1849	Joseph H. STRONG [son of] Humphrey H. & Mary STRONG, resident in Gilead	4:4B
7 Apr 1849	Harriet T. AYERS [dau of] Samuel & Harriet AYERS, resident in Gilead	4:4B
13 May 1849	John GILBERT [son of] Ralph P. & Mary L. GILBERT, resident in Gilead	4:4B

East District per Anson CHAPPEL

29 Jan [1849]	Charles F. BLISS [son of] Samuel (age 35, laborer)& Electa (age 34)BLISS of Hebron	4:4B
29 Apr [1849]	[son of] Solomon (age 50, agriculture) & Matilda (age 38) NORTON of Hebron	4:4B
20 Jan [1849]	Francis LINCOLN [son of] Orrin (age 30, agriculture)& Mary (age 20) LINCOLN of Hebron	4:4B
20 Aug [1849]	Melina LOCKWOOD [dau of] Edward (age 26, cooper) & Elizabeth (age 23) LOCKWOOD of Hebron	4:4B
20 Jun [1849]	[son of] David S. (age 28, agriculture) & Elizabeth (age 22) NORTON of Hebron	4:4B

West District, per Thompson STRICKLAND

1 Jun [1849]	Albert Warner POST [son of] Ichabod (age 33, farmer) & Levina (age 32) POST of Hebron	4:4B
29 Aug [1849]	Mary S. ELLIS [dau of] William L. (age 30, farmer) & Harriet T. (age 27) ELLIS of Hebron	4:4B
24 May [1849]	daughter of Samuel H. (age 24, farmer) & Lucilla (age 23) ELLIS of Hebron	4:4B
1 Oct [1849]	Mary B. HORTON [dau of] William H. (age 48, farmer) & Clarinda (age 32) HORTON of Hebron	4:4B

22 Feb [1849]   Ebn. M. WHITCOMB [child of] Jonathan
                (age 35, farmer) & Harriet M. (age 32)
                WHITCOMB of Hebron   4:4B
                    Hebron Society
              First School District [per] Dwight BLISS
3 Jul 1850   [dau of] Royal A. (age 35, blacksmith)& Sa-
                rah .(age 30) THOMPSON of Hebron   4:5B
              Second School District [per] Abijah PARKS
15 Jul 1850   Justin A. KELLOGG, male, Raimond D. (age
                46, farmer)& Dolly (age 34) KELLOGG   4:4B
              Third School District [per] Gershom BURNHAM
25 Apr 1850   Infants Twins [sons of] Noble E. (age 38,
                farmer) {& Mrs.] (age 32)LORD of Hebron   4:5B
25 Jul 1850   Not named [dau of] Charles L. (age 35, farmer)
                & Malony A.(age 25) DRINKWATER of Hebron 4:5B
              Fourth School District [per] Epaphroditus PORTER
13 Apr 1850   Jane E. EVANS [dau of] Harvey (age 40, far-
                mer) & Adaline (age 40) EVANS of Hebron   4:5B
18 Jun 1850   Hezekiah Asa BISSELL [son of] Hezekiah
                (farmer) & Mary J. BISSELL of Hebron (5
                Aug 1848 in Barbour)   4:5B
              Fifth School District [per] Josiah M. BUELL
22 Dec 1849   Ellen BROWN [dau of] Watson (age 33, far-
                mer) & Eliza (age 25) BROWN of Hebron   4:5B
22 Apr 1850   Emma WHITE [dau of] James (age 32, far-
                mer) & Jerusha (age 32) WHITE of Hebron   4:5B
11 Jun [1850]   John F. TROWBRIDGE [son of Daniel (age
                25, farmer) & Eliza (age 35) TROWBRIDGE of
                Hebron   4:5B
3 Jul [1850]   Fayette LOVELAND [son of] Edwin (age 37, far-
                mer) & Emily (age 38) LOVELAND of Hebron 4:5B
              Sixth School District [per] Hazael GOTT Jr.
18 Dec 1849   Emily NORTHAM [dau of John H. (age 33,
                farmer) & Harriet A. (age 25) NORTHAM of
                Hebron   4:6B
24 Apr 1850   Elizabeth BANNING [dau of] Eliphalet (age
                30, farmer) & Louisa (age 30) BANNING of
                Hebron   4:6B
18 Dec 1849   Samuel THOMPSON [son of] Lothrop (age 26,
                & Emma (age 27) THOMPSON of Hebron   4:6B
                    Hebron Society
              Seventh School District [per] William PORTER 2nd

2 Sep 1850	Charles DENIZON, [son of] Denny D. (age 45, painter & Emily L. (age 39) DENIZON of Hebron	4:7B
29 Jun 1850	[son of] Enoch G. (age 29, mazon) & Emma E. (age 27) WALDER of Hebron	4:7B
29 Mar [1850]	Ellen R. BARBER, [dau of] William M. BARBER (age blank) of New London & Julia R. BARBER (age 25) of Hebron	4:7B

<u>Gilead Society</u>
<u>South School District [per] Ralph P. GILBERT</u>

28 Jan 1850	[son of] John M. WAY (age 41, merchantile) of New York City & Elizabeth J. WAY (age 37) of the Gilead Society in Hebron	4:7B
27 Feb [1850]	Eliza Jane HIGGINS [dau of] Henry (age 34, carriage maker) & Lucinda E. (age 32) HIGGINS of Gilead Society in Hebron	4:7B

<u>West School District [per] David E. HUTCHINZON</u>

27 Apr 1850	[dau of] David (age 24, farmer) & Laura L. (age 23) HUTCHINSON of Gilead	4:7B
9 May [1850]	[dau of] Thompson (age 36, farmer) & Matilda (age 39) STRICKLAND of Gilead	4:7B
9 Jul [1850]	[son of] William L. (age 30, farmer) & Harriet (age 30) ELLIS of Gilead	4:7B
11 Apr 1849	Emma Elizabeth LOCKWOOD [dau] of William (age 34, farmer) & Jerusha LOCKWOOD of Hebron	4:7B
21 Jan 1850	Calvin Andrew PRENTISS [son of] Andrew age 34, farmer) & Clarissa V. (age 26) PRENTISS	4:7B
24 Jun [1850]	Harriet Jane BLISS [dau of] Samuel W. (age 36, cooper) & Electa M. (age 35) BLISS of Hebron	4:7B

<u>North-West School District [per] James BROWN</u>

29 Nov 1849	[son of] Alfonso K. (age 37, farming) & Almira (age 31) POST of Gilead	4:7B
30 Aug [1850]	Ellen Jennette BROWN [dau of] James (age 35, farming) & Jennette (age 34) BROWN of Gilead	4:7B

<u>Hebron Society</u>
<u>First School District [per] Jared C. KELLOGG</u>

19 Aug 1850	Caroline E. HARRIS daughter [of] George W. (age 28, blacksmith) & Caroline M. (age 25) HARRIS of Hebron	4:8B

1 Sep [1850]	G. Bird WOODWARD, son [of] Elijah A. (age 34, physician) & Mary (age 30) WOODWARD of Hebron	4:8B
30 Jan 1851	Wm. Worthington MANN son [of] Cyrus (age 54, farmer & Elizabeth E. (age 35) MANN	4:8B
13 Mar [1851]	Anrius Merrell DOOLITTLE son [of] Edgar J. (age 40, minister) & Jane E. (age 35) DOOLITTLE of Hebron	4:8B
5 Jul [1851]	Harriet AUSTIN daughter [of] Samuel A. (age 37, farmer) & Harriet E. (age 37) AUSTIN of Hebron	4:8B
26 Jul [1851]	Laura Louisa KELLOGG, daughter [of] James C. (age 39, blacksmith) & Frances M. (age 31) KELLOGG of Hebron	4:8B

Third School District [per] Roger L. PHELPS

5 Apr 1851	Irene R. LEWIS [dau of] Sylvanus (age 42, collier) & Helena (age 45) LEWIS of Hebron	4:8B

Fifth School District [per] James A. WHITE

5 Nov 1850	Charles S. STANTON [son of] Albert L. (age 36, farmer) & Lavina (age 35) STANTON of Hebron	4:8B
12 May 1851	[dau of] David (age 44, farmer) & Elizabeth (age 31) PHELPS of Hebron	4:8B

Seventh School District [per] Enoch G. WALDO

28 Nov 1850	George L. WHITE [son of] Joseph W. (age 34, manufacturer) & Laura Ann (age 32) WHITE of Hope Valley	4:8B
27 Jun 1850	Susan Elizabeth, COATS [dau of] Lyman (age 32, turning iron) & Laura (age 29) COATS of Hope Valley	4:8B

Records of Births in the Town of Hebron for the Year Next Proceeding the 1st Day of August A.D. 1851

Gilead

South School District [per] Stephen PAYNE

22 Jul [1850?]	Willard F. HUTCHINZON [son of] George C. (age 23, farmer) & Mary (age 22) HUTCHINZON of Gilead	4:8B
20 Jul [1851]	Franklin H. STRONG [son of] Humphrey H. (age 32, farmer) & Mary E. (age 25) STRONG of Gilead	4:8B
14 Jul [1851]	William E. LATHAM [son of] William E. (age 26, wagon maker) & Ann (age 27) LATHAM of Gilead	4:8B

East School District [per] Andrew PRENTICE

24 Jul [1851]	[son of] Norman P. (age 35, joiner) & Lydia Ann (age 34) WARNER of Gilead	4:8B
10 Mar [1851]	[dau of] David S. (age 29, farmer) & Elizabeth (age 25) WOODWARD NORTON of Gilead	4:8B
27 Oct [1851]	Rosaltha A. LOCKWOOD [dau of] Edwin (age 26, cooper) & Elizabeth (age 23) LOCKWOOD of Gilead	4:8B

Northwest School District [per] Ezekiel WEBSTER

6 Jun 1851	Emily WATROUS [dau of] Leverete T. (age 28, farming & couling) & Emily (age 27) WATROUS of Gilead	4:8B
27 Apr [1851]	Chauncey W. GAY [son of] Henry C. (age 29, farming) & Chiffonett (age 20?) GAY of Gilead	4:8B

West School District [per] James TALCOTT

15 Feb 1851	Laura TRUMBULL [dau of] William H. (farmer) & Clarissa TRUMBULL of Gilead	4:8B
11 Oct 1851	Julia Elizabeth [dau of] Simion F. (farmer) & Julia WATROUS of Gilead	4:8B
29 April 1851	Clara Cordelia [dau of] Jon^n C. (farmer cowler & Harriet M. WHITCOMB of Gilead	4:8B
6 Oct 1851	Charles B. [son of] Benjn S (farmer) & Mary E. SUMNER of Gilead	4:8B
6 Nov 1851	Harley C. BUELL [son of Joseph W. (farmer) & Mary Ann (POST) BUELL of Gilead	4:8B
14 Sep 1852	Hettie Elisabeth [dau of] Alfrede R. & Martha E. STRICKLAND	4:8B
4 Aug 1851	Trumbull BURNHAM [son of] Griswold (farmer) & Elizabeth Swan BURNHAM of Hebron	4:8B
9 Mar 1852	Frank Rollo POST [son of] Abel P. & Sarah A. (ROLLO) POST	4:8B

[No school districts specified]

9 Oct 1853	[son of] Wm P. (age 40, paper maker) & Amanda COOK of Hebron	4:9B
10 Oct [1852]	[son of] Lyman HUTCHINZ (house painter) of Hebron	4:9B
10 Oct [1852]	[son of] Edwin (collier) & Emily LOVELAND of Hebron	4:9B
5 Nov [1952]	[son of] Wm H. (age 32, laborer) & Emily (age 29) WEIR of Hebron	4:9B
9 Dec [1852]	[dau of] Wm L. (farmer) & Harriet R. ELLIS of Hebron	4:9B
11 Dec [1852]	Mary Jane RATHBONE [dau of] Charles C.	

	(age 21, wagon maker) & Angeline (age 25) RATHBONE of Hebron	4:9B
12 Dec [1852]	[dau of] Browning D. (age 42, farmer) & Dorothy O. (age 39) [KELLOGG] of Hebron	4:9B
14 Dec [1852]	[dau of] Jonah C. (farmer) & Sarah L. GILBERT of Hebron	4:9B
14 Dec [1852]	[dau of] John R. (age 34, farmer) & Harriet G. (age 27) NORTHAM of Hebron	4:9B
17 Dec [1852]	[dau of] Leverate (age 30, black laborer) & Hannah (age 36) PETERS of Hebron	4:9B
18 Dec [1852]	[son of] Henry & Abby J. WATROUS of Hebron	4:9B
22 Dec [1852]	[dau of] Leonard & M.N. DOWD of Hebron	4:9B
27 Dec [1852]	[dau of] Harry (age 33, black laborer) & Emily (age 31) PETERS of Hebron	4:9B
9 Jun 1853	[dau of] Horace (age 42, farmer) & Lucy (age 39) HILLS of Hebron	4:9B
26 Jun [1853]	[son of] Levarate & Emily WATROUS of Hebron	4:9B
28 Dec 1852	[dau of] James BROWN of Hebron	4:9B
12 Feb 1853	Eva Josephine PHELPS [dau of] David (age 45, farmer & Elizabeth (age 32) PHELPS of Hebron	4:9B
13 Feb [1853]	[son of] Jon^n (age 38) & Harriet (age 34) WHITCOMB of Hebron	4:9B
2 Mar [1853]	Warren Phelps BUCK [son of] George H. (age 26, farmer) & Emily G. (age 20) BUCK of Hebron	4:9B
10 Mar [1853]	[son of] Henry (age 22, laborer) & Louisa (age 19) HILLS of Hebron	4:9B
7 Mar [1853]	Norton POST [son of] Norman P. (34, joiner) & Lydia (age 34)	4:9B
25 May [1853]	[son of] Russell C. (age 35, laborer) & Eliza (age 32) POST of Hebron	4:9B
1 Aug [1853]	[son of] David E. (age 27, farmer) & Laura HUTCHINZON (age 26) MACK of Hebron	4:9B
15 Aug [1853]	[son of] James A. (age 36, farmer) & Jerusha (age 35) WHITE of Hebron	4:9B
8 [Aug 1853]	[son of] Stephen (age 39, tanner) & Heamon T. (age 34) PAYNE of Hebron	4:9B
5 Sep 1853]	[dau of Charles (age 44, laborer) & Mary (age 44) MORGAN, black of Hebron	4:9B
5 Sep [1853]	[son of] Eliph^t (age 33, laborer) & Louisa T.	

	(age 33) BANNING of Hebron	4:9B
16 [Sep 1853]	[son of] Edward (age 47, laborer) & Betsy R. (age 43) PETERS of Hebron	4:9B
29 [Sep 1853]	[son of] Thomas BROWNHURST, silk dyer of Hebron	4:9B
11 Oct [1853]	[son of] Jeah? L. (age 29, laborer) & Emily (age 30) THOMPSON of Hebron	4:9B
16 Oct [1853]	[dau of] Elias (age 27, farmer) & Sarah (age 34) THOMPSON of Hebron	4:9B
23 [Oct 1853]	[son of] Daniel L (age 28, laborer) & Emma (age 24) NORTON of Hebron	4:9B
1 Nov [1853]	[son of] Lyman (age 32, laborer & Sarah (age 30) COATS of Hebron	4:9B
14 [Nov 1853]	Ely Warner HUTCHINSON [son of] Geo C. (age 25, farmer) & Mary (age 24) HUTCHINZON of Hebron	4:9B
11 Dec [1853]	Mary [dau of Geo W. (age 32, mechanic) & Martha A. (age 26) HARRIS of Hebron	4:9B
15 Dec [1853]	Abner HENDEE [son of] Lucius J. (age 33, merchant) & Adaline E. (age 27) HENDEE of Hebron	4:9B
28 [DEC 1853]	[DAU of] Samuel A. (farmer) & Electa BLISS of Hebron	4:9B
3 [Dec 1853]	[dau of] Benj T. (age 49, farmer) & Mary F. (age 43) SUMNER of Hebron	4:9B
14 Jan 1854	Frederic B. POST, male, Abel P. (age 28, farmer) & Sarah A. (age 27) POST	4:10B
16 [Jan 1854]	{dau of} Sam¹ A. (age 40, mechanic) & Harriet E. (age 39) AUSTEN	4:10B
25 Feb [1854]	Carrie Martha, {dau of} Alfred R. (age 25, farmer) & Martha E. (age 24) STRICKLAND	4:10B
27 [Feb 1854]	[son of] Egbert (age 30, farmer) & Jane E. (age 28) BROWN	4:10B
2 Mar [1854]	[dau of] David (age 25, farmer) & Genette (age 26) MAN	4:10B
6 [Mar 1854]	[son of] Griswold (farmer) & Eliza BURNHAM	4:10B
2 Apr [1854]	[dau of] Wm M. (age 43, clergyman) & Mary (age 32) BURNHAM	4:10B
4 [Apr 1854]	[son of] Edwin W. (age 40, shoemaker) & Sarah (age 42) STRONG	4:10B
18 [Apr 1854]	[son of] Peter (age 21) & Hannah H. (age 16) KELDER[?]	4:10B

27 May [1854]	[son of] Edwin (age 27, mechanic) & Eliza Ann (age 25) BALEY	4:10B
18 July [1854]	[son of] Wm W. (age 34, laborer) & Emily (age 31) WEIR	4:10B
26 [Jul 1854]	[son of] ____ (laborer) & ____ WHEATON	4:10B
7 [Jul 1853]	[son of] Noble (farmer) & Lona [blank]	4:10B
17 Aug [1854]	[dau of] Ralph L. (age 33, farmer) & Caroline M. (age 34) BISEL	4:10B
22 [Aug 1854]	[son of] E. Patrick (age 27) & Mary (age 32) ROWLE	4:10B
31 [Aug 1854]	[Arthur Randall GILLETTE [son of] Edwin (farmer) GILLETT & Sarah J. RANDALL	4:10B
[31 Aug 1854]	[dau of] Henry (age 27, farmer) & Abby G. (age 26) WATROUS	4:10B

Section II A (cont)
MARRIAGES – 1847-1854

<u>Hebron Society- 3rd District</u>

30 May 1847   William W. WHITE (farmer, age 25, born & resident in Windsor) m. Mary D. NORTON (age 25, born & resident in Hebron) both previously unmarried, by Rev. F. B. WOODWARD   4:1M[32]

<u>Hebron Society – 4th District</u>

25 Dec 1847   John J. ANDRUS (age 24; born in Marlborough) m. Aurelia N. BABCOCK (age 16; born in Salem), both previously unmarried operatives in a factory & resident in Boxerville, by Rev. Edgar J. DOOLITTLE   4:1M

<u>Hebron Society – 7th District</u>

26 Sep 1847   Levi BAILEY (Farmer, age 24, born in Haddam) m. Maria HILLS (age 20, born in Hebron) both previously unmarried residents of Hebron, by Rev. E.J. DOOLITTLE   4:1M

24 Oct 1847   George PHELPS (farmer) m. Abbey WARNER, both born & resident in Lyme. His 2nd & her 1st marriage, by Rev. Walter WILKIE   4:1M

28 Nov 1847   Selden T. PORTER (joiner, age 20, born in Hebron) m. Sarah A. DENISON (age 17, born in Goshen) both previously unmarried & resident in Glastonbury, by Rev. Walter WILKIE.   4:1M

<u>Gilead Society – East District</u>

11 May 1848   Mosello L. PERRY (merchant, age 28, born in Augusta NY, resident in Manchester) m. Abby Jane HAUGTON (age 21, born & resident in Hebron). His 2nd & her 1st marriage, by Rev. S.G. HITCHCOCK   4:1M

20 Apr 1847   Orrin A. LINCOLN (hatter, age 28) m. Mary P. KINGSLEY (age 19) both previously unmarried, born in Columbia & resident in Hebron, by Rev. James WOODWARD   4:1M

24 Nov 1847   William E. LATHAM (mechanic, age 23, born in Hebron) m. Huldah Ann RATHBONE (age

---

[32] The Town Clerk's system of pagination begins anew with page one of marriages.

	25, born in Colchester) both previously unmarried residents of Hebron, by Rev. Henry BAILIES	4:1M

<u>Gilead Society N.West District</u>

9 Mar [1847]	Nelson KEENY (farmer, age 42, born & resident in Coventry) m. NancyL. SUMNER (tailoress, age 32, born & resident in Hebron) his 2nd & her 1st marriage, by Charles NICHOLS	4:1M

<u>Hebron Society</u>
<u>First District [per] Royal A. THOMPSON</u>

20 Aug 1848	John A. FULLER (farmer, age 29, born & resident in Ludlow Ms) m. Lavina P WARNER (age 24, born & resident in Hebron) their 1st marriages, by Solomon G. HITCHCOCK	4:2M
~10 Apr 1848	Hosea C. WARNER (basket broker, age 59, born in Springfield Ma., resident in Columbia) m. Philadelphia BEACH (age 48, born & resident in Hebron) their 2nd marriages, by Rev. Mr. BOWLES	4:2M
29 Oct 1848	William L. CONE (farmer, age 24, born & resident in East Haddam) m. Emily B. CARVER (age 26, born & resident in Hebron) their 1st marriages, by Solomon G. HITCHCOCK	4:2M
[1848?]	Egbert BROWN (joiner of Columbia, age 25) m. Jane A. WRIGHT (age 23, of Hebron) both born in Hebron & previously unmarried, by Edgar J. DOOLITTLE	4:2M
[1848?]	George MACK (Black farmer, age 22, born & resident in Coventry) m. Harriet BARBER (Black, age 23, born & resident in Hebron) their 1st marriages, by Solomon G. HITCHCOCK	4:2M

<u>Second District [per] David NILES & Timothy F. JONES</u>

~3 Sep 1848	William W. WEIR (collier, age 28, born & resident in Glastonbury) m. Emily STAPLES (age 24, born in Windham) their 1st marriages. By Walter WILKIE	4:2M

<u>Fourth District [per] Joel WILLCOX</u>

17 Oct 1848	Jasper PORTER (age 52) m. Mary C. BUELL (age 45) (Bissell in Barbour)) both previously unmarried natives & residents of Hebron, by Rev. Edgar J. DOOLITTLE	4:2M

[1848]	Egbert BROWN (farmer of Columbia, age 26) m. Elizabeth WRIGHT (age 23, of Hebron) both previously unmarried natives of Hebron, by Rev. Edgar J. DOOLITTLE 4:2M
21 Jun 1849	George R. BESTOR (farmer, age 28, born & resident in Columbus NY) m. C. Jane STRONG (age 19, born & resident in Hebron) by Rev. Abel GARAMON 4:2M

Fifth District [per] David PHELPS

none

Gilead Society First District [per] John P. FORD

6 Jun 1849	George H. LORD (farmer, age 34, born & resident in Marlboro) m. Anna E. HUTCHINZON (age 24, of Gilead) by Rev. Charles NICHOLS 4:2M
5 Aug 1849	Ebenezer GEER (manufacturer, age 24, born & resident in Stonington) m. Laura L. STAPLES (age 18, born in Hebron) their 1st marriages By Rev. Aaron SNOW 4:2M

East District [per] Anson CHAPPELL

~6 Sep [1849]	Josiah C. GILBERT (Agriculturer, age 39) m. Sarah POST (age 28) both born & resident in Hebron, by Rev. Charles NICHOLS 4:2M

West District [per] Thompson STRICKLAND

~13 Sep [1849]	David E. HUTCHINZON (farmer, age 22, born & resident in Hebron) m. Laura L. LITTLE (age 21, born in Columbia) first marriages by James WOODWARD 4:2M
31 Dec 1848	Sherwood WHEELER (occupation uncertain, age 30, born in Columbia, resident in Terraqueous Bull) m. Sarah PARISH (age 22, born in Hebron) first marriages by Charles NICHOLS 4:2M

Gilead Society
North West District Gilead

1 Jul 184_	Simeon F. WATROUS (farmer, age 2, born in Gilead) m. Julia DINGLEY (age 19, born in Lebanon) both previously unmarried resident of Gilead, by Rev. Charles NICHOLS 4:3M

Hebron Society
First School District, [per] Dwight BLISS

18 Oct 1849	Daniel H. ELDRIDGE (farmer, born & resident in Manchester, age 23) m. Laura GILLET (born & resident in Hebron, age 22) by Rev.

	Edgar J. DOOLITTLE (their 1st marriages)	4:4M
26 Nov 1849	David T. HEWETT (hemp maker, born in Massachusetts, resident in Washington MA, age 55) m. Frances PORTER (dressmaker, born & resident in Hebron, age 50) by Rev. Edgar J. DOOLITTLE (his 3rd, her 1st marriage)	4:4M

Fourth School District [per] Epaphroditus PORTER

25 Jul 1850 Samuel F. JONES (mason, born & resident in Hebron, age 35) m. Hannah A. TIFFE (born in Scituate RI, resident in Hebron, age 23) by Rev. Edgar J. DOOLITTLE (their 1st marriages)　4:4M

Fifth School District, [per] Josiah M. BUELL

~10 May 1850 Enoch JONES (farmer, age 21) m. Emelene PALMER (age 19) by Rev Walter WILKIE (both born & resident in Hebron & not married before)　4:4M

~[1850?] Henry COLEMAN (farmer, born in Marlborough, age 23) m. Laura BROWN (born in Columbia (age 19) by Rev. Alfred F. PARK (both previously unmarried residents of Hebron)　4:4M

Seventh School District, [per] William PORTER 2nd

~19 Apr 1850 Charles H. TISDALE (mazon of New London, age 26) m. Almira P. JOHNSON of Hebron (age19) by Rev. W. WILKIE (both born in Hebron & previously unmarried)　4:4M

12 May [1850] Enoch JONES (Hebron school teacher) m. Emeline PALMER, by Rev W. WILKIE (both born & resident in Hebron & previously unmarried)　4:4M

14 Jul [1850] William A. WATROUS (Rector) m. Abby J. DINGBY (born & resident in Hebron) by Rev. W. WILKIE (both previously unmarried)　4:4M

Gilead Society

South School District, [per] Ralph P. GILBERT

22 May 1850 George C. HUTCHINZON (farmer, born in Gilead, age 28) m. Mary E. T. LOOMIS (born in Bolton, age 21) by Rev. Charles NICHOLS (both previously unmarried residents of Gilead)　4:4M

28 May [1850] Peter S. SMITH (Montville farmer, age 36) m. Jerusha A. ROOT of Hartford (age 26) by

	Rev. Abel GARDNER (both born in Hartford & previously unmarried)	4:4M

West School District, [per] David G. HUTCHINZON

1 Jun [1850]	William MIHOTE[?] (Op[ertative] in factory, age 24) m. Mary DAVIS (born & resident in Glastonbury, age 20) by William BROWN Esq. (his 2nd & her 1st marriage)	4:4M
7 Jul [1850]	Henry WATROUS (farmer born in Gilead, age 23) m. Abby DINGLY (born in Lebanon, age 23) by Rev. Walter WILKIE (both previously unmarried residents of Gilead	4:4M

Hebron Society
First School District, [per] James C. KELLOGG

24 Nov [1850]	George W. HARRIS (blacksmith, born in Hebron, age 29) m. Martha A. NORTON (born in Andover, age 24) by Abel GARDNER (both residents of Hebron, his 2nd & her 1st marriage)	4:5M
15 May [1851]	Amassa A. TOPLIFF (farmer, born & resident in South Coventry, age 23) m. Mary E. BASCOM (born in Hebron, age 26) by Rev. Edgar J. DOOLITTLE (their 1st marriages)	4:5M

Fourth School District, [per] Ralph D. BROWN

22 May 1851	Jesse H. WILLCOX (school teacher of Middletown NY, age 22) m. Jane GILLETTE (born & resident in Hebron, age 21) by Rev. Edgar J. DOOLITTLE (their 1st marriages)	4:5M

Sixth School District, Nathan BOLLEN

24 Apr 1851	Salmon A. JONES (mason, born & resident in Hebron, age 35) m. Sarah MORSE (age 22) by Walter WILKIE (their 1st marriages)	4:5M

Gilead Society
South School District, Stephen PAYNE

13 May [1851]	James M. HURLBURT (farmer, born in Chatham, resident in Portland, age 28) m. Jane JOHNZON (born in Middletown, resident in Hebron, age 28) by Rev. Charles NICHOLS (their 1st marriages)	4:5M

East School District, Andrew PRENTICE

4 Jun [1851]	Abel P. POST (farmer, born & resident in Gilead, age 26) m. Sarah A. ROLLO (age 25) by Rev. Charles NICHOLS (their 1st marriages)	4.5M
5 Dec 1852	Charles CARR (age 24, black, clothes dea-	

	den, born in Wethersfield, resident in Hartford) m. Swan E. MORGAN (age 23, black, born & resident in Hebron) by Rev. Walter WILKIE (his 2nd & her 1st marriage)	4:6M
13 Feb 1853	Linus FOOTE (age 40, mechanic, born in Marlborough, resident in Colchester) m. Adelaide L. ADAMS (age 20, born & resident in Colchester) by Rev. William WARLAND (their 1st marriages)	4:6M
3 Jul [1853]	Orlando MIDDLETON (age 30, carpenter) m. Mary WOODWORTH (age 17, spinster) by Rev. Walter WILKIE (born & resident in New London, his 2nd & her 1st marriage)	4:6M
14 Sep [1853]	William T. WARNER (age 23, farmer, born in Bolton, m. Olive M. HUTCHINZON (age 19, born in Hebron, by Rev. Charles NICHOLS (both previously unmarried residents in Hebron)	4:6M
30 Oct [1853]	Thomas TRUDE (age 40, papermaker, born in England, resident in East Hartford) m. Esther LOOMIS (age 39, born in Manchester, resident in Hebron) by Rev. Walter WILKIE, (his 1st & her 2nd marriage	4:6M

[certificate not specifying school district]

11 Sep [1853]	Horace COLEMAN &. Mis Louisa BRAINED, both of Marlborough, were married by Wm WARLAND, Rector of the Hebron Episcopal Church. Signed 28 July 1864.	4:6M
26 Mar 1854	Lyman SMITH (age 24, harness trimmer) m. Mary E. SAWTELLE (age 17) by Wm H. BURCHARD (both born & resident in Hartford & previously un-married)	4:6M
11 Apr [1854]	Geo. H. LOOMIS (age 28, blacksmith, born & resident in Lebanon) m. Amy L. BABCOCK (age 26, milliner, born in Rhode Island, resident in Colchester) by Wm H. BURCHARD (their 1st marriages)	4:6M
12 [Apr 1854]	Walter WILKIE (age 41, clergyman, born in Norwich) m. Laura A. WHITE (age 34, teacher, born in Hebron) by Wm H. BURCHARD (his 3rd & her 2nd marriage, to reside in Westbrook)	4:6M
16 Apr [1854]	Alfred CHITTENDEN (age 27, mechanic, born & resident in Killingworth) m. Emily M. ROOT	

	(age 27, born in Marlboro, resident in Hebron) by Rev. Anthony PALMER (his 2nd & her 1st marriage, to reside in Colchester)	4:6M
8 Jun [1854]	Samuel l. OTIS (age 21, manufacturer of Stockinett, born in Montville, resident in Manchester) m. Maria L. WEST (age 18, born & resident in Hebron) by Rev. Charles NICHOLS (their 1st marriages)	4:6M
23 Aug [1854]	Charles BROUNHURST (age 23, silk dyer, born in England) m. Harriet GORDON (age 23, born in Mansfield) by Rev. Wm WARLAND (both previously unmarried & of Hebron)	4:6M
17 Sep [1854]	Samuel H. SMITH (age 21, clerk of Hebron) m. June CUSON (age 20, domestic of Hartford) by Rev. Merrick KNIGHT (both born in Ireland & previously unmarried) to dwell in Hartford	4:6M
12 Oct [1854]	Elisha HOUZE (age 37, farmer, born in Glastonbury) m. Delia A. BIDWELL (age 27, paper maker, born in Manchester) by Rev. Charles NICHOLS (both of Hebron; his 2nd & her 1st marriage)	4:6M
[12 Oct 1854]	William CARVER (age 51, farmer, born in Hebron, resident in Allen [Co.] Indiana) m. Agnes BUELL (age 52, born & resident in Hebron) by Rev. Merrick KNIGHT (his 2nd & her 1st marriage)	4:6M
18 [Oct 1854]	Carlos H. WEBSTER (age 26, farmer) m. Lucy A. PHELPS (age 27) by Rev. Merrick KNIGHT (both born & resident in Hebron & previously unmarried)	4:6M

Marriages Recorded from St. Peters Church

1 Dec 1850	James H. TOWNSEND m. Lucy Ann FRANKLIN in Ch by Rev. C.R. TISHER	4:25M
~9 Mar 1851	Cyrus COOK m. Sarah FOOTE	4:25M
10 Mar 1851	Elisha T. BAKER m. Adelaide BRAGG (BRIGGS in Barbour)	4:25M
7 Mar 1852	Henry TINNEY of Plymouth Mass m. Mary Ann BARBER (FINNEY in Barbour)	4:25M
~26 May 1853	Thomas B. CHENEY of Middleborough m. Frances E. FOOTE of Marlborough	4:25M
~10 Oct 1855	Albert HARVEY m. Mary E T. FOOTE	4:25M
~29 Jan 1856	David R. MCCALL m. Caroline FOOTE	4:25M

31 Dec 1857	James H. TOWNSEND m. Susan PERRY	4:25M
5 Apr 1859	Edwin P. HANKS m. Susan A. ALLEN	4:25M
6 Mar 1861	Chauncey E. KNOX m. Rachel C. FOOTE	4:25M
24 Dec 1862	James H. NASH m. Anna E. POST	4:25M
5 Oct 1864	Wm. FRENCH m. Maria GELSTON	4:25M

Section II A (cont)
DEATHS – 1847-1854

Hebron Society 1st Dist.

18 Feb 1848	David GILLETT, age 49. Farmer born in Hebron. Died by the fall of a tree.	4:1D[33]
7 Jul [1848]	Oliver PHELPS, age 71. Hatter born in Hebron. Died of Lung Complaint.	4:1D
11 Feb [1848]	Infant child of Lyman BARBER, black, age one day.	4:1D

Hebron 2nd District

28 Apr 1848	Mary A. FREEMAN, age 76. Seamstress born in Hebron. Died of Liver Complaint.	4:1D
[28 Apr 1848]	Sarah ROOT, age 68. Seamstress born in East Haddam. Died of Consumption.	4:1D
4 Sep [1848]	Samuel ROGERS, age 24. Pauper born in Hebron. Died of Consumption.	4:1D
[1848?]	George CULVER. Pauper born in Hebron. Died of Fits.	4:1D

Hebron Society, 3rd District

29 Aug 1847	Prudence LORD, age 6 mos. Born in Hebron	4:1D

Hebron Society 4th District

29 Oct 1847	Dorcas WILCOX, Age 91. Born in Colchester. Died of Old age.	4:1D
26 May 1848	Uzziel PHELPS, age 76. Shoemaker born in Hebron. Died of Old age.	4:1D

Hebron Society 5th District

22 Jun 1848	Benjamin FREEMAN, age 43. Farmer born in Colchester. Died of Fit.	4:1D
30 Jul [1848]	Prouda CHAPMAN, age 67. Housekeeper. Birthplace unknown. Died of Dropsey.	4:1D

Gilead Society Center District

15 Sep 1847	Jerusha CASE, age 78 born in Hebron. Died of Bowel Complaint.	4:1D
12 Feb 1848	Aurelia CASE, age 23 born in Coventry. Cause of death unknown.	4:1D
12 Jun 1847	Thomas WEBSTER, age 84 Mechanic born in Hebron. Died of Old age.	4:1D

---

[33] The Town Clerk's system of pagination begins anew with page one of Deaths.

Gilead Society, East District

15 Nov 1847	Louisa H. GILBERT, age 38. born in Bolton. Died of Consumption.	4:1D
11 Aug 1847	Mary E. BROWN, age 39. born in Hebron. Died of Dropsy Consumption.	4:1D
6 Nov 1847	Betsey H. NORTON, age 55. born in New Hampshire. Died of Dropsy on the heart.	4:1D
11 Apr 1848	John F. NORTON, age 22. born in Hebron. Died of Consumption.	4:1D

Gilead Society, West Society

12 Jul [1848]	Jonathan STRICKLAND, age 69. Farmer born in Glastonbury. Died of Dropsy.	4:1D
18 May [1848]	Anna LOOMER, age 81. born in Hebron. Died of Dropsy.	4:1D
11 Sep [1848]	John L. HORTON born in Hebron. Died of Hooping cough.	4:1D
11 Feb [1848]	Julia D. POST born in Hebron. Died of Consumption.	4:1D
26 Jan [1848]	Catherine TALCOTT, age 12. Died of Fever.	4:1D

Hebron First District, [per] Royal C. THOMPSON

~[18__]	Pauline GILLETT, age 16, born in Hebron, Died of inflammation of the bowel.	4:2D
23 Feb 1849	Lucy BINDELL, age 82 born in Hebron. Died of Old age. (Bissell age 81)	4:2D
~28 Apr 1849	Sally GILBERT, age 54, born in Norwich. Died of Lung fever.	4:2D
~22 May 1849	Child of John SWAN, born in Hebron, stillborn	4:2D
~19 Jun 1849	Abby A. RANDALL, age 23, born in Hebron. Died of Consumption	4:2D
~22 [Jun] 1849	Abby S. RANDALL, age 27. Tailoress born in Hebron. Died of Hooping cough	4:2D

Second District [per] David NILES {&} Timothy F. JONES

1 Sep 1848	Samuel JONES, age 29. Farmer born in Hebron, attacked at Rockville & removed to Hebron. Died of Dysentery or a cholera variation.	4:2D
25 Dec 1848	Erastus DANIELS, age 60. Farmer born in Hebron. Died of Typhus fever.	4:2D

Third District, [per] George W. BARBER

1 Dec 1848	William B. GRAVES, age 34. Born in Hebron, 3rd dist.. Died of Consumption	4:2D
14 May 1849	John C. PHELPS, age 24. born in Hebron. Died of Plursey	4:2D

Fifth District, [per] David PHELPS

10 Mar 1849	Olive WHITE, age 94. Born in Lebanon. Died of Old age.	4:2D

Gilead Society
First District, [per] John P. FORD

29 Aug 1848	Abigail MERRELL, age 82. Spinster born in Gilead. Died of Dysentery	4:2D
18 Oct 1848	Franklin C. HUTCHINSON, age 5. Born in Gilead. Died of Croup	4:2D
28 Jan 1849	Daniel WAY, age 34. Farmer born in Gilead. Died of Pluresy	4:2D
16 Mar 1849	George BUTTON, age 62. Cooper born in Sterling. Died of Lung fever.	4:2D

East District, [per] Anson CHAPPELL

23 Sep 1848	Hiram H. MARTINDALE, age 43. Agriculturer born in Hebron. Died of Lung Fever.	4:2D

West District, [per] Thompson STRICKLAND

13 Jul 1849	Bishop CURTICE, age 54. Farmer born in Hebron. Died of Dropsy on the heart.	4:2D

Hebron Society
Second School District [per] Abijah PARKS

28 Oct 1849	Jonathan DANIELS, age 89. Farmer born in Colchester. Died of Old age	4:3D
10 Jul 1850	Malvia A. DRINKWATER, age 25. Farmer's wife. Died in Childbirth.	4:3D
1 May 1850	Infant [son] of Noble & Lora [blank], age 6 days	4:3D

Fourth School District, [per] Epaphroditus PORTER

27 Dec 1849	Laura WRIGHT, age 58. born in Hebron. Died of Inflamation of the Bowels.	4:3D
6 Aug [1849]	Hezekiah A. BURRELL, age 1 year. born in Hebron. Cholera inflammation.	4:3D
12 Jul 1850	Anna PORTER, age 70. born in Hebron. Died of Inflamation of the Bowels.	4:3D

Sixth School District [per] Hazael GOTT

14 Mar 1850	Samuel THOMPZON, age 2 mos, 24 days. Born in Hebron.	4:3D
4 May [1850]	Delendia TENANT, age 42. Born in Hebron. Died of Consumption	4:3D

Seventh School District, [per] William PORTER 2nd

27 May 1850	Henry M. COATS, age 3 years. Born in Hebron. Drowned	4:3D

Gilead Society

East School District, [per] Alfred A. JONES

27 May 1849	Mary P. RISLEY, age 1 year. Born in Manchester. Died of Dysentery.	4:3D
7 Sep [1849]	Nancy A. BLISS, age 66. Weaver born in Hebron. Died of Dysentery.	4:3D
12 Sep [1849]	Harriet L BLISS, age 3 {years]. Born in Hebron. Died of Dysentery.	4:3D
17 Sep [1849]	Charles F. BLISS, age 7 months. Born in Hebron. Died of Dysentery	4:3D
5 Jun 1850	Spencer RATHBONE, age 78. Cooper born in Salem. Died of Old Age	4:3D

North-west School District per James BROWN

29 Nov 1849	Infant [son] of A.K. POST. Born in Gilead.	4:3D

Hebron Society

First School District per James C. KELLOGG

28 Aug [1851]	Caroline M. HARRIS, age 25. Born in Chatham. Died of Puerferal fever	4:4D

Second School District per Asa A LATHAM

12 Oct 1850	Alfred F. WIER, age 3 months. Born in Hebron. Died of Scarlett fever.	4:4D
14 Jul 1851	Jedediah JONES, Age 89. Born in Hebron. Old age	4:4D

Third School District per Roger S. PHELPS

30 Nov 1850	Ozias PHELPS, age 85. Farmer born in Hebron. Died of Palsy	4:4D

Fourth School District per Ralph G. BROWN

24 Dec 1850	Mary A. BURELL, age 18. School teacher born in Hebron.	4:4D
[1850]	Augustus BERRILL. Farmer born in Hebron.	4:4D

Fifth School District per James A. WHITE

30 Jan [1850]	Charles S. STANTON, age 2 mos, 25 days. Born in Hebron. Died of croup	4:4D

Seventh School District per Enoch G. WALDO

23 Mar 1850	Joseph W. WHITE, age 34. Manufacturer born in Hebron. Resided in Hope Valley. Died of Typhus fever	4:4D
7 Jan [1850]	George L. WHITE, age 1 mo. Born in Hebron. Resided in [Hope Valley]. Died of Incephalitus	4:4D

Gilead Society

South School District, per Stephen PAYNE

30 Jul [1850]	John H. W. WAY, age 12 yrs. Farmer born

	in Gilead. Died of Inflamation of the bowel	4:4D

<u>North-west School District per Ezekiel WEBSTER</u>

1 Jul 1850	Alfred K. POST, age 31 yrs. Farmer born in Columbia. Died in Gilead of consumption.	4:4D
9 Oct 1852	Philatheda WARNER, age 82. Born in Hebron. Married.	4:5D
13 Oct [1852]	Esther ROOT, age 60 yrs, 4 mos, 5 days. Born in Glastonbury. Died of Heart & Liver complt, Married.	4:5D
19 Oct [1852]	Mary I. MALONEY, age 8 mos, 4 days. Born in Hebron. Single. Died of Disease of Brain.	4:5D
1 Nov [1852]	Dan PHELPS, age 93 yrs, 9 mos, 24 days. Farmer born in Hebron. Born in Hebron. Died of Old age. Married.	4:5D
3 Dec [1852]	Sarah BERRELL, 71 yrs, 3 mos, 24 days. Died of Consumption. Married.	4:5D
18 Dec [1852]	____ ____, male, age 1 mo. 14 days. Born in Hebron. Single. Died of Calanch fever.	4:6D
19 Dec [1852]	Mary A. BLISS, age 42. Born in Hebron. Widow. Died of Consumption.	4:6D
3 Feb 1853	Maria K. BUELL, 18 yrs, 9 mos, 9 days. Born in Marlboro. Single. Died of Billious Pneumonia.	4:6D
5 Feb [1853]	George GILLETT, age 82. Surveyer born in Hebron. [Single]. Died of Old Age.	4:6D
9 Feb [1853]	Clarinda BROWN, 70 yrs, 11 mos, 14 das. Born in Hebron. Married. Died of Consumption.	4:6D
12 Feb [1853]	Dwight BLISS, 38 yrs, 3 mos, 6 days. House joiner born in Hebron. Married. Died of Billius pneumonia	4:6D
2 Apr [1853]	Philance JOHNZON, 66 yrs, 2 mos. Born in Lebanon. Married. Accidental Death	4:5D
5 Apr [1853]	Joel JOHNZON, age 66. Married farmer. Died of Sun affliction.	4:5D
30 Mar [1853]	Caroline WILKIE, age 41. Born in Lyme. Married. Died of Lung fever.	4:5D
7 May [1853]	Electa CARVER, 40 yrs, 3 mos, 4 days. Born in Hebron. Married. Died of Consumption.	4:5D
29 May [1853]	Homer BEACH, 90 yrs, 5 mos. Born in Glastonbury. Widowed. Died of Old age.	4:5D
29 Jun [1853]	Rachel WILLCOX, age 70. Born in Hebron. Married. Died of Dropsy.	4:5D

12 Aug [1853]	Charles H. WARNER, 2 yrs, 11 mos. Born in Hebron. Single Died of Marasmus..	4:5D
20 Aug [1853]	Caroline PETERS, age 85. Born in Bolton. Widow. Died of Old age.	4:5D
1 Sep [1853]	Louisa PHELPS, 48 yrs, 7 mos, 8 days. Born in Hebron. Residing at Oswego B_y. Widow. Died of Fever.	4:5D
6 Sep [1853]	Wiley W. WALDEN, 1 yr, 11 mos, 1 day. Born in Hebron. Single. Died of Billeous fever.	4:5D
[1853]	Rhoda SMITH, black, age 70 yrs. Widow.	4:5D
Jun [1853]	Henry HILLS, age 56. Laborer born in Lebanon .Married. Died of Consumption.	4:5D
Oct [1853]	Chauncey STRONG, age 35. Farmer born in Hebron. Married	4:5D
Oct [1853]	Mary BEACH, age 18. Born in Hebron. Single. Died of Typhus fever.	4:5D
Oct [1853]	George R. BEACH, age 54. Farmer born in Hebron. Married. Died of Typhus fever.	4:5D
13 Nov [1853]	Lovina BISSELL, 65 yrs, 10 mos. Born at Hebron. Married. Died of Desicated lungs.	4:5D
8 Apr [1853]	Wm J. ANNABLE, age 34. Born at East Haddam. Single Died of Lung fever	4:5D
Oct [1853]	Nancy J. LATHAM. Born in Hebron. Died single, a resident of Colchester	4:5D
18 Mar 1854	Elijah BEACH. Age 77. Born in Hebron. Married. Died of Encephalitus.	4:6D
19 [Mar 1854	Martha PHELPS. Age 57. Born in Hebron. Single. Died of Fever.	4:6D
20 [Mar 1854]	Lude BARBER. Male. Black. Age 70. Laborer born in Rhode Island. Widow. Died of Fever	4:6D
12 May [1854]	Herbert W. BARBER. Age 2 yrs.4 mos. 20 days. Born at New London. Widowed. Died of Dropsy on the Brain.	4:6D
21 [May 1854]	Sarah STRONG. Age 42. Born in Hebron. Married. Died of Hydrothorax.	4:6D
20 {May 1854}	Almire P. TISDALE. 23 yrs. 6 mos. Born in Hebron. Married. Died of Consumption.	4:6D
5 Jul [1854]	Abigail A.C. GRAVES. Age 8 yrs. 9 mos. Born in Hebron. Single. Died of Fever.	4:6D
5 Jul [1854]	Louisa NORTON. Age 50. Born in Hebron. Single. Died of Epilepsy.	4:6D
27 [Jul 1854]	Jerusha SMITH. 60. Married. Died of Con-sumption.	4:6D

24 [Jul 1854]	Mrs. STAPLES. Aged 60. Died of Consumption. Married.	4:6D
9 Nov [1854]	Lucy Ann WILLCOX. Age 36. Born in Hebron. Married. Died of Fever.	4:6D
21 Dec [1854]	Hannah WALDO. Age 70 yrs. 2 mos. 21 days. Born in Hebron. Married. Died of Cancer tumor.	4:6D
[1854]	Lucy Ann BROWN Born in Hebron. Married. Died of Epilepsy.	4:6D

Section B
Certified Marriages not in Borbour[34]

[fourth from last past of unpaginated volume]

Apr 1799 — John WHITE of ____ State of Vermont & Betsey ARCHER of Colchester, were married by Salmon CONE, Minister of the Gospel. "[signed] Colchester June 1st 1801.:

19 Jul 1818 — John ANDREWS & Hannah H. GARDNER, both of Hebron, were married at Hebron, by Stuart BEEBE, Justice Peace.

9 Feb 1817 — James SPARROW of Colchester & Abigail STRONG of Hebron were married at Hebron by Stuart BEEBE, Justice Peace.

[third from last past of unpaginated volume]

21 Mar 1818 — Ozias PHELPS & Therzy BROWN, both of Hebron, were married by Stuart BEEBE Justice Peace.

26 Dec 1816 or 1817 — Augustus KINGSBURY & Sally LOOMIS, both of Coventry were married in Coventry by Stuart BEEBE Justice Peace. [Signed] "Coventry Decemr 26th 1817."

22 Jul 1816 — Andrew WELLS & Martha TRUMBULL, both of Hebron, were married by Stuart BEEBE Justice Peace

[second from last past of unpaginated volume]

1 Jul 1817 — William OLCOTT of East Hartford & Patience ROOT of Hebron, were married in Hebron by Stuart BEEBE Justice Peace.

25 Jan 1818 — Lewis ROUVIERE & Huldah HOWARD, both of Hebron, were married by Stuart BEEBE Justice Peace.

[[next to last past of unpaginated volume]

27 Nov 1817 — Zelotes RIDER of Vernon & Amy BILL,[35] both of

---

[34] Each of these certificates is extracted from a separate scrap of paper pasted into a book entitled and cataloged by the FHL as Hebron Town Clerk, Marriage certificates, 1827-1854, 1814-1819 (FHL film 1376166 Item 6) (Includes a typescript listing the name of the groom and bride and the marriage date for most certificates) Marriaqges already indexed by Barbour are not included here even when Barbour has not specified the minister or residences of the couple.

Hebron, were married by Stuart BEEBE Justice Peace.

29 Nov 1814 Simeon DARBY & Roxina COLEMAN, were married at Hebron by Stuart BEEBE Justice Peace.

[last page of unpaginated volume]

2 Nov 1835 Joseph T. BURNHAM (Joseph R. in Barbour) m. Harriet M. GILBERT, both of Hebron, by Sylvester SELDEN

13 Mar 1838 Ira ROOT (POST in Barbour) m. Rhoda FINLEY, both of Hebron, by James SHEPHERD, elder of the Methodist Church

---

[35] Also on file: a scrap of paper implying that bride Amy Bill was underage: "To whom it may concern I hereby certify that my daughter Amy BILL may be joined in marriage with Zelotes RIDER of Vernon. Hebron Nov. 27th 1817 [A/Heidl?] BILL "

Section C
More Records from Barbour's "Book 4"

[Page8]

He's Asa BISSELL Son of
Frederick P. BISSELL & Almira J. BISSELL his wife born May 4th 1848.
Josephine E. PORTER, daughter of Royal PORTER and Fanny his wife born Nov 1st 1847.

[Page 11]

Isabella Saloma WHITE died March 24, 1840
Orrin Bushnell WHITE died March 30, 1844

[Page 12]

James Alexander WHITE born Sept 20. 1847
Jerusha KELLOGG born July 23, 1848
United in marriage May 13, 1845. Children:
Edward James WHITE born Feby 24, 1846
Amanda WHITE [born] Nov. 26, 1847
Emma WHITE [born] Apr. 2, 1850
Sidney WHITE
Fred Kellogg WHITE [born] Aug. 13, 1853
Jerusha wife of James A. WHITE died Aug. 1855
Harriet RATHBONE 2nd wife of James A. White was born Feb 8, 1838. Was married to James A. WHITE Nov. 20 1856.
Children:
Adela WHITE born Jan. 10. 1860
John Bliss WHITE [born] Nov. 26, 1864
Harlan Rathbone [WHITE] [born] July 8, 1866
Deaths Harriet WHITE died May 29, 1885 ae 47
[Deaths] John Bliss WHITE [died] May 29, 1895 ae 30
[Deaths] Fred Kellogg [WHITE] [died] Dec 12. 1808 ae 35
[Deaths] Mary [WHITE] [died] Dec 20, 1900 ae 85
[Deaths] James A. [WHITE] [died] Jan 29, 1901 ae 83
[Deaths] Mrs. Charles [WHITE] [died] Sept 21, 1905 ae
[from JHW Sept 22/06 Copied by Ann C. GILBERT 1924

[Page 15]

Timothy LOCKWOOD, a Revolutionary Pensioner, d. in Hebron 4 Feb 1832, (see file #129 Aug. Co. Const. 1832)
Simeon WRIGHT, a Rev. Pensioner, d. in Hebron 22 May 1832. (see file #118, Co. Cont, Aug 1832) {by F.C. Bissell. Received Feb 18 1922 by Ann C. GILBERT, Asst Town Clerk.

PART III
COMPLETING THE BARBOUR INDEX OF HEBRON VITAL RECORDS
Section A: The Methodology

For Hebron, as for every other early Connecticut town, Barbour insists that his collection of vital records contains errors and requires verification from the original records he cites.[36] This is a relatively simple task when researching one's own family. The goal of finding ALL of the errors and omissions in one of Barbour's Town Collection is a more daunting task. Cross-checking an alphabetized list against a chronological list of the same entries is both time-consuming and difficult to do accurately.

One can, however, approach this goal by comparing Barbour's entries with the similarly alphabetized index of town vital records which virtually every Connecticut town prepared in about the middle of the 19th Century. The relatively few discrepancies between Barbour's data and the index entries can then be compared with the original record and recorded as additions or corrections to the Barbour Collection only where the town index reveals a more accurate extraction of the vital record.

Applying this technique to the Hebron Vital Statistics Index[37] proved extraordinarily productive:

- Sixty-nine marriages by Justice of the Peace Elihu Marvin between 1785 & 1812 are entered into the Hebron Vital Records for the first time within this volume between the letters "O" and "P," and then indexed citing to these pages numbered 167-172.[38]

---

[36] See, e.g., text at note 14 above.

[37] Hebron Town Clerk, [Index to] Births, Marriages, Deaths in v. 1-3 [sic], (original in Hebron Town Hall) (FHL film 1376165, Item 3).

[38] These marriages records are deciphered in detail in Linda MacLachlan, "Marriages by Elihu Marvin, J.P., of Hebron, Connecticut, 1785-1812," *NEHGR*, 161:175-80 (Jul 2007). The findings are summarized here so that this book, when combined with Barbour's

137

- A two-page spread in the First Book of Deaths was simply skipped over by Barbour's indexer.

- Hebron's TILLETSON family records are inexplicably truncated by the Barbour Collection.

While these results may be unique to Hebron, another equally important finding is probably common to all Connecticut Town Indexes: the index is full of enries not made by the indexer which supplement the records entered. Most frequently, they cross-reference other town records or report where a Hebron family came from or where they next settled when they left Hebron. Such information should lead to additional vital records for the family being researched.

In Section B, below:

- The page of the Index referenced is cited first in *italics* at the right margin, along with the identity of the Book (if any) from which the entry beneath comes.

- The page in that book where the cited entry may be found is noted at the right hand margin.[39]

- All writing that appears to be in a hand other than the indexer's is <u>underlined</u> and transcribed verbatim.

- Each entry that is not in Barbour at all is highlighted in **bold face.** Other entries describe the variance from Barbour in brackets.

- All entries by the indexer are verified by comparison with the original record cited.

- Citation to the First Book of Births, Deaths or Marriages also cite the entry in the recopy of the first book.

- All records which clearly should be primary to the town records of another Connecticut town are extracted here only if they contain information omitted from that town's Barbour Collection.

Hebron Collection, will provide a complete picture of all available Hebron vital records.

[39] Citations to the First Book of Births, Deaths or Marriages also cite the page number of the entry in the recopy of the first book.

Section B
Additions and Corrections to Barbour from the Vital Statistics Index & underlying records, 1708-1854

1st page of Index containing writing
Oliver DAVIS died March 26 1786.
Anne Daugh of Stephen & Susannah SAWYER **was born 4th of May 1761.**

2nd page of Index with handwriting (before page numbered 1)
Widow Hannah SHALER died May 16 1770.
Nathaniel Son of Nathaniel SHIFFORS J & Rachel his wife **born May 4 1761.**

Page 1, First Book of Births

		Page
24 Oct 1747	ARCHER Anna daug of Benjamin ARCHER	
27 Oct 1747	ARCHER Anner [daug of Benjamin ARCHER]	
5 May 1721	ASTON Hanah [dau of Robert ASTIN] [1725 in Barbour]	
22 Feb 1725/6	Hannah, dau of Robert ASTEN [1725 in Barbour]	1/1
10 Apr 1727	ASTON, Azor [A[a]ron in Barbour] son of Robert ASTON	1/1

Page 1, Second Book of Births

8 Feb 1767	ALLEN Ahincias [Ahimas in Barbour] son of Wm [&] Mahitable	
29 Jan 1758	**ANNABLE Anselon**	142
27 Apr 1769	ANNABLE Anna [child of] Anslen & Betty [1767 in Barbour]	143

Page 2, Second Book of Births

[Not stated]	AISCRAFT Robert Bastard son of Ann [illegitimacy not in Barbour]	

Third Book of Births

13 May 1806	AYUEL Benjamin [son of] Joseph & Ruth PERKINS his wife [relationship not in Barbour]	[2]

Page 3, Second Book of Marriages

16 Apr ___	ALLEN William & Mehit [page torn] [Merrit in Barbour]	1
12 Apr 1771	ARCHER Benjamin 2^d [m.] Wid. ___ ___	1

Page 5, First Book of Births

18 Jul 1748	David BARBER's fifth child still born (1st in Barbour]	52/12
9 May 1727	**BARBER, Joseph, son of Thomas BARBER**	6/5
10 July 1722	**Samuel, son of David BARBER**	1/3
17 Feb 1716/7	BARBER ____ son of David & Hannah POST (**David B[ARBER] died 1801** Aged 69) [birthday, mother's name & and father's death not in Barbour]	3/1
9 ___ 1762	BARBER daughter [of David & Hannah POST] [mother not in Barbour]	3/1
8 Aug 1718	BARBER Temperance [daughter to] David & Hannah (POST) [mother not in Barbour]	3/1
26 Apr 1715	**BARBER David** second daughter was **born. Died 10 May 1715**	3/1
10 Jul 1722	**BARBER Samuel** son of David, BARBOUR & Hannah POST	3/1
2 Jun 1742	BARBER Oliver [son of David 2nd & Patience CASS] [mother & suffix not in Barbour]	8/35
Mar 1 1743/4	BARBER Mary dau [of David 2nd & Patience CASS] [mother not in Barbour]	-/38
26 Mar 1746	BARBER Liddy [dau of David 2nd & Patience CASS] [mother not in Barbour]	10/43
13 Mar 1748	BARBER Aless [dau of] Capt. Stephen & Alice CASS [mother & father's rank not in Barbour]	12/51
5 Jan 1749/50	BARBER Abigill daug David [1749 in Barbour]	12/53
18 Jul 1748	BARBER 5th child stillborn [1st child in Barbour] [of] David	12/52
6 Feb 1729	BIRGE Coziah [Caziah in Barbour] daug [Daniel BIRGE]	4/15
10 Jan 1744	BIRGE Elizabeth [daug of Daniel BIRGE] [1744/5 in Barbour]	10/40

Page 6, First Book of Births

13 Jan 1748/9	BISSEL Leah [dau of Benjamin [1749/9 in Barbour]	11/50
4 Oct 1718	BLISS Mary [__ry in Barbour] [daug of Mr. John	3/1
20 Jan 1723	BLISS (not readable) ____ e [child of] John ([&] Constant?) ["Constant?" not in Barbour]	3:1

140

	Page 7, First Book of Births, after Neziah BLISS:	
_____	son of Rev. John (see Land records, Vol. 5, p. 324) [title & source not in Barbour]	6/22
23 May 1738	BLISS Anna [daug of] John Jr. [May 28 in Barbour]	7/25
	Page 7, First Book of Births	
26 Apr 1730	Abiel, son of Mr. John BLISS [no title in Barbour]	17/6
1 Mar 1717	Anna, dau of Mr. John BLISS [no title in Barbour]	1/3
19 Feb 1747	BLISS Anna [dau of John Jr.] [1742 1747/8 & John in Barbour]	11/50
5 Oct 1746	BLISS, Constant [dau of John Jr.) {John in Barber]	10/45
14 Dec 1711	Elizabeth, dau of Mr. John BLISS [no title in Barbour]	1/3
25 Feb 1733	Ellis, son of Mr. John BLISS [no title in Barbour]	14/6
22 Dec 1712	John, son of Mr. John BLISS [no title in Barbour]	1/3
21 Mar 1736	Neziah, son of Mr. John BLISS [no title in Barbour]	22/6
23 Jan 1721	dau of Mr. John BLISS [no title in Barbour]	1/3
20 ___ 1728	dau of Mr. John BLISS [no title in Barbour]	1/3
26 Jan 1727/8	Silvanus, son of Mr. John BLISS [Siluanus & no title in Barbour]	1/3
20 Nov 1731	BLISS ____ child of John Jr. [last child of John in Barbour]	1/11
27 __ber 1722	dau of Nicholas BOND [29 __ber in Barbour]	1/5
13 Jan 1725/6	Niclos, son of Niclas BOND [17 Jan in Barbour]	3/4
21 Jan 1721/2	dau of Nicholas BOND [1720 in Barbour]	1/3
4 Sep 1750	Anner, dau of Nathaniel BROWN [9 Sep in Barbour]	57/13
14 May 1716	**BROWN Nathan** son of Thomas	3/1
27 Oct 1742	BROWN Dorithy [dau of Azariah] [Dority in Barbour]	8/36
	Page 9, First Book of Births	
29 Apr 1751	**BUCK, Abel, son of Benjamin**	12/56
24 Nov 1736	BLACKMAN Samuel [of] Abraham [1786 in Barbour]	7/31

Page 10, Second Book of Births

7 Apr 1767   Lydia BARBER dau [of Capt. David 2nd & Abigail] m.Lawrence POWERS

Page 19

Rev. John Flavel BLISS went to State of N. Y. Cong. Church

Page 20

From records of Elmer T. BEACH, Kalamazoo, Mich, descendant of Appollos BEACH:

1775   **Elijah BEACH**, son of Azariah & Elizabeth
1778   **Apollos [BEACH**, son of Azariah & Elizabeth]
1782   **Joseph [BEACH**, son of Azariah & Elizabeth]
1786   **Chauncey [BEACH**, son of Azariah & Elizabeth]
1789   **Lucy [BEACH,]** dau [of Azariah & Elizabeth]
1793   **William R. [BEACH,]** son [of Azariah & Elizabeth]

Page 21, Fourth Book of Births

Date	Entry	Ref
16 Aug 1747	BANNING L. Jennette [dau of] Eliphalet & Louise [1847 in Barbour]	9x
4 Mar 1820	BUELL, Josiah M., son of Joseph & Mary [1821 in Barbour]	7
25 Apr 1834	BUELL. Maria K. [Maria H. in Barbour], dau of E. P. & Lucy	7

Page 22, First Book of Marriages

Date	Entry	Ref
19 May 1737	BEACH Unice, HORSFORD & Joseph HOSFORD [1734 in Barbour]	4/141
30 Oct 1746	BLISH [BLUSH in Barbour] Hannah & Edward NELAND	52/149
10 Jul 1730	BROWN Dinah & Thomas POST [July 1 in Barbour]	27/154
4 Mar 1747	BILL Phillap & Mercey TILDEN [Phillop & Marcey in Barbour]	51/134

Page 23, First Book of Marriages

Date	Entry	Ref
24 Aug 1794	BROWN Azariah & Lydie BLISS [Lydia in Barbour]	33/134
2 Dec 1750	BROWN Stephen & Sarah [Jerusha & 12 Dec in Barbour] LEE	55/134
11 Oct 1743	**BURAS John (died in Col. Co. N.Y.)** [death not in Barbour] [m.] Rebeckah BIRGE	44/134
4 Oct 1727	BURNHAM Annie & Samuel FILER [BURNBURNHAM in Barbour]	7/139

14 Jul 1714	BRONZON Martha [Marthar in Barbour] & Samuel PALMER	153

Page 23 (cont.)

William BROWN & Betsey TRUMBULL were **married October 1802** as per Gilead Church Records
Simeon BAXTER & Abigail MAN were **married April 6th 1721** from Lebanon Records

Page 24, Second Book of Marriages

6 Oct 1768	BAXTER Aaron & Mercy MENTER [MENTON in Barbour]	2:5

After Azariah BEACH m. Elizabeth SKINNER: Removed to 1805 Westfield Mass.

Page 26, above marriage of David BROWN & Lydia SWETLAND:
[David Brown] died in Peru Mass May 28 1830. [Lydia (Swetland) Brown] died March 28, 1814.

Page 30, Book 2 of Deaths

18 May 1782	BARBER **Dudly**, son of Stephen Jr. & Desire	275
5 Oct 1751	BARBER **Stephen,** son of Stephen	274
21 Feb 1762	BALDWIN **sixth child** of Benjn	274
23 Aug 1777	BAXTER **Lydia**	275
26 Dec 1778	BAXTER **Simon,** Aged 81	275
24 Oct 1748	BEACH **Abel,** son of Benjamin	274
30 Jun 1752	BEACH **Sary,** Daughter of Benjamin	274
16 June 1754	BEACH **Daniel,** son of John & Ann	274
22 Jun 1754	BEACH **Jedediah,** son of John & Ann	274
5 Aug 1756	BEACH **John,** son of John & Ann	274
1 Sep 1775	BEACH **Ann,** wife of John	275
7 Aug 1779	BIRGE **Daniel**	275
12 Feb 1776?	BIRGE **Elizabeth**, "aged 50," wife of Daniel	275
17 May 1773	BIRGE **Daniel, Jr.,** 22 years, 3 mo. 25 days. [but 12 May in index]	275
10 Apr 1759	BIRGE **Jonathan,** son Daniel & Elizabeth, 6 years, 2 mo.	274
30 Aug 1758	BILL **Samuel,** son of Samuel & Sarah	274
15 Sep 1758	BILL **Rachel**, Daugh. of Samuel & Sarah	274
20 Feb 1761	BILLINGS **Oliver**	274
22 Mar 1770	BINGHAM **Stephen**, aged 89	275
14 Dec 1735	BINGHAM **Benjamin** [son of] Benjamin & Elizabeth BISELL?	274
26 Aug 1755	BLISS **Abiel**	274
20 Nov 1769	BLISS **Thoner**, wife of Ellis "at night &	

	their infant was christened in the morning of this same day"	275
7 Jun 1775	**BLISS Hannah**, dau. of Doct. Neziah and Martha [father read as "Joel Maj" by indexer]	275
22 Oct 1776	**BLISS Anna**, dau. of Ellis & Grace [20 Oct in index]	275
9 Dec 1747	**BLACKMAN Elizabeth**, Aged 57, Mother of Abraham [age only in index]	274
25 Jul 1778	**BOLTON Mary**, widow	275
26 Jun 1758	**BOND Mahitabel**, wife of Nicholas, Jr.	274
11 Jul 1758	**BOND Joseph**, son of Nicholas, Jr.	274
10 Apr 1761	**BOND Nicholas** [indexer reads: no day of month & BOND _____, son of Nicholas, Jr.]	274

Page 31, (2nd Book of Deaths, cont.)

21 Apr 1761	**BOND Anne**, wife of Nicholas	274
28 Jul 1763	**BOND Joseph** son of Stephen & Mary	275
4 Jan 1757	**BROWN Thomas,** dau of John & Abigail	274
3 Jun 1757	**BROWN Sarah**, dau. of Jonathan & Abigail [read "John" by indexer]	274
22 Dec 1759	**BROWN Samuel**, son of Abner & Sarah	274
26 Oct 1760	**BROWN John**	274
1 Mar 1762	**BROWN David**, son of David & Lydea	274
20 Sep 1770	**BROWN Azariah**	275
29 Nov 1775	**BROWN Lucinda**, Daughter of Abner & Hannah	275
12 Jan 1753	**BUSHNEL Daniel**	274
26 Apr 1779	**BUSHNELL Mindwell**	275
22 Dec 1784	**BUSHNELL Sarah**, aged 73, Relict of Daniel	275
8 June 1772	**BUSHNEL Jonth**	275
5 Dec 1783	**BURROWS Isaac**, aged about 90	275
18 Jul 1754	**BUEL Mary**, wife of Samuel	275
6 Dec 1753	**BUEL Mary**, wife of Benjamin	274
22 Jul 1772	**BUEL Cybel**, wife of Benjamin "his child was born the 20th of the same"	274
20 Jul 1772	**BUEL child** of Benjamin & Cybel. Born & died same day	275
22 Jul 1778	**BUEL Abigail**, daug. Capt Benjamin & Abigail	275
20 Oct 1777	**BUEL William**, son of William Jr. & Abigail ['Jr.' not in index]	275
15 Oct 1751	**BUCK Sary**, wife of Thomas	274

27 Feb 1756	BUCK Eunice, Daughter of Thomas Jnr	274
14 Dec 1755	BISSELL Benjamin, son of Benjamin & Elizabeth[40]	274

Page 32, added at bottom of page

[See book 3 pages 145 x 146 of Land Records of Thos. BUCK of Hebron

I am very certain that CASE and CASS are of the same family.

Gerre BELNAP born Aug 31 – 1760 as per family record Mr. Hyram BELNAK has [in] Ogden Utah

Page 33, after CASS/CASE births:

Moses CASE married Mary HOSKINS probably of Lebanon Settled in Hebron? H[ebron] Land Records Vol 1 P 216

Page 34, First Book of Births

24 May 1728	CHAPWELL, Rachell [daug of Jonathon]	10/16

Page 35, Above birth of Caleb CURTICE:

Richard CURTICE was of Southold Long Island N Y

Page 36: After birth of Abner CURTICE:

Caleb went to Sharon Conn.

Page 38: Second Book of Births:

For Abner HOWARD see _____

At bottom

CHAMBERLIN went to Hartford & Stratford NY about 1762

Page 48, added to birth of Oliver S. DAVIS:

1st son Oliver Died Mar 26 1786

Page 50, Second Book of Births

7 Sep 1784	DARBE Sally daug of Joseph & Charity	169
21 Oct 1786	DARBE Mary [daug of Joseph & Charity]	169

Page 50

H. DANIK m. Elihu McKALL of Salisbury 1777   167

Marriage of Calvin DUNHAM to Ruth NOBLE was recorded in Pittsfield Mass in 1773

Page 57, at top of page

Thomas CARTER Sr. & sons went to Kent & Warren Ct. in 1750-6

Page 65, First Book of Births

---

[40] For some unknown reason, this death is not actually recorded on pages 274 or 5 or 6 of the original vital record book as implied in the index.

Feb 19 1709   FILER John son of Samll [Feb 17 in Barbour]   33
Capt Jacob FORD born Apr 22, 1744 moved to Austerlitz NY
                in 1766. Was Captain in Rev. War 1775 in Col.
                Peter SAMPSON's Reg. Lieut. Col. in 1778.

Page 66, First Book of Births

21 Jul 1747   FULLER Roger, son of Ebenezer & Mary (see below) (Vol. 1 of the FULLER Genealogy. Pages 143-5 give **birth of Roger FULLER at Hebron, Conn** (Concord. NH Historical Society))

Page 68, Second Book of Births

23 Jul 1789   FORD Gilbert son of Luther & Lucy [1787 in Barbour]   179

Page 72, First Book of Marriages

Did Amos FULLER marry 2nd Mary TAYLOR? L. K. HAMBLIN

4 Oct 1727   FILER Samuel & Anne BURNHAM [BURNBURNHAM in Barbour]   139

13 Mar 1749/50 FILER Amey & ~~Joseph CARRIER~~ David CARVER (Error: CARVER instead of CARRIER in copy) [CARDER in Barbour]   136

Page 73 [in p. 66 hand]

4 Jun 1810   **FULLER Roger [m.] Susanna KEENEY**. FULLER Genealogy

Asa son [of] Shubael of Coventry & Sarah (SCOTT) MELLTREE? (Hawkins) TAYLOR [MELLTREE? (Hawkins) TAYLOR not in Barbour] of Coventry

25 Nov 1787   **FILER Anna [m.] Dan ROOT**   87

Page 80

Joel GILLET went to Franklin in 1801.

Page 91

Lydia daug of Samuel **GILBERT Baptized in Gilead 1764**
                (from Gilead Church Records)

Page 90, Third Book of Deaths

30 Oct 1806   **GILBERT Cloe** a Negro girl brought up by Sylvester GILBERT   35

23 Oct 1809   **GARDNER Milley** their Negro girl   35

Page 91

William BUELL from Wales England settled at Windsor Conn.

with his two sons W^m & Peter Stiles History of Windsor.

Lydia daug of Samuel GILBERT Baptized in Gilead 1764 (from Gilead Church Records)

Page 92

Samuel GILBERT [not **Abilena**'s twin] was **born May the first A.D. 1712** copied from certified copy from Town Clerk of Lebanon [**birth not in Barbour for Hebron or Lebanon**]

Page 92, First Book of Births

15 May 1749   HOUGHTON Joel son of Ebenezer & Abigail MATION   1:44

Page 104, added to birth record of **Sarah HORTON:**

My great grandmother who **Mar John HIGH**

Page 105

Sarah HORSFORD b. June 12 1770 m. John TAINTOR?

Page 106

Talcot HORSFORD to Rutland Vermont

Page 108

HEATON, Samuel & Sarah HAWS married in Wrentham Mass See Vol 1 Page 202 H2 from Mrs E.R. STARR Sanborn N.Y.

Page 109, Fourth Book of Births

19 Mar 1821   HARRIS, George W., son of Joseph [1812 in Barbour]   1x

Page 113

Record of Marriage of **Daniel HORSFORD & Hanna DAY on Nov 9, 1780 in Colchester** records v. 3

2 Oct 1768   [MENTER!) HUNTER Mary & Aaron BAXTER [only under Baxter 1812 in Barbour]   3:5

Page 122 First Book of Births

25 Feb 1728   **JONES Samuel** son of Samll **died 1733**   49
Feb. 18 1735   **JONES Samuel** Jones Street Cemetery Land Rec. Am. Hist Soc. NJ
Anna JONES dau. [of] Ezekiel & Mindwell (BEACH) JONES was **born Mar 20, 1765,** married Roger PHELPS, Jr. not of Hebron records

Page 125, Fourth Book of Births

13 Apr 1848   JOHNSON Wm. K. [Wm. N. in Barbour], son
               of David & Piercy   10

                              Page 126, Second Book of Marriages
6 Apr 1762   JONES Jedediah son of Joel & Margaret
               PORN   Rec. Fam. [No day of birth in Barbour]
7 Jul 1785   **JONES Samuell 3rd (born in Lebanon
               [in] 1759)** & Talatha [Tabitha in Barbour]
               BISHOP of Bolton   2:50

                               Page 133, First Book of Marriages
15 Nov 1737   KENNY (Keny & 1739 in Barbour] Susannah
               & Joseph KELLOGG   145
10 Oct 1771   KNEELAND David & Marcy KNEELAND of
               Colchester (Mercy & no town in Barbour]   145
3 Jun 1754   KELLOGG Elisha [Elijah in Barbour] &
               Hannah ADAMS of Colchester   145

                  Page 134, First Book of Marriages [in indexer's hand]
15 Jun 1751   KELLOGG Susannah & Hozea CURTICE Jun[r]
               [No suffix in Barbour]   56
21 Aug 1777   KELLOGG Hannah & Jonathan HALL
               [20 Aug in Barbour]   56

                                 Page 136, First Book of Births
[n.d.]   **Ebenezer** son Rev Benjamin **LORD** of Norwich

                                  Page 141, across top of page
Will of Micah MUDGE in Vol. II Early Connecticut Probate
               Records in Vault
                                           First Book of Births
30 Mar 1711   MUDG, Mary, [Marcey in Barbour] dau of Ebene-
               zer MUDG   66/59
16 Jun 1715/16 MAN, Nath[ll], [16 Jan in Barbour] son of Nath[ll]
               MAN   61/60
                       (After the birth of John MANN, Jr.):
(Capt.) John[5] MANN Jr. (John[4], Nathaniel[3], Richard[2],
               Richard[1]) removed 178- to Oxford VT. Others
               went to Hartford & Strafford VT & Fairfield NY
               & Del Co NY

                                  Page 142, First Book of Births
9 May 1720 MACK, Luise, dau of Orlandder MACK   2/60

                       Page 149, Fourth Book of Births (in indexer's hand)

Who was Mary MARKS Father? where did she come from.
Joseph MARKS lived in North Brookfield Mass. Mary MARKS his
daughter was married in North Brookfield Mass
[not Hebron, as Barbour implies] to John PETERS.

Page 153, Second Book of Marriages

15 Dec 1785	MCKALL (ROCKWELL) [maiden name not in Barbour] Lucy 2d wife & Joel POST.	
__ Apr __	[MCKALL] Mehit[torn] & William ALLYN	1
__ __ __	[MCKALL] Mary & Samuel ALLEN	1
__ Apr __	[MCKALL] Mehitabel & Matthew ALGER	

Page 160, Second Book of Marriages

Capt Obidiah NEWCOMB & Mrs. Mary POST   214

Page 163, First Book of Births

6 Jun 1675   Josiah OWEN of Windsor John (1) of Windsor Jonah (2) Jonah (3) Hebron

Page 168: all marriages by Elihu MARVIN, J.P.[41]

No 11	**7 Mar 1789 - Amasa ARCHER m. Mrs Sibel RAYMOND** both of Hebron.	168
No 12	**2 Jul 1789 - Mr George CULLUM** of Glosenbury m. **Mrs Lucy RAYMOND** of Hebron.	168
No 13	**4 Oct 1789 - Richard TUCK m. Lidia PERRIN** both of Hebron.	168
No 14	**25 Mar 1790 - Gershom HOLDRIDG** of Lebanon m. **Rebeccah CROUCH** of Hebron.	168
No 15	**25 Apr 1790 - Asa DAY** of Colchester m. **Anna MARVIN** of Hebron.	168
No 16	**May 12th 1790 - Hazael GOTT to Abigail PHELPS** both of Hebron. [By Elihu MARVIN not in Barbour]	168
No 17	**13 May 1790 - Daniel NILES** of Colchester m. **Abigal BEACH** of Hebron.	168

Page 169, all marriages by Elihu MARVIN, J.P.

No 1	6 Feb 1785 - Col Jo[hn PETERS] m. Mrs Elisabeth MURREY. [Murry in Barbour]	169

---

[41] Wherever there is a difference between the index and the original record now in the CSA, the original record is presented above and the indexer's reading in a footnote. See also, Linda MacLachlan, "Marriages by Elihu Marvin, J.P., of Hebron, Connecticut, 1785-1812," *NEHGR*, 161:175-80 (Jul 2007).

No 2	8 Sep 1785 - Obadiah ARCHER of East Haddam m. Mrs Elizabeth FITCH of Hebron.	169
No 3	18 Dec 1785 - Joshua PALMER m. Mrs Sarah TAYLOR both of Hebron.	169
No 18	6 Feb 1791 - Mr John Wilks PARKER m. Rebeccah STILES both of Hebron.	169
No 19	6 Feb 1791 - Mr Warren CARVER m. Sarah STILES both of Hebron.	169
No 20	20 Jun 1791 - Nehemiah DANIELS Junr m. Elisabeth FREEMAN both of Hebron.	169
No 21	14 Mar 1792 - Mr Amasa HOLDRIDGE of Spencertown, New York m. Mrs Experience JONES of Hebron.	169
No 22	27 Jul 1792 - Mr Abijah ROOT m. Mrs Charity JONES both of said Hebron.	169

Page 170, all marriages by Elihu MARVIN, J.P.

No 23	13 Dec 1792 - Mr Jonathan ROOT m. Mrs Levina GILLET both of Hebron.	170
No 24	20 Dec 1792 - Mr John DAY of Colchester m. Mrs Catharine JONES of Hebron.	170
No 25	19 Oct 1793 - Bartholomew TIERNER or FIERNER[42] m. Lydia JONES both of Hebron.	170
No 26	21 Oct 1794 - Henry a Negro man m. Betty a Black Girl both Resident in Hebron.	170
No 27	26 Apr 1795 - Silas PERRY [a] Transient Person m. Mary RAYMONT of Hebron.	170
No 28	10 Sep [1795] - Zophrastes GEE of Lyme m. Lara JONES of Hebron.	170
No 29	27 Jan 1796 - Elihu PHELPS m. Elizabeth BEACH both of Hebron.	170
No 30	13 Apr 1796 - Joseph BURNHAM of Colchester m. Jerusha KELLOGG of Hebron.	170

Page 171, all marriages by Elihu MARVIN, J.P.

No 31	7 Sep 1796 - Mr John FELSHOW m. Mrs Desiah BEACH both of Hebron.	171
No 32	8 Jun 1797 - George OWEN m. Sibbll HORSFORD both of Hebron.	171
No 33	9 Aug 1796 - Joseph MORE m. Mrs Abigail ROOT both of Hebron.	171

---

[42] Read as FRIERER by indexer.

No 34	16 Nov 1797 - Mʳ Moses COUDRE of Hartland m. Mʳˢ Zeruah PHELPS of Hebron.	171
No 35	23 Nov 1797 - Mʳ Ezekiel FULLER m. Mʳˢ Esther CHAPMAN both of Hebron.	171
No 36	8 Feb 1798 - Mʳ Philip BROWN m. Mʳˢ Sally SALLET [then corrected to VALLET in another hand] both of Hebron.	171
No 37	1 May 1798 - Mʳ Joseph WILLCOX of Tidinham [sic] Massachusetts m. Mʳˢ **Sebbel**[43] WRIGHT of Hebron.	171
No 38	31 May 1798 - Mʳ Adniram BISSELL m. Mʳˢ Salla PORTER both of Hebron.	171

Page 172, all marriages by Elihu MARVIN, J.P.

No 39	1 Jul 1798 - Mʳ Wm. SKINNER of New London m. Anna WHITE of Hebron.	172
No 40	25 Oct 1798 - Mʳ Allen HILLS of Chatham m. Temprance JONES of Hebron.	172
No 41	5 Nov 1798 - Mʳ Aaron PHELPS m. Mʳˢ Thankfull POST both of Hebron.	172
No 42	26 Nov 1798 - Mʳ Samuel LOOMIS [Jr.] of Colchester m. Mʳˢ Anna HORSFORD of Hebron.	172
No 43	21 Feb 1799 - Fortune m. Sibel both free Negro persons now resident in Hebron.	172
No 44	3 Mar 1799 - Mʳ ___ BECKWITH of Lyme m. Wihay [or Wethay] GAY of Hebron.	172
No 45	22 Aug 1799 - Henory CURTICE m. Elisabeth WRIGHT, both of Hebron.	172
No 4	9 Sep 1787 - Moses KELLOGG Jnr. m. Abigail MARVIN both of Hebron	172

Page 173, all marriages by Elihu MARVIN, J.P.

No 5	18 Feb 1788 - Mʳ Zenus WATERS m Mʳˢ Seenah[44] PHELPS both of Hebron.	173
No 46	7 Sep 1799 - Mʳ Anson GILLETT m. Mʳˢ Mary WASHBURN both of Hebron.	173
No 47	10 Sept 1799 - Mʳ William HEBERD m. Mʳˢ Rachel BARBER both of Hebron.	173
No 48	13 Nov 1799 - Mʳ Rozel BOWLS m. Mʳˢ Lois NOR-	

---

[43] Read as Mʳˢ Silbel WRIGHT by indexer.

[44] Read as Adeenah PHELPS by indexer.

	THAM both of Hebron.	173
No 49	23 Feb 1800 - Mr Oliver OLCOTT of East Haddam m. Mrs Jerusha DANIELS of Hebron.	173
No 50	3 Sep 1800[45] - Mr Ebenezer STRONG of Bolton m. Polly DAY of Hebron.	173
No 51	17 Jun 1801 - Mr Elisha STRICKLAND of Glosebury m. Mrs Polley ROOT of Hebron.	173

Page 174, all marriages by Elihu MARVIN, J.P.

No 52	4 Oct 1801 - Mr Daniel OLCOTT of Litchfield m. Mrs Theodore GAY of Hebron.	174
No 53	21 Nov 1802: Mr Benoni WRIGHT now Resident in Hebron m. Dorathy SHORT Now Resident in Hebron.	174
No 54	10 Feb 1802 - Mr Adonijah DAY of Elington m. Elisabeth MARVIN of Hebron.	174
No 55	25 Mar 1802 - Joseph WATERS Junr of Franklin State of New York m. Huldah JONES Junr of Hebron	174
No 56	29 Mar 1802 - Mr Zadock SMITH of Colchester m. Mrs Lura JONES of Hebron.	174
No 57	6 Jun 1802 - Aaron PHELPS Jr m. Eunice GURLEY both of Hebron.	174
No 58	14 Apr 1803 - Elisha FARBOX [indexed under TARBOX] m. Lidia PORTER both of Hebron.	174
No 59	2 Oct 1803 - Shubel PERKINS m. Cloha MANLY both of Hebron.	174
No 60	23 Dec 1804 - ___ GATES of East Haddam m. Mrs Prudence TAYLOR of Hebron.	174

Page 175, all marriages by Elihu MARVIN, J.P.

No 61	2 Oct 1805 - Calvin MANNING m. Mrs Desiah ROSE both of Coventry.	175
No 62	7 Nov 1805 - James SUMMERS of Hebron m. Phena THOMAS of Columbia.	175
No 63	25 Jan 1806 - [Timothy][46] JONES m. Nancy TAYLOR both of Hebron.	175
No 64	15 Oct 1806 - Oliver SKINNER m. Salla BROWN both of Hebron.	175

---

[45] 30 Sep 1800, as read by indexer

[46] To the entry in Vital Statistics Index, p.175, has been added: "The above is Timothy JONES from family record." The original manuscript is torn where this name should be.

No 65	16 Oct 1806 - ___ [Edward][47] ASHCRAFT to Salla TAYLOR both of Hebron.	175
No 66	22 Oct 1807 - ___ ___ m. ___ ___ [48]	175
No 67	4 Feb 1808 - Mr George WASHINGTON of Franklin New[tear] m. Mrs Welthy CHAMBERLIN of Hebron.	175
No 68	18 Feb 1808 - Robert TAYLOR, a Negro Man m. Polly WONKS both of Colchester.	175
No 69	1 May 1808 - Mr Brabras NILES of Colchester m. Mrs Anna SKINNER of Hebron.	175
No 70	22 May 1809 - Mr Daniel DOUBLEDAY m. Mrs Sally DEAN[49] of Hebron.	175

Page 176, all marriages by Elihu MARVIN, J.P.

No 71	18 Apr 1810 - [___ MOSYER][50] m. Margaret STONE.	176
[72]	8 Oct[51] 1810 - Ebenezer SNOW of Vernon m. Lucinda GOTT of Hebron.	176
[73]	3 Feb 1811 - Dan JONES m. Cornelia MANLEY both of Hebron.	176
[74]	18 Jan 1812[52] - Charles FOLEMAN of Colchester m. Betsy TISDALE of Lebanon [Jan 18th 1812 and Betsy TISDALE of Hebron in original].[53]	176

---

[47] Where this record is indexed under A (p. 4), the Town Clerk added: "As it is stated in a letter I received from Alice Budduck HIBBARD of Brockford, NY the above Ashcraft name was Edward ASHCRAFT who married Sarah TAYLOR."

[48] This "marriage" never included any names, but the original is explicitly dated 22 Oct 1807

[49] Read as DOAN by Indexer.

[50] Jno JAGER/JAGGER as read by Indexer. If the surname was actually Mosier or Mosier, the groom may have been Stephen MOSHER of Hebron in 1810 or his son (U.S. Census, Hebron, Tolland County, Connecticut, roll 3, p. 292). Original manuscript says ___ MOSYER.

[51] "1 Oct" as read by indexer.

[52] "18 Feb 1813" as read by indexer.

[53] The last three known (but largely illegible) entries in the original record, now at Connecticut State Archives are not reproduced by the Hebron Town Clerk:

75 23 ___ 1812 ___ [EVERTON?] S___ [to] Charity FOX.
76 28 Apr 1812 ___ BROWN? [to] ___ ___.
77 7 Dec 1812 ___ ___NATHY [to] Sarah CHEHEN?

Page 178

1. "Nicholas **NORTON** b. 1610, d. 1690. wife Elizabeth --
2. **Joseph**, son of Nicholas, **b. 1651, d. 1741** ae 87 years. His first wife was **Mary BOYES**; second wife Anne **TRAPP**.
3. **John**, son of ²Joseph , **b. 1674, d. 1730** wife Mary--
4. **John**, son of ³John, **b. about 1700. m. Nov. 3, 1724 Hepzibah**, daug. of Enoch & Beulah (EDDY) **COFFIN** of Marthas' Vineyard. She was **b. Sep. 7, 1704.**
5. **Francis**, son of ⁴John, **b. Feb 7, 1745. m.** (dau. Malatia DAVIS) **Lydia DAVIS, "Dec. 15, 1769 She died Feb. 21, 1797, ae 51. m. 2nd Tabitha DARMAN April 18, 1798. She died Aug. 17, 1803,** ae 41. m. 3rd Mrs. Thalia HAYDEN. She died Apr. 11, 1846 [Tabitha in Barbour], ae 81. **Francis NORTON d. Aug. 14, 1813."** The above record between quotation marks was sent to me by a professional genealogist.

The following copied from Family Bible. Leaf Torn. Marthas Vineyard

Francis NORTON. b. 7 Feb 1745, m. Dec 15, 1769 Lydia DAVIS. b. Feb. 5, 1746
Anna. (leaf torn) b. Nov. 12, 1770
Jemima. b. Aug 4, 1773
Lydia. b. Nov 5, 1775
Francis. b. Oct. 20, 1777.
Joseph. b. June 26 1780
Mary. b. [June 26 1780]
Davis. b. Apr. 24, 1782.
Betsey. b. Aug. 24 1786

Page 189

Sarah POST, dau of Joel & Sarah (BUSHNELL) POST Born Dec 21ˢᵗ 1765. **Mar Dr. Fred ROSE** of Coventry

Page 190, First Book of Births

27 Mar 1725	PALMER, Marthar, [1723 in Barbour] dau of Samuell PALMER	80/74
Mar ____	**PALMER, Mary, dau of Samuell PALMER**	80/74
1 Jan 1739/40	**PERRIN, Thomas, son of James**	30/80

Page 191, First Book of Births

7 Feb 1749/50	PETERS, Marcey, [9 Feb in Barbour] dau of John Junior PETERS	53/86

13 Feb 1741/2	POST, sixth [fifth in Barbour] child of Thomas POST, d. 13 Feb 1741/2	81
30 Jun 1726	PORTER, Daniell, second son of John Jr. (Daniell 2nd in Barbour]	61/75

Page 192, First Book of Births

16 Feb 1724	PORTER, Daniel, [1724/5 in Barbour] son of John Junior PORTER	61/75
~~19 Jan 1743/4~~	~~PORTER, Mary dau of John Jr.~~	38/82
24 Nov 1745	PORTER, Hannah, dau of John 2nd (1746 in Barbour]	44/84

Page 193, First Book of Births

11 Nov 1724	PHELPS, Freny, [Ireny in Barbour] dau of Cornelas PHELPS	65/75
11 Apr 1721	PHELPS, Abigill, dau of Nath^ll PHELPS, "the 3rd day of the month, the 3rd day of the week, at 5 of the clock afternoon." [time not in Barbour]	70/76
31 Jul 1724	PHELPS, Elisah [Elijah in Barbour] son of Noah	67/76
3 Jul 1734	**PHELPS, Asell, son of Asell**	19/79

Page 194, First Book of Births

2 Dec 1743	PHELPS, Hannah, dau of Timothy PHELPS 3RD [29 Dec in Barbour]	28/80
8 Feb 174_	PHELPS, Abitha, dau of Ichabod [1740/1 in Barbour]	33/81

Page 195, First Book of Births

5 Aug 1751	PINNEY, Oliver, son of Isaac of Windsor [6 Aug in Barbour]	87

Page 196, First Book of Births

10 Oct 1708	~~PORTER, Mercy~~, [name not crossed out in Barbour] dau of Thomas	76

<u>POMPSON see letter T</u>

Page 202

<u>POST Joel son of Joel & Sarah (BUSHNELL) POST [maiden name not in Barbour)</u>

page 221, over Ezekiel POST's birth record
<u>blurred the Records might ___ in effort to erase it</u>

Page 204, Second Book of Births

5 Nov 1762/3   POLLY Hannah dau [of Daniel & Rachel]
[1762 in Barbour]   230

Page 210

b Timothy Dammick PERKINS moved to Lee, Mass

Page 212, Fourth Book of Births
17 Jul 1839   PERKINS Mary Eliza dau of Wm A. & Eliza ___
BOYNTON of Coventry (mother's maiden name
& origin not in Barbour)   5x

Page 219, above POST *Eldad m. Hannah* CASE:
moved to Oxford NH

Page 220, Second Book of Marriages
15 Dec 1 785   POST Joel & Lucy ROCKWELL MCKALL of Lebanon
[bride's first surname not in Barbour]   2/85

Page 225, Second Book of Deaths, added to death of Oliver PINNEY:
Was lost in a Storm at sea in a voyage from Jamaica to New York

Page 230, Second Book of Deaths, added to death of Asabel PHELPS:
Buried in Marlboro Cemetery

Page 225, Second Book of Births
15 May 1753   **RYLE Jonth** son of Jonth & Hulda   236

Page 225, Second Book of Births
6 Jun 1809   RUDE Betsey daug of Storan [Horace in
Barbour] & Sukey   309

Page 242, by John ROW m. Mary WILLIAMS:
See Vol. 3, p. 152, Hebron Land Records.

Page 246

Rorss of B. M. & D. 163
See Land Records Book 3 page 153
of BENJAMIN Robinson of Hebron & Lyme.

Page 250

Jacob SAWYER, b. Gloucester Mass. **d 1687** A.L.G.

Page 251, First Book of Births
14 Jul 1721   SAWYER, Isaac, son to Edward SAWYER [17

	Jul in Barbour]	70/99

First Book of Deaths

8 Jul 1707	SAWYER, Moses, son of Moses SAWYER [30 Jul in Barbour]	8/205
16 Jan 1736/37	SAWYER, John, son of John SAWYER [1737 in Barbour]	24/206
4 Jun 1731	**SAYER, John, son of Moses SAYER**	6/205

Page 252, First Book of Births

| 1 Oct 1742 | [SWETLAND], Noah, son of Jonathan SWETLAND [4 Oct in Barbour] | 35/106 |

Page 254, First Book of Births

| 23 Aug 1738 | [SILLS] [STILES in Barber] Abigill, dau of Nathan SILLS [STILES in Barber] | 26/104 |

Page 255,..First Book of Births, added to Seth Sutton's children' births:
[John SUTTON] died Jan 1824 ae 91
[David SUTTON] died Jan 20 1804

Page 256, First Book of Births

| 25 Apr 1745 | [STUARD] John, son of Thomas STUARD [James in Barbour], but son of James is also indexed for same date | 42/108 |

For Nath<u>ll</u> SHEPERSON's ch. see vol 3, p. 96, Land Records.

Page 262, Second Book of Births

| **Aug 1773** | Dorcus [daug of] Cesar & Loice Negros | 268 |
| Aug 1783 | Ziba [Zilba in Barbour] [daug of] Cesar & Loice | 268 |

Page 281

~~Rowleys~~ ~~Fuller~~ Elizabeth FULLER Daughter of Dr. Matthew FULLER **Married Moses ROWLEYS** in History of Barnstable Mass. Notes by Otis. Also see records of Haddam & East Haddam Taintor's Colchester.

Page 330, First Book of Births.

29 Apr 1731	[TILLETSON] Darckis, [24 Apr in Barbour] dau of Joshua TILLETSON, died 16 Apr 1725	17/114
30 Mar 1725	[TILLETSON] Darkis, [21 Mar in Barbour] dau of Joshua TILLETSON, died 16 Apr 1725	69/113
22 Feb 1746/7	**[TILLETSON] Freny, dau of Isaac TILLETSON, Junior**	46/115
15 Jun 1729	TILLETSON Lazir [son of] Jonathan Ju-	

	nior]	29/[115]
30 Jul 1726	TILLETSON Sarah daug of Joshua. **Died Aug the 27 1726**	69/113
29 Dec 1727	TILLETSON Sarah [daug of Joshua] **Died Feb 4, 1727-8**	8/[113]
8 Mar 1734/5	TILLETSON Sarah [daug of Joshua]	20/[114]
26 Aug 1748	TILLOTSON Sary daug [of] Abraham	54/[116]
23 Apr 1750	TILLOTSON Zeruiah [13 Apr in Barbour] daug of Jonathan	[116]

Page 331

	TILDEN, Ann	249

Page 332

2 Jan 1761	TALCOT Anne [daug of] **John dec'd** & Abiah [**father's death not in Barbour**]	[247]

Page 333, Second Book of Births

6 Dec 1756	TILLETSON Abram [son of] Abraham & Sibil [mother not in Barbour]	163

Page 334, Second Book of Births

6 Dec 1756	TILLETSON Sarah [dau of] Joshua & Elizabeth	248
12 Aug 1765	TILLETSON Zerujah [son of] Elezur & Content	248
4 Feby 1766	TILLETSON Sibil [dau of] Abr^m & Sybil	248
10 June 1753	TILLETSON Sarah [daug of] Abraham & Cybil	248

Page 336, First Book of Marriages

21 Jul 1713	TILLETSON Morris & Not Stated <u>Martha</u> Gilead Ch rec p 74 [Bride not in Barbour]	163

Page 337, First Book of Marriages

11 Nov 1743	TILLETSON Isaac Juner & Irene PHELPS	163
	[in a faint hand]	

<u>Samuel TARBOX es Birth about 1770 [birth not in Barbour]</u>

Page 338, Second Book of Marriages

10 Mar 1773	TILLETSON Sarah & Enos WRIGHT	259

Page 341, First Book of Deaths

19 Sep 1735	TILLETSON Sarah daug of [Joshua]	209
4 Aug 1750	TILLETSON Sary wife [of] Abraham	209

Second Book of Deaths

24 Nov 1751	TILLETSON **Sarah** daug of Abraham & Sarah	356
22 Aug 1753	TILLETSON **Rebecca (Chamberlin)** wife of Jonathan	356
24 Aug 1753	TILLETSON **Sibil** wife of Abraham	356
25 Jul 1776	TILLETSON (Martha Gilead Ch. Rec p. 74) Relict of Capt. Morris [1st name not in Barbour]	356

Page 342, after death of John TALCOTT

Son of **John decd & Abiah wife of Simon** DURHAM [marriage(s) not in Barbour]

Lawrence TAYLOR mar Martain RICHISON? step daughter of Roger FULLER of Hebron. This family of TAYLORs was of Coventry.

Page 343

John THOMPSON Buried in Old Cemetery in Gilead East St near Many Lords in Andover Over the Town Line

By Will of Abraham TILLETSON
    Executed March 26 1791
    Probated August 24 1796
    David TILLOTSON Executor
    He bequeaths to the following
    Abraham Junr.
    To daughters Sarah & Elisabeth
Rachel, Margery & Cybil & his wife Elinor & son David Vol. 2. Page 20. Andover Probate Records Distribution of said Estate Vol. 2. Page 145. Andover P.R.

Page 344

Who was Samuel WATERS Sr.'s wife? Who were his parents? Apr 12 1911 H Water SHELDON, Yonkers N.Y.
    [in another hand]: **[births and marriages not in Barbour?]**
Samuel [Waters] son of James & Mary (STALLWORTHE) of Topsfield Mass. **b. 1679**
James son of Richard WATERS of Salem Mass.
Richard, son of James WATERS m Phebe MANNING of St. Botolph's Eng. (Prof TUBBS, Bates College, Me.)

Page 345, First Book of Births

10 Feb 1717	WILLIAMS **Mary** daug [of] Nathaniel **died Mar 10 following**	[120]

159

Added to Steven WILLCOX birth:
Buried in South Fairlee Vt.

Page 346, First Book of Births
14 Nov 1737   RIGHT **Aaron** son of Aaron & Elizabeth
              BLISS   [120]

Page 347
Obidiah WILCOX removed to Surrey NH about 1765. This from
    W. E. BRITTON, 296 McKinley Ave., N. Haven,
    by F.C.B. Anne C. GILBERT

Page 348
Nov 14, 1744 WALTERS (WATERS) Mary dau of Adam & Mary
    [mother not in Barbour]
Dec. 28 1746 WALTERS (WATERS) Oliver s of Adam & Mary
    [mother not in Barbour] Moved to Halifax VT,
    Bennington VT. Bur at Horsick Falls NY.
Note by H. Waters SHELDON of Yonkers NY April 1921.
    Adam & Mary WATERS buried at Horsick Falls
    NY. Oliver married Theoda ROGERS, d. of
    Nathaniel & Theoda MINER ROGERS of New
    London & Lebanon. Children born at Halifax —
    Adam — Elisha — 1784 —**Oliver m. second**
    Phoebe JUDD. Children: Worthy, Theda, Mary,
    Sophia, Hiram —Family later settled in
    Bennington.

Page 350, Second Birth of Births
14 Apr 1752   **WILLIAMS James**, son of Edmond   254
              [but index says in another hand]:
This James may not be Williams check

Page 355, added to the births of James & Rachel WHITE's children:
Also **Joseph** and **Alexander** not on record.
Mary WHITE married Edward SIMS.
Cheney WHITE, daughter of Ebenezer WHITE **married John**
    LONDON of Norwich. As per Deed in Book 4 page
    97.
James WHITE Sr. that came to America had 3 sons — James
    Samuel & William. Also a daughter whose name
    is not known.

Page 358

20 Sep 1818	WHITE, James Alexander, b. Lebanon, Conn.
24 Feb 1846	WHITE, Edward James, son of James Alexander & 1st wife
26 Nov 1847	WHITE, Amanda, dau. of James Alexander & 1st wife
2 Apr 1850	WHITE, Emma, dau. of James Alexander & 1st wife
WHITE, Sidney, son of James Alexander & 1st wife	
12 Aug 1852	WHITE, Fred Kellogg, son of James Alexander & 1st wife
10 Jan 1860	WHITE, William Allen, son of James Alexander & 2nd wife
24 Oct 1861	WHITE, Adela, dau of James Alexander & his 2nd wife
26 Nov 1864	WHITE, John Bliss, son, of James Alexander & 2nd wife
8 July 1866	WHITE, Harlan Rathbone, son of James Alexander & 2nd wife

Page 359, First Book of Marriages

Isaiah WRIGHT of Hebron m. Sarah PAYNE 1868
b. 1750 d. 1813   b. 1745 d. 1829
by Mrs. Floyd E. COLE, Granville NY

Page 359, added to Saloma HIBBARD's marriage from South Windham (Hebron in Barbour]
Added to Mary BINGHAM's marriage: of Windham [no residence in Barbour]

Page 362, Fourth Book of Marriages
23 Nov 1856   **WHITE James Alexander & Harriet RATHBONE**

Page 362, Third Book of Deaths
Should be Mercy [on line preceeding Mary]
WOODWARD Mary 3d wife of Lieut Henry WOODWARD   x
former wife of Capt. Joseph SWETLAND **Died Aug 26 1761** in 83 years. Buried in Townsend Cemetery Andover Corner. She was daughter of Jonathan BABCOCK of Williams City.

Followed by entries in another hand:

Aug 1855	WHITE, Jerusha, wife of James A. age 37
May 29 1885	[WHITE,] Harriet, [Wife of James A., age] 47
May 29 1895	[WHITE,] John Bliss son of James & Harriet [age] 30

Dec 20 1888   [WHITE,] Fred Kellogg [son of James &] Jerusha [age] 35
Dec 20 1900   [WHITE,] Mary aged 85
29 Jan 1901   [WHITE,] James Alexander [aged] 83
Sept 21 1905   [WHITE,] Mrs. Charles [aged] 83

Page 366, First Book of Births [in another hand]:
Eliphalet YOUNGS son of Joseph YOUNGS see Hebron Land Records Vol. 3 page 255-6. **14 June 1750**. Also Ephriam YOUNGS

Page 366, Third Book of Marriages
26 Nov 1797 YOUNGS Constantia & Isaac W. CRANE   233

Page 384
Joel POST Married Sarah BUSHNELL Daughter of Daniel BUSHNELL and Daniel was the son of Daniel [I] think Daniel was the son of William.
Letters from Ellis BLISS Bradford [Vt?] to Ellis Bliss or Benjamin BLISS of Hebron – write [_] W. Bliss 145 Lasalle St. Chicago.

Loose Page 1[54]
John **SPRAGUE** from Lebanon before 1789 – had son Benjn Buell [middle name not in Barbour] & **Oliver Crouch** from Heirs of Joseph SKINNER Book 16 Page 250. **Buell Crouch to Joseph Skinner 1832** Book 16 Page 71.

Loose Page 2
Mrs. Hill
Did I give you these marriages of Hebron people not of town?
Lisbon   Daniel GOTT of Hebron and Charity RUSS of Canterbury. Aug. 13. 1760. [not Lisbon in Barbour]
Lebanon   Daniel POLLY of Hebron and Rachel LOOMIS Aug. 20. 1741 [not Lebanon in Barbour]

Levi CASE of Hebron and Hannah PIERCE May 29 1777 [m. 7 Feb 1771 in Barbour]

---

[54] The following seven pages are characterized as "loose" because they are not now in the Vital Statistics Index volume in Hebron, but in a separate notebook labeled "Hebron records in other towns."

Dick STARK of Hebron and Hannah ROSE May 29. 1777
Leonard HILLS & Eleanor ROOT of Hebron Aug. 28. 1754
Daniel ALLEN of Hebron & Mary BOSAM Nov. 21. 1754
Elisha D[UN?] of Hebron & Esther PORTER Jan. 10. 1760 [DUNK m. 23 Jun 1755 in Barbour]
Ebenezer COLEMAN of Hebron & Beulah BRISCO July 1. 1756
Caleb ROOT of Hebron & Patience PORTER Jan. 10. 1760 [not in Barbour's Hebron]
John STRONG of Hebron & Thankful BROWN [BASCOM of Hebron in Barbour] Mar 13. 1764.
Zebulon GAY of Hebron & Lydia TYLOR April 3. 1764
Benjamin ARCHER Jr. of Hebron & Jerusha ARCHER [Jerusha ____ in Barbour] Oct. 8. 1764
David WEBSTER [Daniel & 30 Oct 1765 in Barbour] & Bridget HOLDRIDGE of Hebron Jan. 1. 1768
Samuel H[EWIT] & Betty ARCHER, both of Hebron Jan 1. 1768
If not given before, copy in list with others. F.C. BISSELL

Loose Page 3

John ASHCRAFT of Hebron, made will 4 Apr 1755 ----tuted of Jan 1745/61, "being listed to go upon dangerous expedition to an enemies land", his wife Mary
Ch. Anne, Samuel, Timothy, d. by a former wife, Abigail, John, Jedediah, Desire. His inventory taken 22 June 1745/6 considted of English & latin books, m--- ---ticed works ----, no ---- estate.
--- an additional inventory 3 Nov 1746 in
"John ASHCROFT   ----   £ 50..13..0
his part of the plunder   7. 3. 0"
Samuel C[HAMBLIN?] was apptd guardian to 3 children
Probably the John ASHCROFT, who was a Corporal in 5th Co. Conn. Regt. "as this reduction of ----burg", Col. Simon LATHROP," died North 45" according to Conn. Hist Socy Coll. 12, -- 1 p. 71.

Loose Page 4

Ogden l--- to P.W. ---- Page 62 clute Sept 17 – 1853 Book
    20 Wm E. BUCKLEY to Ogden CROUCH[?] Page 8   1851-
    Book 20
Find the line between Elisha WRIGHT and Joseph SKINNER

163

Look for Solomon TARBOX sold to Elisha WRIGHT he thinks T-----ace property.

Separate piece of paper on page:

Anne [BROWN dau of Abner & Hannah Born] Aug 2~~1~~ 1762 [22 in Barbour]

Ammer [BROWN] Daug of Nathaniel BROWN [born] September 4 [9 in Barbour] 1751

David [BROWN] son of David & Lydia Died Mar 1, 1762

Loose Page 5

Marriages from Cong. Church Records E. Hampton

Nov. 20 1785 Geo. HALL of Hebron in ___ & Eunice ROLLO, Hebron

Dec 7 [1795] John CURTIS, Hebron & Sarah A _CLEY

Dec 9. 1800   Amaziah ARCHER, Hebron & Sarah SWETLAND

Nov. 22. 1801 Ezekiel SKINNER, Hebron & Sarah WIATT

Oct. 9. 1803   Ebenezer ROLLO, Hebron & Susannah USHER

Feb. 14. 1813 Henry PETERS, Hebron & Lydia ADAMS colored

Loose Page 6

Lydia [Jonathan TARBOX's] wife born March 7th 1792 [birth may not be in Barbour]

Aaron TARBOX, son of Jonathan TARBOX who was born Septemr 25th 1790 [1780 in Barbour] now assumes the name of Aaron Donelson TARBOX April 12th 1802

Loose Page 7, all entries in the same hand & ink:

Isabella Saloma WHITE Born Sept 14 1834. **Died March 24 1840.**

Orrin Bushnell WHITE Born Feb 8 1841. [18 in Barbour] **Died Mar 30 1844.**

~~Sept 1 1845~~	Aug 29 1875[55]
~~August 1 1894~~	Sept 1 – 1845
Mar 4 – 1895	Aug 16 - 1804

---

[55] These three sets of entries seem to have been made contemporaneously with the rest of the page, but are unexplained

INDEX

This index includes all people and places named, except Hebron itself. Surname spellings are grouped together, following the practice of Lucius Barbour in his collection of Connecticut Town Records. Each surname spelling thus absorbed by another index entry is cross-indexed: For example, because Barbour groups "Lothrop" with "Lathrop," our index groups both spellings under the category **LOTHROP, LATHROP** but also says

LATHROP, *See* **LOTHROP** at that point in the index.

Wives and widows identified only by their husband's name are indexed as **[MARRIED NAME]**, ____ (___). Married women whose maiden names are unknown are listed as

[MARRIED NAME], [Christian name] (___),

to distinguish them from similar entries for females listed under what is believed to be their maiden name. Married women whose maiden names are known are listed as

[MARRIED NAME], [First name] [(Maiden name)] and as

[MAIDEN NAME], [First name] *wed* [MARRIED NAME].

Women known to have been married more than once are indexed in this manner under each known surname. In the few instances where an entry is ambiguous as to whether a given surname is a maiden name of the name of a prior husband, it is indexed with a question mark, both ways.

Because "Mrs." was a term of status – like Mr. – when these records were created, women who are identified in these records only as Mrs. [First name] [Surname] may not be married. They are therefore indexed only as Mrs. **[First name] [SURNAME]**

Children and/or infants identified only by their surname are so indexed, unless their gender is specified, in which case, he or she is indexed as a son or daughter.

African-Americans are indexed as written: sometimes under their own surname, sometimes under their master/owner's , surname and sometimes without any surname. But they are all also indexed as "**RACE IDENTIFIED**," for the convenience of African-American genealogists.

____
    ____ (____), 11
    ____ (____) *wed* ARCHER, 139
    ____*wed* BROWN, 153
    Adam, 75
    Benjamin, 94
    Betsey, 95
    Betty, 29
    Betty (____), 150
    Betty *wed* ____, 150
    Cesar, 157
    Charles, 94
    Charles's infant, 93
    Chloe (Cook), 75
    Dorcus, 157
    Eleazer, 33
    Fortune, 151
    Henry, 150
    Jethro, 94
    Joel, 55
    Loice (____), 157
    Lona, 116
    Lora (____), 127
    Lu____ *wed* STRONG, 81
    Martha, 87
    Nathan, 94
    Noble, 116, 127
    Pomp, 9
    Pomp's wife, 9
    Primus, 92
    Prince, 86
    Richard, 22
    Roman, 55
    Sampson, 11
    Sibel (____), 151
    son, 116, 127, 129
    Susan, 91
    Ziba, 157
____GER, 11
____ININ, 11
____NATHY
    ____, 153
    Sarah (Chehen), 153

A____CLEY
    Sarah *wed* CURTIS, 164
ABBY
    Abigail *wed* POST, 80
ABENS
    Dorothy (Post), 77
    Mary (Ingham), 73
    Samuel, 73, 77
ADAMS
    Adelaide L. *wed* FOOTE, 122
    Amasa, 55
    Catharine *wed* TURNER, 80
    Cynthia, 28, 29, 93
    David, 52
    Hannah, 53
    Hannah (Yeamen), 73
    Hannah *wed* KELLEGG, 148
    Jerusha (Strong), 82
    Jonathan, 52, 53, 55, 73, 85
    Lydia *wed* PETERS, 164
    Phila Martha, 70
    William, 82
AISCRAFT. *SEE* ASHCRAFT
ALGER
    Matthew, 149
    Mehutabel (McKall), 149
ALLEN, ALLIN, ALLYN
    ____ (____), 11, 14, 15, 19
    Aaron, 66
    Ahimas, 139
    Ahincias, 139
    Barbarry *wed* ROLLO, 78
    Cyrus, 92
    Daniel, 163
    Eunice, 36
    Hiram, 14, 15
    Lenoris (____), 18
    Mahetable *wed* ROSELL, 77
    Mahitable (____), 139
    Mary (Bosam), 163
    Mary (McKall), 149
    Mehit____ (____), 139
    Mehitable (McKall), 149
    Merrit (____), 139

Phineas, 22
Phinias, 23
Samuel, 149
Sarah *wed* HITCHCOCK, 78
Susan A. *wed* HANKS, 124
Willard, 92
William, 10, 11, 15, 18, 19, 66, 139, 149
ALLIN. *SEE* ALLEN
ALLYN. *SEE* ALLEN
ALVORD
   Louisa *wed* GILBERT, 39
AMBROS
   Eliza *wed* WRIGHT, 80
AMHERST
   Gen'l, 5
AMOS
   Eliza *wed* POWERS, 79
ANDOVER SOCIETY, 3, 7
ANDREWS, ANDREW
   ____ (____), 32
   Hannah H. (Gardner), 133
   John, 133
   Loren, 32
ANDROUS. *SEE* ANDRUS
ANDRUS, ANDROUS
   ____ (____), 33
   Aurelia N. (Babcock), 117
   John J., 117
   Loren, 33
ANIBAL. *SEE* ANNABLE
ANNABLE, ANIBAL
   Anna, 139
   Anselon, 139
   Anslen, 139
   Betty, 139
   J., 36
   Levi A., 36
   William, 43
   William J., 42, 130
ARCHER
   ____ (____) (____), 139
   Amasa, 149
   Amaziah, 164
   Anna, 139

Anner, 139
Benjamin, 90, 139
Benjamin 2d, 139
Benjamin Jr., 163
Betsey *wed* WHITE, 133
Betty *wed* HEWIT, 163
Jerusha (Archer), 163
Jerusha *wed* ARCHER, 163
Mrs. Elizabeth (Fitch), 150
Obadiah, 150
Sarah (____), 90
Sarah(Swetland), 164
Sybel (Raymond), 149
ARMS
   Hiram P., 3
ARNOLD
   ____ (____), 25
   ____ (Thomas), 24
   Arethusa (____), 41
   Charles, 24, 25
   Dan, 7, 44, 45
   Dr. Dan, 41
ASHCRAFT, ASHCROFT, AISCRAFT
   Abigail, 163
   Ann, 139
   Anne, 163
   Desire, 163
   Edward, 153
   Jedediah, 163
   John, 163
   Mary (____), 163
   Robert, 139
   Salla (Taylor), 153
   Samuel, 163
   Sarah (Taylor), 153
   Timothy, 163
ASHCROFT. *SEE* ASHCRAFT
ASTEN. *SEE* ASTIN
ASTIN, ASTEN, ASTON
   Aaron, 139
   Azor, 139
   Hannah, 139
   Robert, 139
ASTON. *SEE* ASTIN

ATHERTON
   ____, 79
   Sally (Phelps), 79
AUSTEN. *SEE* AUSTIN
AUSTIN, AUSTEN
   daughter, 115
   Harriet, 112
   Harriet E. (____), 112, 115
   Samuel A., 112, 115
AVERILL
   Jasper, 15
AYERS
   Harriet (____), 109
   Harriet T., 109
   Samuel, 109
AYUEL
   Benjamin, 139
   Joseph, 139
   Ruth (Perkins), 139
BABCOCK
   Amy L. *wed* LOOMIS, 122
   Aurelia N. *wed* ANDRUS, 117
   Horace, 82
   Jonathan, 161
   Mary *wed* SWETLAND, 161
   Rhoda (Root), 82
BACKUS
   ____ (____), 24, 25, 26, 27
   E.B., 26
   Ezra, 20, 21
   Ezra L., 108
   Hannah (Bissell), 80
   J., 25
   Jabez, 24
   Jabez L., 44
   Jane A.(____), 108
   Lucy A., 108
   Nathaniel, 80
   Susan C. (Phelps), 37
   Welthy, 14, 15
BAILEY, BALEY
   ____ (____), 28, 93
   Edwin, 116
   Eliza Ann (____), 116
   Levi, 117

   Maria (Hills), 117
   Mrs., 29
   son, 116
BAILIES
   Henry, 118
BAKER
   Adelaide (Bragg), 123
   Elisha T., 123
   Lydia, 88
BALDWIN
   Benjamin, 74, 143
   child, 143
   Lydia (Peters), 74
   Thankful *alias* TRUMBUL, 18
   Thankfull, 19
   Thankfull (____), 19
BALEY. *SEE* BAILEY
BALLSTONE
   Clarinda *wed* PETERS, 35
BANNING
   ____ (____), 41
   Eliphalet, 107, 110, 114, 142
   Elizabeth, 110
   Henry, 41
   L Jennette, 107, 142
   Louisa (____), 107, 110
   Louisa T.(____), 115
   Louise (____), 142
   son, 115
BARBER, BARBOUR
   ____ (____), 22, 23
   Aaron, 15
   Abigail, 140
   Abigail (____), 10, 142
   Aless, 140
   Alice (Cass), 140
   Alice *wed* BISSEL, 37
   child, 15
   daughter, 140
   David, 7, 8, 12, 13, 140
   David 2nd, 140, 142
   Desire (____), 143
   Dudly, 143
   Ellen R., 111
   family, 3

George W., 126
Hannah (Post), 140
Harriet *wed* MACK, 118
Herbert W., 130
Hiram, 22, 23, 44
infant, 125
Joseph, 140
Josiah, 10
Julia R. (____), 111
Leude, 43
Lewd, 42
Liddy, 140
Lude, 130
Lydia *wed* POWERS, 142
Lyman, 125
Lyman's child, 107
Mary, 140
Mary Ann *wed* TINNEY, 123
Mrs Rachel *wed* HEBERD, 151
Mrs. Abijah (____), 11
Oliver, 14, 15, 140
Oscar, 42
Patience (Cass), 140
Sally (____), 44
Samuel, 140
son, 140
Stephen, 8, 14, 15, 22, 23, 35, 140, 143
Stephen Jr., 143
stillborn, 140
Temperance, 140
Thomas, 140
William M., 111
BARBOUR. *SEE* BARBER
BARNETT
   Ann *wed* PETERS, 74
BASCOM
   Mary E. *wed* TOPLIFF, 121
BASSET. *SEE* BASSETT
BASSETT, BASSET
   ____ (____), 15
   A., 14
   Amos, 3, 15
   J.W., 12
   Mary *wed* TOWNSEND, 77

Rev. Dr. Amos, 7
Sally (____), 14
BAXSTER. *SEE* BAXTER
BAXTER, BAXSTER
   Aaron, 30, 31, 93, 143, 147
   Abigail, 48
   Abigail (Man), 143
   John, 49
   Lydia, 143
   Mary (Hunter (Menter), 147
   Mercy (Menter), 143
   Richard, 47, 48, 49, 50
   Sarah, 50
   Simeon, 143
   Simon, 143
BEACH
   ____ (____), 24, 25, 32, 33
   Abel, 143
   Abigal *wed* NILES, 149
   Ann (____), 143
   Appollos, 142
   Azariah, 66, 142, 143
   Benjamin, 143
   Chauncey, 142
   Daniel, 143
   Desiah *wed* FELSHAW, 150
   Elijah, 32, 33, 42, 43, 130, 142
   Elisha, 24, 25, 33
   Elizabeth (____), 142
   Elizabeth (Skinner), 143
   Elizabeth *wed* PHELPS, 150
   Elmer T., 142
   George, 42
   George R., 42, 130
   Homer, 129
   Jedediah, 143
   John, 143
   Joseph, 142
   Lucy, 66, 142
   Mary, 42, 130
   Mindwell *wed* JONES, 147
   Philadelphia *wed* WARNER, 118
   Sary, 143

Unice *wed* HOSFORD, 142
William, 66
William R., 142
BECKWITH
   Emma (Way), 80
   Mr., 151
   Solomon, 80
   Wilhay (Gay), 151
BEEBE, BEBE, BEEBEE
   Mercy (Peters), 76
   Phoebe *wed* JUDD, 160
   Ruel, 35, 76
   Stuart, 133, 134
BELNAP, BELNAK
   Gerre, 145
   Hyram, 145
BENJAMIN
   Ben, 82
   Benjamin, 79
   Betsey (Dix), 79
   Harriet (Watson), 82
BENNET, BENNETT
   Mr., 13
BENTON
   Anna (Post), 2
BERRELL. *SEE* BERRILL
BERRILL. *SEE ALSO* BURRELL
BERRILL, BERRELL
   Augustus. *See also* BURRELL
   Sarah (____), 129
BESTOR
   C. Jane (Strong), 119
   George R., 119
BETTIS
   Elizabeth, 53
   Simeon Marten, 53
BIDWELL
   Delia A. *wed* HODGE, 83
   Delia A. *wed* HOUZE, 123
   Henrietta M. (Post), 82
   Mary (Wilcox), 81
   Russell, 81
   Stephen W., 82
BILL, BILLS
   A/Heidl?, 134

Amy *wed* RIDER, 133, 134
David, 47
Ebenezer, 75
Elisabeth *wed* ROW, 75
Fanny *wed* THOMPSON, 82
Joshua, 26, 27
Mercey (Tilden), 142
Patience, 50
Patience *wed* WRIGHT, 76
Phillap, 142
Rachel, 49, 51, 143
Rachel (Root), 75
Samuel, 47, 49, 50, 51, 53, 143
Sarah (____), 143
Sarah *wed* KILBORN, 74
Thomas, 15
BILLINGS
   ____ (____), 13
   Oliver, 143
BINDELL
   Lucy, 126
BINGHAM
   ____ (____), 22, 23, 37, 89
   Albert, 84
   Alexander, 54
   Benjamin, 143
   Elizabeth (Bisell), 143
   Eunice (Taylor), 84
   Mary *wed* ---, 161
   Oliver, 66
   Samuel, 66
   Stephen, 143
BIRD
   Rev. Mr., 20, 21
BIRGE, BURGE
   Anna, 66, 67, 90
   Caziah, 140
   Content, 67
   Coziah, 140
   Daniel, 140, 143
   Daniel, Jr., 143
   Elizabeth, 140
   Elizabeth (____), 143
   Ezekiel, 16, 17

Jonathan, 143
Julia *wed* SPRAGUE, 36
Marvin, 81
Rebeckah *wed* BURAS, 142
Sally (Hutchinson), 81
William Augustus, 66, 90
BISEL. *SEE* BISSELL
BISHOP
  Levi, 79
  Lucy (Root), 79
  Lydia (Craft), 79
  Talatha *wed* JONES, 148
  Thomas, 79
BISSEL. *SEE* BISSELL
BISSELL, BISSEL, BISEL
  ____ (____), 27, 28, 29, 32, 33, 40, 41, 43
  Abel, 40
  Abel S., 81
  Adam, 43
  Adniram, 151
  Adoniram, 41, 44
  Adoniram N., 22
  Alice (Barber), 37
  Almira (____), 107
  Almira J. (____), 135
  Anna, 28, 29
  Asa, 135
  Benjamin, 140, 145
  Betsey, 16, 17
  Capt., 37
  Caroline M. (____), 116
  Caroline W. (____), 107
  Clarissa *wed* STRONG, 80
  dau, 116
  Elihu R., 43
  Elizabeth (____), 145
  Elizabeth *wed* BINGHAM, 143
  Elizabeth *wed* POST, 2, 73
  F.C., 135, 163
  Frederic C., 107
  Frederic P., 107
  Frederick P., 135
  Hannah *wed* BACKUS, 80
  Hezekiah, 8, 27, 30, 31, 32, 33, 107, 110
  Hezekiah Asa, 107, 110
  Hiram, 23
  Ira, 2, 28, 29, 42, 43
  Israel Augustus, 41
  John, 75
  Laura (Trumbull), 81
  Lavina (____), 42
  Leah, 140
  Levi, 28, 32, 33
  Lovina (____), 130
  Lucy, 126
  Maria, 40
  Mary A., 40
  Mary C. *wed* PORTER, 118
  Mary J. (____), 107, 110
  Phebe, 22, 23, 28, 29, 65
  Phebe (Post), 26
  Ralph L., 116
  Ralph R., 107
  Ralph S., 107
  Salla (Porter), 151
  Susannah (Youngs), 75
BLACKMAN
  ____ (____), 22, 23
  Abraham, 141, 144
  Elizabeth (____), 144
  Samuel, 141
BLACKMER
  Elisha, 35
BLISH. *SEE* BLUSH
  Hannah *wed* NELAND, 142
BLISS
  ____ (____), 97
  ____ (Porter), 43
  ____ e, 140
  ____ *wed* DANIEL, 24
  __ry, 140
  Abial, 76, 97
  Abiel, 35, 95, 141, 143
  Abigail (____), 86
  Abigail *wed* DANIELS, 80
  Amelia, 28, 29
  Anna, 35, 141, 144

Anna (Brown), 76
Anna (Case), 76
Benjamin S., 44
Charles F., 109, 128
child, 141
Constant, 140, 141
daughter, 115, 141
Dwight, 42, 43, 108, 110, 119, 129
Electa (____), 109
Electa G. (____), 115
Electa M. (____), 111
Elizabeth, 141
Ellis, 22, 23, 52, 64, 86, 141, 143, 144
F., 42
Flavel, 43, 64
Florinda (Strong), 82
Grace, 144
Hannah, 64, 144
Harriet I., 128
Harriet Jane, 111
Joanna wed BROWN, 82
John, 3, 48, 52, 140, 141
John Flavel, 142
John Jr., 141
John Jr.), 141
John P., 82
Lydie wed BROWN, 142
Marcy (____), 108
Martha (____), 144
Mary, 140
Mary A. (____), 129
Mary Ann, 41
Mary Ann (____), 42
Nancy, 40
Nancy A., 128
Nathan, 95
Neziah, 141, 144
Samuel, 39, 48, 109
Samuel A, 115
Samuel W., 111
Silvanus, 141
Simeon, 76
son, 108

Thoner (____), 143
BLOSSOM
   Enos, 75
   Mary (Ellis), 75
BLUSH. *SEE* BLISH
   Hannah wed NELAND, 142
BOHAM
   Thomas, 17
BOLLEN
   Nathan, 121
BOLTON
   ____ (____), 88
   Mary, 60
   Mary (____), 144
   Sarah, 60
BOND
   Ann wed SWETLAND, 73
   Anna, 49
   Anna (____), 85
   Anne (____), 144
   daughter, 141
   David, 50
   Elisabeth, 51
   Elisha Yeamans, 54
   family, 3
   Joseph, 53, 85, 144
   Mahitabel (____), 144
   Mary, 55, 144
   Nicholas, 48, 49, 51, 73, 85, 141, 144
   Nicholas, Jr., 144
   Niclos, 141
   son, 144
   Stephen, 48, 50, 51, 53, 54, 55, 85, 144
   Susanna, 48
   Temperance wed DARBE, 75
   Thankfull (Foot), 73
   William, 51
BOOTH
   Ambrose, 51
   Jonathan, 51, 73
   Joshua, 51
   Oliver, 51
   Tarzo (Noble), 73

BOSAM
  Mary *wed* ALLEN, 163
BOWLES, BOLLES, BOWLS
  Florence *wed* STRICKLAND, 84
  Lois (Northam), 152
  Rev. Mr., 118
  Rozel, 151
BOWLS. *SEE* BOLLES
BOXERVILLE, 117
BOYES
  Mary *wed* NORTON, 154
BOYNTON
  Eliza *wed* PERKINS, 156
BRADLEY
  Harriot (Wells), 80
  Joseph, 80
BRAGG. *SEE ALSO* BRIGGS
  Adelaide *wed* BAKER, 123
  Emeline M. (___), 41
BRAINED. *SEE* BRAINERD
BRAINERD, BRAINED
  Edmund R., 95
  Louisa *wed* COLEMAN, 122
BRAY
  Amelia R. (Webster), 82
  David C., 82
BRIANT
  Betty, 52
  Betty *wed* HALL, 74
  Jesse, 52
BRIGGS. *SEE ALSO* BRAGG
  Adelaide *wed* BAKER, 123
BRISCO
  Beulah *wed* COLEMAN, 163
BRITTON
  Delia C. *wed* LEE, 82
  W. E., 160
BROCKWAY
  Lavina *wed* DEAN, 80
  Sena *wed* POST, 80
BRONSON, BRUNSON, BRONZON
  Martha *wed* Palmer, 143
  Tollotson, 4
BRONZON. *SEE* BRONSON

BROOKER
  Elisabeth *wed* TILLOTSON, 73
BROOKS
  Asahel H., 82
  Sally (Brown), 82
BROWN
  ___, 153
  ___ (___), 9, 92, 97, 153
  Aaron, 44
  Abigail (___), 144
  Abner, 144, 164
  Almira (Norton), 82
  Amasa, 38
  Ammer, 164
  Ann, 92
  Anna, 22, 23
  Anna (Horton), 81
  Anna (Phelps), 76, 97
  Anna *wed* BLISS, 76
  Anner, 141
  Asa, 60, 67, 75
  Azariah, 51, 57, 58, 141, 142, 144
  Betsey (___), 32
  Betsey (Trumbull), 79, 94, 143
  Candace, 34
  Charles N., 83
  Chester, 64, 80
  Clarinda (___), 129
  Clarissa, 43
  Clarissa (___), 42
  Clarissa (Post), 79
  Clarissa *wed* POST, 81
  Cynthia Ann *wed* LEWIS, 82
  Daniel, 62, 63, 64, 65, 76, 88, 95, 97
  Daniel Bishop, 62
  Daniel W., 83
  daughter, 114
  David, 67, 74, 79, 107, 143, 144, 164
  David T., 82
  Deborah, 66, 89
  Deborah (Tarbox), 38, 76

173

Deborah *wed* HALING, 82
Dinah *wed* POST, 87, 142
Dorithy, 141
Dorithy *wed* DAVIS, 75
Dority, 141
Ebenezer, 51
Ebenezer Rockwell, 67
Egbert, 115, 118, 119
Elisabeth, 60
Elisabeth (Dunham), 75
Elisabeth *wed* TILDEN, 77
Eliza, 28, 29, 93
Eliza (___), 110
Elizabeth (Ticknor), 83
Elizabeth (Wright), 119
Elizabeth F. *wed* GILLET, 41
Ellen, 110
Ellen Jennette, 111
Emma (Ellis), 83
Ephriam, 64
Eunice (White), 84
Ezekiel, 9, 34, 37, 77, 97
Ezra, 63
family, 3
George Dexter, 107
Hannah, 23
Hannah (___), 22, 144, 164
Henry, 65
Hervy, 68
Hiram, 39
Isaac, 56
James, 30, 31, 38, 61, 62, 63, 64, 66, 67, 68, 76, 89, 93, 111, 114, 128
Jane A. (Wright), 118
Jane E. (___), 115
Jennette (___), 111
Jeremiah, 38, 96
Joanna (Bliss), 82
John, 144
Jonathan, 144
Julia, 72
Laura *wed* COLEMAN, 120
Levi, 60
Lovina *wed* THOMAS, 74

Lucinda, 144
Lucy, 57
Lucy (Ford), 79
Lucy A., 45
Lucy Ann, 69
Lucy Ann (___), 131
Luta (Horton), 80
Lydia (___), 144, 164
Lydia (Swetland), 74, 143
Lydie (Bliss), 142
Mansel, 16
Manson, 91
Martha (___), 9
Martha (Horton), 77
Martha P. *wed* GOODELL, 81
Mary (Lothrop), 76
Mary E., 126
Mary E. (___), 39
Munsel, 17
Nathan, 141
Nathaniel, 141, 164
Neziah, 42, 43, 44, 63, 79
Pemberton, 16, 17
Philip, 151
Prudence (Sawyer), 75
Ralph D., 121
Ralph G., 128
Rebekah *wed* WEBSTER, 74
Ruel, 41
Russel, 82
Salla, 67
Salla *wed* SKINNER, 152
Sally (Sallet/Vallet), 151
Sally *wed* BROOKS, 82
Samuel, 44, 56, 62, 75, 88, 144
Samuel Augustus, 67
Sarah, 65, 144
Sarah (___), 144
Sarah (Lee), 142
Sarah F. *wed* GILLET, 41
Sarah L. *wed* GILLETTE, 82
Sarah Louisa, 70
son, 115
Stephen, 142

Temperance (Pettice), 79
Thankful, 163
Therzy *wed* PHELPS, 133
Thomas, 9, 12, 13, 41, 45, 63, 69, 70, 76, 79, 141, 144
Thomas L., 72, 84
Thomas Leverett, 69
Thomas' dau, 41
Watson, 110
William, 32, 33, 44, 45, 58, 62, 79, 81, 94, 121, 143
BROWNHURST, BROUNHURST
  Charles, 123
  Harriet (Gordon), 123
  son, 115
  Thomas, 115
BUCK
  Abagail (Palmeter), 78
  Abel, 141
  Anna (Talcott), 77
  Benjamin, 141
  Daniel, 48
  David, 78
  Deborah *wed* ROOT, 74
  Ebenezer, 47, 53, 77
  Ebenezer's child, 85
  Emily G. (____), 114
  Enoch, 51
  Eunice, 49, 145
  Eunice *wed* HOW, 77
  George H., 114
  Jane, 54, 86
  John, 47
  Persis, 53
  Persis *wed* WOOD, 77
  Sarah *wed* ROBINSON, 74
  Sary (____), 144
  Sibil, 47
  Thomas, 47, 48, 49, 51, 53, 54, 86, 144, 145
  Thomas Jnr, 145
  Warren Phelps, 114
  Zurviah, 53
BUEL, BUELL
  ____ (____), 19

Abby (Ellis), 84
Abigail, 20, 21, 144
Abigail (____), 144
Abigail (Bartlett), 18, 20
Abigail E. *wed* GILLETT, 82
Abigail *wed* WARNER, 81
Agnes *wed* CARVER, 123
B., 18
Benjamin, 10, 18, 19, 20, 144
Cybel (____), 144
Deborah, 50
Delight (Finley), 79
E. P., 142
Elisebeth *wed* WICKUM, 79
Hannah, 50
Harley C., 113
Hubbell, 18, 19
infant, 144
John H., 20, 21, 84
John W., 82
Joseph, 142
Joseph W., 113
Josiah M, 110, 120, 142
Laury, 43
Levi, 10, 11
Lucy (____), 142
Maria H., 142
Maria K, 42, 142
Maria K., 129
Mary, 41
Mary (____), 142, 144
Mary Ann (Post), 82, 113
Mary C. *wed* PORTER, 118
Mary E. *wed* SUMNER, 108
Peter, 147
Rebecca *wed* CROUCH, 18
Samuel, 144
Sybil, 10
Timothy, 8, 9, 50
William, 9, 26, 27, 79, 144, 146, 147
William Jr., 144
BURAS
  John, 142
  Rebeckah (Birge), 142

BURCHARD
William H., 122
BURDIT
Mrs., 97
BURDON
Jerre, 78
Sliva (Morgan), 78
BURELL. *SEE* BURRELL
BURGE. *SEE* BIRGE
BURNHAM
____ (____), 13, 24, 25
Anne *wed* FILER, 142, 146
Capt J., 25
Catherine (____), 12
daughter, 109, 115
Eliza (____), 109, 115
Elizabeth Swan (____), 113
Gershom, 110
Griswold, 109, 113, 115
Harriet (____), 44
Harriet M. (Gilbert), 134
J. T., 12
Jerusha (____), 12
Jerusha (Kellogg), 150
Joseph, 150
Joseph R., 134
Joseph T., 24, 41
Martha *wed* YOUNGS, 74, 88
Mary (____), 115
Moses K., 81
Mr. J., 13
Susannah (Norton), 81
Trumbull, 44, 113
William M., 115
BURR
Aaron, 15
BURRELL. *SEE ALSO* BERRILL
BURRELL, BURELL
Hezekiah A., 127
Mary A., 128
BURRORS. *SEE* BURROWS
BURROWS. *SEE ALSO* BARROWS
BURROWS, BURRORS
Daniel, 4
Isaac, 144

BURT
Albert P., 84
Sarah H. (Prentice), 84
BUSHNALL, BUSHNEL[L]
____ (____), 89
Daniel, 26, 27, 93, 144, 162
Jonathan, 86
Jonth, 144
Josiah, 50
Lydia, 94
Mindwell, 88, 144
Sarah (____), 144
Sarah *wed* POST, 74, 88, 154, 155, 162
son, 50
BUSHNEL. *SEE* BUSHNALL
BUTTON
George, 40, 127
CALDWELL
Elizabeth (Lockwood), 84
William M., 84
CALKINS, CAULKINS
James, 49, 50, 73
Jedediah, 14, 15
Mary (Man), 73
Rhoda, 50
CANDALL
Melora *wed* DRINKWATER, 40
CARD
Charles, 81
Mercy (Perry), 81
CARDER
David, 146
CARPENTER
Benjamin, 82
Betsey (West), 82
Ralph M., 83
Sarah J. (Root), 83
CARR
Charles, 121
Susan *wed* MORGAN, 42
Swan E. (Morgan), 121
CARRIER
Amey (Filer), 146
Ebenezer, 76

Jemima (Sumner), 79
John, 79
Joseph, 146
Prudence (Wells), 76
CARTER
   Mary *wed* TALCOT [T], 57, 58, 59, 60, 62, 63
   Sarah *wed* WELLS, 76
   Thomas Sr, 145
CARVER
   ____ (____), 20, 21, 30, 31
   Agnes (Buell), 123
   Aldric, 30
   Aldrich, 31
   Amey (Filer), 146
   David, 20, 21, 146
   David T., 39, 107
   Electa (____), 129
   Emily B. *wed* CONE, 118
   Flavel A., 107
   Henry O., 42
   John S., 39
   Joseph, 39, 43, 44
   Mary E. (____), 107
   Sarah (Stiles), 150
   Sarah Electa (____), 42
   Warren, 150
   William, 123
CASE. *SEE ALSO* CASS
   ____ (____), 17
   A. (____), 91
   A___ (____), 16
   Anna *wed* BLISS, 76
   Aurelia, 125
   Azubah, 57
   Azubah (Phelps), 75
   Azubah *wed* MARVIN, 76
   family, 145
   Frances *wed* ____, 83
   Hannah (Pierce), 162
   Hannah *wed* POST, 156
   J.W., 17
   Jerusha, 125
   Joseph W., 16, 91
   Levi, 162
   Martha, 59, 88
   Mary (Hoskins), 145
   Molly, 88
   Moses, 145
   Roger, 64, 65
   Russel, 64, 65
   Zia, 57, 58, 59, 75, 88
   Zia's infant, 87
   Zia's son, 88
CASS. *SEE ALSO* CASE
   Alice *wed* BARBER, 140
   family, 145
   Patience *wed* BARBER, 140
CAULKINS. *SEE* CALKINS
CELLOGG. *SEE* KELLOGG
CHAMBERLIN, CHAMBERLEIN
   family, 145
   Rebecca *wed* TILLETSON, 159
   Welthy *wed* WASHINGTON, 153
CHAMBLIN. *SEE ALSO* CHAMPLIN
   Samuel, 163
CHAMPION
   Col, 11
   Henry, 10
CHAMPLIN. *SEE ALSO* CHAMBLIN
   Jemima (Loveland), 75
   Thomas, 75
CHAPEL. SEE CHAPPEL
CHAPMAN
   Daniel, 60, 61, 62, 75
   Ezra, 59
   Ichabod, 61
   Lucy, 62
   Lucy (Tallcott), 75
   Martha, 91
   Mrs Esther *wed* FULLER, 151
   Patty, 14, 15
   Prouda, 125
   Prudence (____), 39
CHAPPEL, CHAPEL[L]
   ____ (____), 20, 21, 32, 33
   Anson, 82, 108, 109, 119, 127
   Caleb, 47
   Ceasar, 95

Ester, 47
Harriet N. (____), 108
Harriet N. (Hutchinson), 82
Jane, 108
John, 38
Jonathan, 30, 31
Mary M. *wed* WEBSTER, 82
Nancy (Norton), 80
Seaser, 31
Zenas, 20, 80
Zenus, 21
CHAPWELL
   Jonathon, 145
   Rachell, 145
CHASE
   Mary *wed* POST, 2
CHEHEN
   Sarah *wed* ____NATHY, 153
CHENEY
   Frances E. (Foote), 123
   Thomas B., 123
CHESEBRO
   Kate *wed* WAY, 83
CHITTENDEN. *SEE* CHITTENDON
CHITTENDON, CHITTENDEN
   Alfred, 122
   Emily M. (Root), 122
CHURCH
   Hattie *wed* ROOT, 83
CLARK
   ____ (Eldridge), 83
   Anson, 22, 23
   Joseph, 76
   Olin, 83
   Submit (Dunham), 76
COATES, COATS
   ____ (____), 41
   child, 17
   Harry, 26, 27
   Henry M., 127
   Laura (____), 112
   Lyman, 112, 115
   Nathan P., 34, 41
   R., 26
   Rufus, 16, 17, 27, 28, 29

Sarah (____), 115
son, 115
Susan Elizabeth, 112
COFFIN
   Beulah (Eddy), 154
   Enoch, 154
COLBURN
   Daniel, 76
   Daniel's child, 88
   Roxelanie (Phelps), 76
COLE
   Mrs. Floyd E., 161
COLEMAN, COLMAN
   ____ (____), 38
   Beulah (Brisco), 163
   Ebenezer, 163
   Eleazer, 38
   Ephraim, 97
   Henry, 120
   Horace, 122
   Laura (Brown), 120
   Louisa (Brained), 122
   Maria *wed* WELLES, 81
   Mr.'s infant, 95
   Richard's infant, 92
   Roxina *wed* DARBY, 134
COLLINS
   ____ (____), 28, 29
   Abelene (Curtice), 78
   Augustus, 3
   Charles, 78
   Deborah (Culver), 75
   Florilla S. (Root), 83
   Julius, 75
   Levi, 28, 29
   Seth, 30, 31
   William A., 83
COLMAN. *SEE* COLEMAN
COLTON
   George, 18, 19
CONE
   Caroline *wed* PETERS, 42
   Emily B. (Carver), 118
   Esther, 68
   Esther *wed* MACK, 81

Esther *wed* WARREN, 79
Fanny Post, 69
Hannah (____), 94
Hannah Emely, 68
Jerusha, 69
Jerusha *wed* WILLIAMS, 81
John, 16, 17, 68, 69, 91, 94
Mary (____), 34
Mary *wed* ROWLEY, 34
Rev. Mr., 67, 68
Salmon, 133
Sarah Bingham, 68
Sarah *wed* HUTCHINSON, 81
William L., 118
CONNECTICUT, 5
    Warren, 145
    Coventry, 156
    Andover, 12, 26, 121, 159, 161
    Bethlehem, 104
    Bolton, 13, 18, 19, 20, 21, 24, 25, 76, 90, 97, 120, 122, 126, 130, 148, 152
    Boxerville, 117
    Bridgeport, 39, 104
    Bristol, 104
    Canaan, 104
    Canterbury, 162
    Chatham, 128, 151
    Cheshire, 104
    Colchester, 10, 31, 41, 68, 118, 122, 123, 125, 127, 130, 133, 147, 148, 149, 150, 151, 152, 153, 157
    Colebrook, 104
    Columbia, 15, 26, 104, 117, 118, 119, 120, 129, 152
    Coventry, 118, 125, 133, 146, 152, 154, 159
    Coventry, South, 121
    Danbury, 104
    Darien, 104
    Derby, 3
    Durham, 104
    East Haddam, 118, 125, 130, 150, 152, 157
    East Hampton, 164
    East Hartford, 122, 133
    Eastberry, 26
    Ellington, 152
    Exeter?, 26
    Fairfield, 104
    Farmington, 104
    Franklin, 146
    Glastonbury, 10, 11, 38, 117, 118, 121, 123, 126, 129, 149, 152
    Goshen, 117
    Greenwich, 104
    Groton, 104
    Haddam, 117, 157
    Hartford, 10, 11, 41, 121, 122, 123, 145, 148
    Hartland, 151
    Hebron, 12
    Hope Valley, 4, 112, 128
    Kent, 145
    Killingworth, 104, 122
    Lebanon, 119, 121, 122, 127, 129, 130, 143, 145, 147, 148, 149, 153, 156, 160, 161, 162
    Lisbon, 162
    Litchfield, 152
    Lyme, 117, 129, 150, 151, 156
    Manchester, 38, 40, 117, 122, 123, 128
    Mansfield, 123
    Marlboro, 12, 26, 28, 32, 35, 96, 97, 119, 123, 129, 156
    Marlborough, 27, 104, 117, 120, 122, 123
    Middle Haddam, 4, 16, 18
    Middleton, 41
    Middletown, 104, 121
    Milford, 104
    Montville, 123
    N[ew] Haven, 40

New Britain, 105
New Hartford, 104
New London, 120, 122, 130, 151, 160
North Branford, 104
Norwalk, 105
Norwich, 3, 122, 126, 148, 160
Portland, 121
Rockville, 126
Rocky Hill, 105
Roxbury, 105
Salem, 117, 128
Salisbury, 105, 145
Saybrook, 2, 3, 34
Seymour, 105
Sharon, 145
Simsbury, 105
South Coventry, 121
South Windham, 161
Southbury, 105
Southington, 105
Stamford, 105
Sterling, 127
Stonington, 105, 119
Stratford, 22, 23
Suffield, 3
Tolland, 105
Trumbull, 105
Vernon, 134, 153
Washington, 105
Waterbury, 4, 105
Watertown, 105
Westbrook, 122
Weston, 105
Westport, 105
Wethersfield, 10, 122
Willington, 105
Winchester, 105
Windham, 118, 161
Windsor, 2, 117, 146, 149, 155
Wolcott, 105
COOK
    ____ (____), 40

Amanda (____), 113
Chloe *wed* _____, 75
Cyrus, 123
Elisabeth (Sumner), 76
George O., 10, 11
Mr., 13
Oliver, 76
Sarah (Foote), 123
son, 113
William, 40
William P., 113
COOLEY
    Jane (, Wills), 83
    John, 83
COOPER
    Eunice *wed* ROWLEE, 76
COOX. *SEE* COX
CORKINS. *SEE ALSO* CALKINS
    Nancy *wed* WELLS, 80
CORNWELL
    Edmund, 68
CORWIN
    David, 17
    son, 17
COUDRE
    Moses, 151
    Zeruah (Phelps), 151
COUZENS
    ____ (____), 40
COVEL
    Anna (Mack), 75
    Hannah (Goodrich), 77
    Henry, 77
    Samuel, 75
COX, COOX
    Ann (Polly), 73
    Armindwell, 53
    James, 51, 52, 53, 54, 73, 85
    Melisena, 54
    Ruth *wed* HUTCHINSON, 28, 73
    Sarah *wed* HORTON, 73
CRAFT
    Lydia *wed* BISHOP, 79
CRAIG

A.G., 7
CRANE, CRAIN[E]
  Constantia (Youngs), 162
  Eunice, 30, 31
  Isaac, 38
  Isaac W., 162
CROCKER
  Lucinda (Kelley), 78
  Richard, 78
CROUCH
  ____ (____), 19
  A., 36
  Christopher, 18, 19, 37, 77, 93
  Christopher, Jr., 27
  family, 3
  Franklin, 36
  Lydia (Hutchinson), 77
  Rebecca (Buel), 18
  Rebecca wed HOLDRIDG, 149
CULLUM
  George, 149
  Mrs. Lucy (Raymond), 149
CULVER
  ____ (____), 95
  Abigail, 63, 66, 90
  Alleson, 65
  Anson, 80
  Asahel, 66
  Barzellial, 49
  Benjamin, 56
  David, 22, 23, 51, 52, 53, 54, 55, 56, 63, 64, 65, 66, 90, 92
  David Curtice, 64
  David's infant, 87
  Deborah, 47
  Deborah wed COLLINS, 75
  Dinah (Post), 77
  Elisabeth, 51
  Elisabeth wed POST, 76
  Elisabeth wed ROWLEE, 76
  Eunice wed SKINNER, 74
  George, 125
  Hannah, 56

Henry, 54
Ira, 65
Isabella (Horton), 80
James, 55, 95
Jeremiah, 53
Jerusha, 63
John, 52, 77
Joseph, 39, 56
Mary, 52, 57, 63
Melisent, 50, 54, 85
Nathan, 48
Obadiah, 47, 48, 49, 50, 51, 52, 54, 55, 56, 57, 85
Sarah wed MERREL, 74
Sarah wed MERRILS, 94
William, 63
CURTICE. SEE CURTIS
CURTIS, CURTICE, CURTISS
  ____ (____), 13, 22, 35
  Abelene wed COLLINS, 78
  Abigail Elisabeth Martha, 60
  Abner, 145
  Bishop, 40, 127
  Caleb, 145
  David, 37, 60, 67, 68, 74, 87
  David Bishop, 67
  David's child, 87
  Deborah wed POST, 86
  Elisabeth, 60
  Elisabeth wed YOUNGS, 73
  Elizabeth (____), 87
  Elizabeth (Wright), 151
  family, 3
  Hannah wed ROWLE, 73
  Henory, 151
  Henry, 85
  Horace, 67
  Horace's child, 96
  Horace's infant, 96
  Hozea Junior, 148
  John, 16, 18, 19, 91, 164
  John Ephriam Henry, 60
  Jonathan, 89
  Judith, 90
  Judith (____), 60

Judith (____)) (____), 12
Judith (Wright), 74
Lavina, 95
Martha, 60, 87
Mr, 23
Richard, 145
Sarah (A_cley, 164
Sarah (____), 16, 91
Selden, 35
Susannah (Kellogg), 148
Wealthy *wed* HODGE, 81
Welthy, 68
CURTISS. *SEE* CURTIS
CUSON
  June wed Smith, 123
CUSTER
  ____ (____), 17
  John, 17
DANIELS, DANIEL
  ____ (____), 25, 92
  ____ (Bliss), 24
  Abigail (Bliss), 80
  Elisabeth (Perrin), 77
  Elizabeth, 94
  Elizabeth (Freeman), 150
  Elizabeth (Leonard), 80
  Erastus, 126
  Ezekiel, 77, 95
  Ezekiel's infant, 88
  Jerusha *wed* POST, 81
  Jerusha *wed* OLCOTT, 152
  Jonathan, 127
  Lucy *wed* PIPER, 78
  Nehemiah Junr., 150
  Simeon, 24, 25, 80, 92
DANIK
  H. wed MCKALL, 145
DARBE. *SEE* DARBY
DARBY, DARBE
  Charity (____), 145
  Joseph, 145
  Mary, 145
  Nathaniel, 75
  Roxina (Coleman), 134
  Sally, 145

Simeon, 134
Temperance (Bond), 75
DARMAN. *SEE ALSO* DORMAN
  Tabitha *wed* NORTON, 154
DARROW
  ____ (____), 26, 27
  Pierce, 26
DART
  Charlotte (Perrin), 77
  William, 77
DAVIS
  Allin, 54
  Azubah (Wilcox), 79
  Betsey (Wilcox), 79
  Bildad, 52
  Daniel, 53
  Dorithy (Brown), 75
  Israel, 62, 90
  Israel Austin, 68
  Joel, 62, 79
  John, 30, 31
  Joseph, 75, 86, 88
  Keziah, 56
  Lydia *wed* NORTON, 10, 154
  Malatia, 154
  Mary, 55
  Mary C. *wed* GILBERT, 84
  Mary *wed* MIHOTE, 121
  Nathaniel, 55, 74, 75, 88
  Oliver, 63, 65, 89, 139, 145
  Oliver S., 145
  Rachel, 61
  Rachel (Rollo), 74
  Sibil (Mack), 75
  Thomas, 52, 53, 54, 55, 56
  Worthy, 65
  Zepheniah, 61, 62, 63, 65, 68, 79, 89, 90
  Zerubabel, 55
  Zilpah, 62
DAY
  Adonijah, 152
  Anna (Marvin), 149
  Asa, 149
  Elizabeth (Marvin), 152

Hanna *wed* HORSFORD, 147
John, 150
Margaret *wed* JONES, 18
Mrs. Catherine (Jones), 150
Polly *wed* STRONG, 152
DEAN. *SEE ALSO* DOAN
DEAN, DEANE
  Amos, 78, 80
  Lavina (Brockway), 80
  Marsilvah (Ingham), 78
  Mary, 37, 94
  Sally *wed* DOUBLEDAY, 153
DEANE. *SEE* DEAN
DEMING
  Henry, 10
DENISON, DENIZON
  Charles, 111
  Denny D., 111
  Emily L. (____), 111
  Enoch G., 111
  Sarah A. *wed* PORTER, 117
DENIZON. *SEE* DENISON
DEWEY
  Apollos, 54
  Charles, 8
  Ebenezer, 48, 52, 53, 54, 73, 85
  family, 3
  Joseph, 47
  Lydia, 49
  Martha (____), 85
  Roger, 47, 49, 50
  Samuel Rollo, 50
  Sarah *wed* SAWYER, 75
  Sarah *wed* WHITE, 74
  Simeon, 48
  Temperance, 52
  Temperance (Holdrige), 73
  Timothy, 48
DIBBLE
  Mary *wed* HUTCHINSON, 96
DICKINSON
  Augusta *wed* SPRAGUE, 83
  Ezra, 108
  Mary (____), 108

Seth B., 108
DINGLEY, DINGLY
  Abby J. *wed* WATROUS, 120, 121
  Julia E. *wed* WATROUS, 83, 119
DIX
  Betsey *wed* BENJAMIN, 79
DOAN. *SEE ALSO* DEAN, *SEE* DOANE
DOANE, DOAN
  infant, 97
  Isaac, 36
  Leonard, 82
  Mary M. (Sumner), 82
  Richard, 10, 11
  Sally *wed* DOUBLEDAY, 153
DONE. *SEE* DOANE
DOOLITTLE
  Anrias? Merrell, 112
  Edgar, 3
  Edgar J., 108, 112, 118, 119, 120, 121
  Henry N., 108
  Jane E. (____), 108, 112
DOOSE
  Charles, 7
DORMAN. *SEE ALSO* DARMAN
  Tabitha *wed* NORTON, 12
DOUBLEDAY
  Daniel, 153
  Sally (Dean), 153
  Sally (Doan), 153
DOW
  James, 7
  John, 93
  Lorenzo, 28
  Mr., 30, 31
  Mrs., 29
  Peggy (____), 28
DOWD
  daughter, 114
  Leonard, 114
  M. N. (____), 114
DOWNER

    Rebeker *wed* SUMNER, 74
DRINKWATER
    Charles, 40
    Charles L., 110
    daughter, 110
    Malony A. (____), 110
    Malvia A. (____), 127
    Melora (Candall), 40
DUN
    Elisha, 163
    Esther (Porter), 163
DUNHAM
    ____ (____), 91
    Abby J? (Horton), 81
    Abiah, 55
    Abiah (____), 91
    Abiaih *wed* WELLS, 78
    Anna, 49
    Betty (Hall), 78
    Calvin, 48, 87, 145
    Calvin Noble, 87
    Chester Hiram, 70
    Content, 51
    Content *wed* MARKS, 77
    Cyrus, 68, 94
    Elijah, 24, 25, 47, 62, 69, 70, 92
    Elijah Hart, 69
    Elisabeth *wed* BROWN, 75
    Esther, 48
    Esther *wed* RUSSELL, 75
    Hannah, 48
    Hannah (Pinneo), 73
    Harvey, 81
    Hersa, 69
    Hervy, 69
    Humphrey Blodget, 70
    Isaac, 47, 50, 51, 54, 67, 68, 69, 90, 94
    Isaac Ansel, 67
    Jerusha, 15, 62, 91
    Jerusha (____), 90
    Jerusha *wed* WRIGHT, 75
    John Talcott, 59
    Lizzie *wed* TRACY, 84
    Mary, 96
    Obadiah, 48, 49, 73
    Obedia, 25
    Obedience, 24, 56, 61, 87, 92
    Patience, 57
    Prudence *wed* MORRISON, 78
    Ruth (Noble), 145
    Simeon, 24, 25, 54, 55, 56, 57, 59, 61, 62, 66, 78, 87, 91, 92
    Simeon Harlow, 69
    Simeon's twins, 87
    Sophia, 68
    Submit, 50
    Submit *wed* CLARK, 76
    Theodosia Harriot, 70
DUNK
    Elisha, 49, 51, 85
    Esther (____), 86
    Hannah, 49
DUNNING
    Mr., 53, 55, 57
DURHAM
    Abiah (____) (Talcott), 159
    Simon, 159
DUTTON
    Lydia *wed* MANN, 78
EATON
    Anna (Hutchinson), 81
    Joshua W., 81
EDDY
    Beulah *wed* COFFIN, 154
ELDRIDGE
    ____ *wed* CLARK, 83
    Daniel H., 119
    Laure (Gillet), 119
ELLIS
    ____ (____), 23
    Abby Lauretta, 69, 95
    Abby *wed* BUELL, 84
    Abigail, 95
    Anna, 60
    Benjamin, 63, 89
    Beula, 61
    daughter, 109, 113

David, 62
Dea., 88
Edward, 95
Edward S., 22, 23, 69, 70, 79, 91, 92
Edward Sawyer, 63
Elijah, 63
Elisabeth, 51, 56
Elisabeth (Sawyer), 74
Emma *wed* BROWN, 83
Hannah (Mack), 78
Harriet (____), 111
Harriet R. (____), 113
Harriet T. (____), 109
Horace, 67
Huldah, 52
Huldah *wed* MERREL, 78
Isaac, 58
Jabesh, 49, 50, 51
Jabez, 52, 53, 54, 56, 58, 61, 63, 73, 78, 89
John, 47, 52, 54, 55, 56, 57, 59, 60, 62, 63, 74, 85, 89
Jonathan, 57
Levi, 62
Lucilla (____), 109
Lydia, 52
Lydia *wed* TALCOTT, 64, 77
Mary, 56
Mary (____), 22
Mary (Hutchinson), 78
Mary (Sawyer), 73
Mary Elvira, 70
Mary S., 109
Mary *wed* BLOSSOM, 75
Mary *wed* HUTCHINSON, 78
Mercy, 50
Mercy (Rollo), 79, 92
Mercy Maria, 69, 95
Molly, 49
Mordica, 67, 78
Mr.'s Black woman, 91
Rebekah, 49
Rese *wed* ISHUM, 76
Rose, 51
Rose (____), 88
Ruhamah, 53
Ruhamah *wed* TAYLOR, 77
Samuel, 49, 50, 51
Samuel H., 109
Sarah, 47, 59
Sawyer, 50, 63, 95
son, 111
Warin, 55
William L., 109, 111, 113
William R., 91
Zilpah (____), 49
ELY
   Henry L., 81
   Mary A., 81
ENGLAND, 122, 123
   London, 3, 4
   St. Botolph's, 159
   Wales, 146
EPISCOPAL SOCIETY, 3
EVANS
   Adaline (____), 110
   Harvey, 110
   Jane E., 110
EVERTON
   Charity (Fox), 153
   S___, 153
EXETER, 26
FALSHAW. *SEE* FELSHAW
FALSHAW, FELSHAW, FELSHOW
   Desiah (Beach), 150
   John, 150
FARBOX. *SEE ALSO* TARBOX
   Elisha, 152
FELLOWS
   Asa, 22, 23
FELSHOW. *SEE* FELSHAW
FERNIER. *SEE* FERRIER
FERRIER, FERNIER
   Bartholomew, 150
   Lydia (Jones), 150
FIELDING
   ____ (____), 90
   Catharine, 67
   Clarissa, 65

Elisabeth, 65
Hannah, 67
Lucy, 69
Lydia (Hildreth), 78
Mariah, 68
Olive, 65
Philander, 69
Sally, 66
Samuel, 65, 66, 67, 68, 69, 78, 90, 91
William, 69
FIERNER. *SEE* TEIRNER
FILER, FILOR
Amey *wed* CARRIER, 146
Amey *wed* CARVER, 146
Anna *wed* ROOT, 146
Anne (Burnham), 142, 146
Elizabeth, 14, 15
John, 146
Samuel, 8, 142, 146
FILOR. *SEE* FILER
FINDLEY, FINLEY
Anna (Morgan), 78, 90
David, 79
Delight *wed* BUELL, 79
Florinda (Risley), 79
Hannah *wed* NICHOLS, 79
John, 18, 20, 21, 76, 78, 79, 89, 90
Lucy *wed* STRONG, 80
Phebe (Ford), 76, 89
Polly (Horsford), 79
Rhoda (____), 20, 21
Rhoda (Morris), 78
Rhoda *wed* LOOMIS, 134
Samuel, 10, 11
FINLEY. *SEE* FINDLEY
FINNEY
Mary Ann (Barber), 123
FISH
Eunice *wed* MACK, 73
FISHER
Mr., 4
FITCH
Elizabeth *wed* ARCHER, 150

FLINT
George, 84
Jennette (Hyde), 84
FOLEMAN
Betsy (Tisdale), 153
Charles, 153
FOOT. *SEE* FOOTE
FOOTE, FOOT
____ (____), 11
Adelaide L. (Adams), 122
Ann (____), 10
Ann (Thompson), 74
Caroline *wed* MCCALL, 123
Frances E. *wed* CHENEY, 123
Habacolm[?], 13
Hezekiah, 12
Joel, 39
John, 10, 11, 26, 27, 74, 93
Linus, 122
Mary E T. *wed* HARVEY, 123
Rachel C. *wed* KNOX, 124
Roger, 32, 33
Sarah *wed* COOK, 123
Sarah *wed* THOMPSON, 78
Thankfull *wed* BOND, 73
FORD
____ (____), 24, 25, 88
Amanda, 38
Betsey Grant, 69
Deacon, 24, 25
Frederic, 50
Gilbert, 68, 146
Hannah, 48
Hannah (Post), 80
Hannah E. *wed* KNEELAND, 82
Hannah Emily, 70
Isaac, 12, 13
Isaiah, 50
Jacob, 146
Jedediah Luther, 71
Jemima, 59
John, 48, 49, 50, 52, 53, 54, 59, 61, 87, 88
John P., 109, 119, 127

John Post, 70
Lucy, 59, 61, 87
Lucy (____), 68, 97, 146
Lucy Amanda, 71
Lucy Luther, 68
Lucy *wed* BROWN, 79
Lucy *wed* LOOMIS, 75
Luther, 35, 37, 53, 68, 69, 70, 71, 80, 97, 146
Mabel *wed* MACK, 34
Mary (____), 86
Mary *wed* GOODRICH, 76
Maryann (Grant), 69
Maryann Grant, 69
Mathew, 86
Phebe, 49, 52
Phebe *wed* FINLEY, 76, 89
Phila *wed* HALL, 80
Susanna, 54
Sylvester Grant, 69
FOX
  Abraham, 52
  Caroline Matilda, 2
  Charity (____), 153
  Elijah, 76
  Matilda C. *wed* TURNER, 82
  Sabra (Nettleton), 76
  Zerabbabel John Rollo, 52
FRANKLIN
  Lucy Ann *wed* TOWNSEND, 123
FREEMAN, FREMAN
  ____ (____), 39, 40
  Benjamin, 40, 125
  Dorothy, 2
  Elizabeth *wed* DANIELS, 150
  Mary A., 125
  Miss ____, 41
  Phebe *wed* WATROUS, 81
FREMAN. SEE FREEMAN
FRENCH
  Maria (Gelston), 124
  William, 124
FRIERER. *SEE* TEIRNER
FULLER

____ (____), 9, 10, 11, 14, 15, 16, 17
Amos, 146
Ebenezer, 146
Elizabeth *wed* Rowley, 157
Ezekiel, 151
Fayette, 36
John A., 118
Lavina P. (Warner), 118
Mary (____), 146
Matthew, 157
Mrs. Esther (Chapman), 151
R.F., 17
Roger, 10, 14, 15, 16, 28, 29, 146, 159
Susanna (Keeney), 146
GARAMON
  Abel, 119
GARDNER
  Abel, 121
  Hannah H. *wed* ANDREWS, 133
  Milley, 146
GARNLEY. *SEE* GURLEY
GATES
  ____, 152
  ____ (____), 37
  Fannie M. *wed* HYDE, 83
  M. L., 84
  Mary A. (Hyde), 84
  Prudence (Taylor), 152
  Thomas, 37
GAY
  Chauncey W., 113
  Chiffonett (____), 113
  Henry C., 113
  Lydia (Tylor), 163
  Mrs., 40
  Mrs. Theodore *wed* OLCOTT, 152
  Wilhay *wed* BECKWITH, 151
  Zebulon, 163
GAYLORD
  family, 3
GEAR. *SEE* GEER

GEE
    Lara (Jones), 150
    Zophrastes, 150
GEER, GEAR
    Abiel Sherman, 2
    Alpheus, 4
    Charles Gilbert, 72
    E C., 72
    Ebenezer, 119
    Edmund C., 34, 71, 96
    Edmund Sylvester, 71
    Frances Elizabeth, 72
    Hannah (____), 68
    Hannah M. *wed* TICKNOR, 82
    Hannah Minerva, 71
    Hannah *wed* PORTER, 80
    Hannah *wed* POST, 24, 92
    Harrier Jerusha, 71
    Laura L. (Staples), 119
    Mary Emily, 37, 71
    Polly (Wells), 79
    Samuel, 14, 15, 19, 68, 91
    Samuel E., 18, 79, 91
GELSTON
    Maria *wed* FRENCH, 124
GILBERT
    ____ (____), 34, 40
    Abby Maria, 70, 95
    Abby Maria *wed* JONES, 80
    Abby Mosier, 45
    Abigail, 47
    Abigail (____), 10, 85, 90
    Abilena, 147
    Ann C., 135
    Anna, 54, 63
    Anna (Lathrop), 76
    Anne C., 99, 160
    Betsey *wed* ISHAM, 79
    Champin, 45
    Champion, 37, 39
    Charles Augustus, 70
    Charles Champion, 67
    Cloe, 146
    daughter, 45, 114
    David, 39
    Deborah (____), 38, 45
    Ebenezer, 48
    Edwin Randolph, 70
    Elisabeth, 62
    Ezekiel, 29
    Florilla, 58
    Gardiner, 50, 62, 63
    Gardner, 64, 76
    George L., 39
    George Oliver, 58
    Harriet M. *wed* BURNHAM, 134
    Henry Champion, 37
    J., 10
    Joel, 69, 91
    John, 8, 9, 90, 109
    John H., 79
    John Henry, 64
    John R., 84
    Jonah C., 114
    Josiah C., 83, 119
    Josiah Champion, 70
    Laura, 64
    Lewis, 40
    Lieut., 60, 87
    Louisa (Alvord), 39
    Louisa H., 126
    Lydia, 54, 146, 147
    Lydia (Post), 58, 73, 87
    Lydia *wed* MACK, 77
    Mary, 62
    Mary C. (Davis), 84
    Mary L. (____), 109
    Mary L. (Hutchinson), 82
    Melissa A. *wed* HALL, 82
    Melissa Ann, 70
    Mr., 58, 59
    Mr.'s Negro child, 86
    Mrs. Abijail, 11
    Nabba Marie, 66
    Nabby (Wells), 79
    Nathan, 2
    Nathaniel, 60
    P. R., 72
    Payton R., 70, 71

Payton Randolph, 64
Peter, 60
Peyton, 45
Peyton R., 45
Phineas, 24
Polly (Root), 79
Prime, 59
Ralph P., 82, 109, 111, 120
Ralph Porter, 71
Rimus, 25
Roseannah *wed* TAYLOR, 75
RoseJannah, 48
S., 91
Sally, 126
Sally (____) *wed* WARD, 40, 60, 68, 72, 80, 83
Sally Theresia, 72
Samuel, 26, 27, 38, 40, 45, 47, 49, 50, 54, 58, 61, 62, 63, 64, 65, 66, 67, 69, 73, 85, 86, 87, 89, 93, 146, 147
Samuel A., 79
Samuel A[u]gustus, 58, 61, 86
Samuel Epaphroditus, 71
Samuel's infant, 88
Sarah, 63, 65, 89
Sarah (Post), 119
Sarah L. (____), 114
Sarah S. (Post), 83
Sarah Theresa, 38
Susan Theresa, 45
Sylvester, 34, 38, 49, 146
Thomas, 59, 60, 87
Tom, 58
GILEAD SOCIETY, 1, 3, 7, 20, 40, 47, 108, 109, 111, 112, 113, 117, 118, 119, 120, 121, 126, 127, 128, 129, 143, 146, 147, 159
GILLET. *SEE* GILLETT
GILLETT, GILET [TE]
____ (____), 30, 31, 32, 38
Abigail E. (Buell), 82

Adaline, 40
Alvin, 30, 31, 34
Amanda Miranda, 69
Anson, 20, 21, 38, 151
Arthur Randall, 116
Betsey (Hutchinson), 81
Clarissa, 20, 21
David, 32, 40, 125
Edwin, 116
Egburt, 29
Eliphalet, 81
Elizabeth F., 41
Ezekiel, 28
George, 42, 43, 129
Henry, 37
J. A., 82
Jane *wed* WILLCOX, 121
Joel, 146
Joel Albert, 71
Laura *wed* ELDRIDGE, 119
Lydia Emeline, 68
Mrs Mary (Washburn), 151
Mrs. Levina *wed* ROOT, 150
N., 1
Nathan, 3, 28, 68, 69, 71, 79, 82, 93
Nathan Edwin, 69
Ozias, 26, 27
Pauline, 126
Ralph Jones, 69
Samuel Egbert, 28, 69, 93
Sarah (Brown) F., 41
Sarah J. (Randall), 116
Sarah L. (Brown), 82
Silas Alfred, 71
GILLETTE. *SEE* GILLETT
GOODALE. *SEE ALSO* GOODELL
Hiram, 97
Lucy Vandelia, 96
GOODELL. *SEE ALSO* GOODALE
Gustavus, 95
Hiram, 36, 81
Martha P. (Brown), 81
GOODRICH
____ (____), 10, 11, 30, 31

Charles Whiting, 56
Craft, 30
Crafts, 31
Mary (Ford), 76
Moses, 76
Samuel, 56
Sarah *wed* COVEL, 77
Welthia *wed* WELLS, 75
GORDON
   Harriet *wed* BROWNHURST, 123
GOSLEE
   Sarah A. (Rollo), 83
   William N., 83
GOSS
   Hubbell, 82
   Nancy (Lockwood), 82
GOTT
   [Charity (Russ)], 16
   ____ (____), 16, 17, 32, 33
   Abbe, 35
   Abigail (Phelps), 149
   Charity (Russ), 17, 162
   Daniel, 16, 17, 26, 27, 162
   Hazael, 32, 33, 44, 45, 127, 149
   Hazael, Jr., 110
   Lucinda *wed* SNOW, 153
   Samuel, 16, 17
GRANNIS
   Edward, 59, 75
   Hannah (Wells), 75
   John, 59
GRANT
   Betsey *alias* FORD, 69
   Maryann *wed* FORD, 69
   Sylvester *alias* FORD, 69
GRAVES
   Abigail A.C., 42, 130
   Caroline, 36, 43
   Elizabeth (____), 37
   J., 37
   William B., 40, 43, 126
GRAY
   Sally *wed* WEBSTER, 80

   Unice *wed* HOUSE, 80
GREEN
   ____ (____), 95
GRIDLEY
   Anna *wed* WAY, 83
GRIFFIN. *SEE* GRIFFING
GRIFFING, GRIFFIN
   ____ (____), 34
   Peter, 4, 34
GRISWOLD
   Alvin, 78
   Anna (Wass), 78
   Carrie (Pinney), 83
   Daniel, 83
   Roger, 20, 21
GROVER
   Phineas, 75
   Ruth (Nichols), 75
GURLEY, GARNLEY
   Eunice *wed* PHELPS, 152
HALING
   Deborah (Brown), 82
   Isaac, 82
HALL
   ____ (____), 10
   Abigail, 67
   Amos, 22, 23, 51, 53, 54, 56, 57, 58, 60, 61, 62, 63, 73, 74, 85, 87, 88, 92
   Anna, 61, 68
   Anna *wed* LOOMIS, 79
   Azubah, 97
   Azubah (Trumbull), 34, 78
   Betsey, 95
   Betty, 57
   Betty (Briant), 74
   Betty *wed* DUNHAM, 78
   Calvin, 60
   Chester, 67, 90
   David, 58, 62, 83, 87
   Dean, 10
   Ebenezer, 49, 73
   Eliza (Tracy), 83
   Eunice (Rollo), 164
   Ezra, 63, 80

George, 34, 35, 54, 78, 97, 164
Hannah, 67
Hannah (Kellogg), 148
John, 68, 87
John Meigs, 82
Jonathan, 47, 67, 90, 148
Lucy *wed* ROLLO, 75, 89
Lydia, 60, 95
Mahetable *wed* MACK, 77, 96
Martha, 51, 88
Martha (____), 85
Martha (Wilcox), 73
Mary (Wadsworth), 73
Melissa A. (Gilbert), 82
Phila (Ford), 80
Prince Briant, 56
Seth, 47, 90
Susanna *wed* WILCOX, 74
William, 67
HALLYE
____ (____), 43
Elijah, 43
HAMILTON
[Alexander], 14
Clarissa, 95
James, 30
Majr Gen, 15
HAMMOND
Betsey wed Perrin, 80
HANKS
Edwin P., 124
Susan A. (Allen), 124
HANMER
Clara E. (Way), 83
Henry, 83
HANNA
Jane *wed* JOHNSON, 83
HARDIN
Jerusha (Lee), 81
Jesse, 23
Nelson A., 81
HARRIS
____ (____), 40
Caroline E., 111

Caroline M. (____), 111
George W., 111, 115, 121, 147
Joseph, 28, 93, 147
Lucy (____), 28, 93
Martha, 115
Martha A. (Norton), 121
Mary, 115
Moses, 3
Mrs., 29
William, 40
HARRIS,
Caroline M., 128
HARRISON
Jesse, 22
HART
Richard W., 34
HARVEY
Albert, 123
infant, 96
Mary E.T. (Foote), 123
HAUGTON, HOUGHTON
Abby Jane *wed* PERRY, 117
Abigail (Mation), 147
Anna *wed* SAXTON, 19
Ebenezer, 147
Joel, 19, 147
HAWS
Sarah *wed* HEATON, 147
HAYDEN
Mrs. Thalia *wed* NORTON, 154
Thalia (Owen) *wed* NORTON, 24, 38
HAYWARD
Esther *wed* HYDE, 83
HEATON
Samuel, 147
Sarah (Haws), 147
HENDEE
Abner Henice, 115
Adaline E. (____), 115
Lucius J, 115
HENDEE
Abner, 39, 41

Elizabeth (____), 39
HEWETT. *SEE* HEWIT [T]
HEWIT [T], HEWET [T]
    Betty (Archer), 163
    David T., 120
    Frances (Porter), 120
    Samuel, 163
HIBARD. *SEE* HIBBARD
HIBBARD, HIBARD, HEBERD
    ____ (____), 24, 25
    Alice Budduck, 153
    Capt, 25
    Lucinda (Jones), 80
    Rachel (Barber), 151
    Saloma *wed* ---, 161
    Salome *wed* WHITE, 24
    Walter, 80
    William, 24, 151
HIDE. *SEE* HYDE
HIGGINS, HIGGINZ
    Abalena (Ticknor), 97
    Eliza Jane, 111
    Henry, 97, 111
    Lucinda E. (____), 111
HIGH
    John, 147
    Sarah (Horton), 147
HILDRETH, HELDRITH
    Lydia *wed* FIELDING, 78
    Miner, 16, 17
HILL. *SEE* HILLS
HILLS, HILL
    ____ (____), 27, 45
    Allen, 151
    Chester, 26, 27
    Chester M., 83
    Clarinda Gypson, 69
    daughter, 114
    Eleanor (Root), 163
    Harry, 42
    Henry, 114, 130
    Horace, 114
    Jared, 45
    Josephine M. (Hutchinson), 83
    Leonard, 49, 163
    Louisa (____), 114
    Lucy (____), 114
    Maria *wed* BAILEY, 117
    Oliver, 69
    Sarah, 37
    son, 114
    Temprance (Jones), 151
    Timothy, 49
HINCKLEY, HINKLEY
    Eunice Dunis, 95
    Henry's child, 94
HINKLEY. *SEE* HINCKLEY
HITCHCOCK
    Daniel, 78
    S.G., 117
    Sarah (Allen), 78
    Solomon G., 4, 118
HODGE
    Daniel, 81
    Delia A. (Bidwell), 83
    Dudley's infant, 95
    Elisha, 44, 83
    Mary L. (____), 44
    Wealthy (Curtice), 81
HOLBROOK
    Huldah *wed* HUTCHINSON, 84
HOLCOM
    Betsey (Post), 79
    Elijah, 79
HOLDRIDG. *SEE* HOLDERIDG[E]
HOLDRIDG[E], HOLDRIGE
    Amasa, 28, 150
    Ammasa, 29
    Aseneth (____), 45
    Bridget *wed* WEBSTER, 163
    Deborah *wed* OWEN, 74
    Experience (Jones), 150
    Gershom, 149
    Rebeccah (Crouch), 149
    Robert, 45
    Temperance *wed* DEWEY, 73
HOLDRIGE. *SEE* HOLDRIDGE
HORSFORD. *SEE* HOSFORD
HORTON

____ (____), 14, 15, 17, 33, 96
Abby J. *wed* DUNHAM, 81
Abby Juliet, 71
Anna, 94
Anna *wed* BROWN, 81
Anna *wed* SEXTON, 18
Annis (____), 13, 34
Annis (Peters), 12
Austin Shipman, 70
Clarinda (____), 109
Clarinda (Wells), 45
E., 16
Ebenezer, 22, 23, 73
Edmund, 95
Elijah, 73
Ellis Luther, 71
Ezekiel, 12, 13, 26, 27, 36, 37
H., 34
Hannah, 16, 17, 91
Hannah (Morris), 76
Hannah *wed* PHELPS, 76
Harry B., 37
Hiram, 38, 96
Isabella *wed* CULVER, 80
J., 18, 30
Joel, 31, 34
John L., 126
Laura T., 38
Lucina *wed* WHITE, 80
Luta *wed* BROWN, 80
Lydia (____), 30, 31
Lydia *wed* MANN, 18
Lydia *wed* PARKER, 77
Mabel *wed* SEELEY, 79
Martha *wed* BROWN, 77
Martha *wed* ROLLO, 81
Mary B., 109
Mary P., 38
Mason, 28, 29
Mr. H., 45
Nancy *wed* WEST, 79
Prudence (____), 32
Rosamond (____), 37
Russel, 14

Sally (____), 45
Salmon, 38
Samuel, 30, 31, 76, 93
Samuel C., 71, 79
Samuel Leonard, 71
Sarah (Coox), 73
Sarah *wed* HIGH, 147
Semantha, 96
Shipman, 36, 40, 45
Sibil (Luther), 79
Stephen, 16, 17, 91
Temperance (____), 16, 17
Temperance (Shipman), 73
William, 38
William H., 109
HOSFORD, HORSFORD
Daniel, 12, 13, 147
Hannah (Day), 147
Harriot Emeline, 70
Joseph, 142
Luna Louisa, 70
Lydia *wed* KELLOGG, 78
Martha *wed* HUTCHINSON, 80, 93
Mrs Anna *wed* LOOMIS, 151
Obadiah, 7, 8
Polly *wed* FINLEY, 79
Roger, 14, 15
Sarah *wed* TAINTOR, 147
Sibbll *wed* OWEN, 150
Talcott, 147
Tallcott, 70
Unice (Beach), 142
HOSKINS
Mary *wed* CASE, 145
HOSMER
Hannah *wed* POST, 2
HOUGHTON. *SEE* HAUGTON
HOUSE, HOUZE
Alexander, 32, 33
Delia A. (Bidwell), 123
Elijah, 32, 33
Eliphalet, 73
Elisha, 123
John, 60

Lucretia (Howell), 73
Salmon, 80
Simon, 37
Unice (Gray), 80
HOUZE. *SEE* HOUSE
HOW
  Asa, 77
  Eunice (Buck), 77
HOWARD
  Huldah *wed* ROUVIERE, 133
  Mr., 45
HOWELL
  Lucretia *wed* HOUSE, 73
HOXEY
  Gideon, 14, 15
HUBBARD
  Betty *wed* LATHROP, 78
  Caleb, 42, 43
  John, 75
  Martha (Jordan), 78
  Roswel, 78
  Thankful (Rowlee), 75
HULL
  ____ (____), 11
  Daniel, 11
HUNT
  Anna (Phelps), 79
  Eliphas, 79
HUNTER
  Mary *wed* MENTER, 147
HUNTINGTON
  ____ (____), 12, 13
  Abigail (Talcott), 78
  James, 31
  Oliver, 78
  Solomon, 10, 11, 12, 13
HURLBURT
  Amos, 64, 65
  Amos' child, 89
  Clarissa, 64
  Esther, 65
  James M., 83, 121
  Jane (Johnzon), 121
  Julia, 64
  Mary Jane (Johnzon), 83

HUTCHINS, HUTCHINZ
  Lyman, 113
  son, 113
HUTCHINSON, HUTCHINZON
  ____ (____), 26, 27, 29
  Aaron, 67
  Abagail, 52, 60
  Abigail (____), 90
  Alfred W., 84
  Amelia Rhoda, 72
  Anna, 56, 69
  Anna E. *wed* LORD, 119
  Anna Elizabeth, 72
  Anna Elizabeth *wed* LORD, 83
  Anna *wed* EATON, 81
  Anna *wed* LOOMER, 78
  Augustus, 67, 90
  Bazaliel, 26
  Betsey, 66
  Betsey *wed* Gillett, 81
  Bezeleel, 27
  Clarissa, 30, 31, 65, 67, 93
  Clarissa V. *wed* PRENTICE, 82
  Clarissa Velina, 72
  Daniel, 35, 66, 78
  David, 27, 71, 72, 80, 81, 93, 95, 111
  David E., 111, 119
  David Edwin, 71
  David G., 121
  E., 27
  Ele, 84
  Eleanor (____), 56, 60, 61, 96
  Eleazar, 97
  Eleazer, 26, 35, 61, 69, 79, 93, 96
  Eleazer's infant, 91, 92
  Elisabeth, 48
  Elisabeth *wed* INGHAM, 76
  Elonor (Post), 74
  Ely Warner, 115
  Experience (Mack), 77
  Ezra, 66
  family, 3
  Franklin C., 127

George C., 83, 112, 115, 120
George Champion, 72
Hannah (____), 13
Hannah Eliza, 72
Hannah *wed* WELLS, 75
Harriet B. *wed* WAY, 82
Harriet Belinda, 72
Harriet N. *wed* CHAPPEL, 82
Harvy, 69
Huldah (Holbrook), 84
Ida B. (Strickland), 84
Ira, 68
Israel, 63, 64, 96, 97
Israel Champion, 71
Israel E., 71, 80
Israel Ele, 64
Jewett E., 83
Job, 49, 64, 65, 77
John, 28, 29, 38, 50, 65, 66, 67, 68, 69, 72, 78, 90, 93
John B., 72, 81
John Bissel, 65
John Calvin, 72
John Cone, 72
Jonathan, 10, 11, 34, 48, 49, 50, 52, 53, 55, 56, 60, 61, 74, 90, 96, 97
Joseph, 56, 63, 66, 76, 94, 95
Josephine M. *wed* HILLS, 83
Josiah Champin, 63
Laura, 66
Laura L. (____), 111
Laura L. (Little), 119
Laura *wed* MACK, 114
Lauretta (Jewett) (Hutchinson), 81
Louisa D. (Root), 83
Lucinda, 64
Lydia, 55
Lydia *wed* CROUCH, 77
Martha (Horsford), 80, 93
Mary, 56
Mary (____), 66, 112, 115
Mary (Dibble), 96
Mary (Ellis), 78

Mary (Warner), 80
Mary L. *wed* GILBERT, 82
Mary Lauretta, 72
Mary T. (Loomis), 83, 120
Mary *wed* ELLIS, 78
Molly, 93
Molly (____), 65, 66, 67, 68, 69, 90
Molly (Post), 28, 93
Moses, 14, 15, 28, 73, 93
Olive M. *wed* WARNER, 83, 122
Polly (____), 67
Polly B. *wed* LUTHER, 80
Polly Belinda, 66
Polly C. (Post), 81
Rachel *wed* SHEPHERD, 73
Ruth (____), 29, 35, 93, 97
Ruth (Cox), 28, 73
Sally, 66
Sally (____), 69
Sally (____)'s infant, 91, 92
Sally (Tal[l]cott), 26, 79
Sally *wed* BIRGE, 81
Sarah (Cone), 72, 81
Sibil (Mack), 76
Sybil (____), 66, 95
Thankful *wed* RAWLIN, 76
Willard F., 112
William, 68, 72, 81
Zilpah, 48, 63
Zilpha *wed* STRONG, 79, 94
HUTCHINZON. *SEE* HUTCHINSON
HUXFORD
   Melissa *wed* ROOT, 84
HYDE, HIDE
   ____ (____), 18, 19
   Charles W., 83
   Esther (Hayward), 83
   family, 3
   Fannie M. (Gates), 83
   Harriet N. (Strong), 82
   Jane L. *wed* JAYCOX, 83
   Jennette *wed* FLINT, 84
   Mary A. *wed* GATES, 84

Samuel S., 82
William, 18, 19
INDIANA
   Allen [Co.], 123
INGHAM. *SEE ALSO* INGRAHAM
   ____ (____), 85
   Alexander, 52, 53, 55, 56, 57, 58, 73, 86
   Betsey, 67
   Capt., 86
   Catherine (Noble), 73
   Daniel, 22, 23, 48, 53, 54, 56, 88, 90
   Elisabeth (Hutchinson), 76
   Erastus, 48, 62, 76
   Eunice (Mack), 77
   Gamaliel, 56
   Huldah, 52
   Katherine, 52
   Mahitable (____), 86
   Mahitable *wed* NORTON, 80, 96
   Marsilvah *wed* DEAN, 78
   Mary *wed* ABENS, 73
   Mehitable, 54
   Micaiah, 53, 64, 77
   Oliver, 56, 67
   Phebe *wed* TOWNZEN, 73
   Rhoda *wed* TOWNZEN, 73
   Samuel, 62
   Samuel A[u]gustus, 64
   Tarza, 53
   Theodora, 57
   Thomas, 55, 58, 86
   William, 62
INGRAHAM. *SEE ALSO* INGHAM
   Daniel, 47, 50, 68
   Jabez, 76
   Naomi (Root), 76
   Oliver, 68
   Samuel, 50
   Solomon, 47
IRELAND, 123
ISHAM, ISHUM
   ____ (____), 28
   Betsey (Gilbert), 79
   Elizabeth (Gilbert), 79
   John, 79
   Joseph, 39
   Mrs., 29, 31
   Rese (Ellis), 76
   Timothy, 20, 21
   Zebulun, 76
ISHUM. *SEE* ISHAM
JACKSON
   Betsey *wed* ROOT, 81
JAGGER
   Aaron Perrin, 61
   Abigail, 57
   Elias, 55, 56, 57, 58, 61, 74, 86
   Elias' child, 87
   John, 153
   Mahetable (Root), 74
   Mehitable, 55
   Mehitable (Root), 86
   Sarah, 56
   Sarah (Perrin), 74
JAMAICA, 156
JARVIS
   Samuel F., 41
   William, 4
JAYCOX
   Gilbert B., 83
   Jane L. (Hyde), 83
JEWETT
   Lauretta *wed* HUTCHINSON, 81
   Mehetable *wed* WITTER, 82
JOHNSON, JOHNZON, JONSTON
   ____ (____), 42, 43
   Almira, 42
   Almira P. *wed* TISDALE, 120
   Charles, 83
   Dan, 22, 23
   David, 42, 108, 148
   Edward, 83
   Ellen (Ticknor), 83
   Jane (Hanna), 83
   Jane *wed* HURLBURT, 121

Joel, 42, 43, 129
Mary Jane *wed* HURLBURT, 83
Philance (____), 129
Pierce, 42, 43
Piercy (____), 108, 148
William K., 148
William M., 108
William N., 148
JOHNZON. *SEE* JOHNSON
JONES
    ____ (____), 12, 13, 17, 26, 27, 35
    Abby Maria (Gilbert), 80
    Alfred A., 128
    Anna, 147
    Anna *wed* PHELPS, 77
    Cornelia (Manley), 153
    Dan, 153
    E. H,, 26
    Ebenezer H., 20
    Ebenezer T'n, 21
    Eliakim, 77
    Elias, 26, 27
    Emeline (Palmer), 120
    Enoch, 120
    Ezekiel, 147
    family, 3
    Gideon, 13
    Hannah A. (Tiffe), 120
    Henry, 37
    Huldah, 28
    Huldah Junr. *wed* WATERS, 152
    Jedediah, 41, 128, 148
    Joel, 9, 18, 19, 30, 31, 148
    L.K., 27
    Lara *wed* GEE, 150
    Lucinda *wed* HIBARD, 80
    Lucius, 39
    Lura *wed* SMITH, 152
    Lydia *wed* FERRIER, 150
    Margaret (____), 19
    Margaret (Day), 18
    Margaret (Porn____.), 148
    Mindwell (Beach), 147
    Mindwell *wed* WATERS, 77
    Mrs Catharine *wed* DAY, 150
    Mrs Experience *wed* HOLDRIDGE, 150
    Mrs. Charity *wed* ROOT, 150
    Mrs. Hulda, 29
    Nancy (____), 39
    Nancy (Taylor), 152
    Oliver, 35
    Polly, 32, 33
    Rachel *wed* TWINING, 81
    Ralph, 16, 17, 69
    Rebekah (Webster), 77
    Reuben, 20, 21
    Salmon A., 121
    Samuel, 12, 13, 20, 21, 22, 23, 28, 80, 126, 147
    Samuel 3rd, 148
    Samuel F., 120
    Sarah, 95
    Sarah (Morse), 121
    Talatha (Bishop), 148
    Temprance *wed* HILLS, 151
    Timothy, 39, 152
    Timothy F., 108, 118, 126
JONSTON. *SEE* JOHNSON
JORDAN
    Martha *wed* HUBBARD, 78
    Mary *wed* POST, 2
JUDD
    Mary (Peters), 74
    Mary (Rollo), 75
    Mary's child, 85
    Philip, 74
    Phoebe (Beebee) *wed* WATERS, 160
    Thomas, 75
KEENEY, KENNY, KEENY
    Gera G., 82
    Harriet M. (Post), 82
    Nancy L. (Sumner), 83, 118
    Nelson, 83, 118
    Susanna *wed* FULLER, 146
    Susannah *wed* KELLOGG, 148

KEENY. *See* KEENEY
KELDER
   Hannah H. (____), 115
   Peter, 115
   son, 115
KELLEY
   Lucinda *wed* CROCKER, 78
KELLOGG, CELLOGG
   ____ (____), 24, 25
   Abigail (Marvin), 151
   Ann *wed* PERRIN, 75
   Browning D., 114
   Charles, 78
   daughter, 108, 114
   David, 108
   Dolly (____), 110
   Dorothy (____), 114
   Elijah, 14, 15, 148
   Elisha, 38, 148
   Elizabeth Septame (Lothrop), 78
   Frances M. (____), 112
   Hannah (Adams}, 148
   Hannah *wed* HALL, 148
   Israel, 24, 25
   James C., 112, 121, 128
   Jared C., 111
   Jerusha *wed* BURNHAM, 150
   Jerusha *wed* WHITE, 135
   Joseph, 148
   Justin A., 110
   Laura Louisa, 112
   Lydia (Hosford), 78
   Mary R. (____), 108
   Moses, 24, 25, 28, 29
   Moses Jnr, 151
   Raimond D., 110
   Samuel, 3, 78
   Susannah (Kenny), 148
   Susannah *wed* CURTICE, 148
KILBORN, KILBURN
   Ebenezer, 74
   Josiah, 47
   Sarah (Bill), 74
   Sarah *wed* PORTER, 73

KILBURN. *See* KILBORN
KIMBALL
   Cynthia, 26, 27, 93
KING
   Elijah Russel, 65
   Seluta, 67
   Seth, 65, 67, 76
   Silence (Lothrop), 76
KINGSBERRY. *See* KINGSBURY
KINGSBURY, KINGSBERRY
   ____ (____), 32
   Augustus, 133
   Hannah *wed* WHITE, 76
   Mrs., 33
   Sally (Loomis), 133
KINGSLEY
   Asahel, 36
   Elizabeth A. *wed* NORTON, 37
   Mary P. *wed* LINCOLN, 117
KNEELAND, NELAND
   Augustine, 82
   David, 148
   Edward, 142
   Hannah (Blish), 142
   Marcy (Kneeland), 148
   Marcy *wed* KNEELAND, 148
KNIGHT
   Merrick, 3, 123
KNOX
   Chauncey E., 124
   Rachel C. (Foote), 124
LAMB
   Bridget, 38
LANGDON
   Chauncey, 65, 66, 78
   Laura Lothrop, 65
   Lucy, 66
   Lucynana (Lothrop), 78
LATHAM. *See also* LUTHAM
   Abby (____), 107
   Acer A., 107
   Ann (____), 112
   Asa A, 128
   Caroline A. (Strong), 81
   Harriet A., 107

Huldah Ann (Rathbone), 117
Joel C., 81
Joseph, 72
Joseph Durfey, 72
Nancy J., 130
William, 30, 31
William E., 112, 117
William E. Jr., 112
LATHROP. *SEE* LOTHROP
LAWRENCE
  Henry's infant, 89
LEE
  Delia C. (Britton), 82
  Elizabeth *wed* TAYLOR, 84
  Esther *wed* TAYLOR, 82
  Henry, 97
  Jerusha *wed* BROWN, 142
  Jerusha *wed* HARDIN, 81
  Sarah *wed* BROWN, 142
  William A,, 82
LENORIS
  Mrs. *wed* ALLEN, 18
LEONARD
  ____ (____), 34
  Elizabeth *wed* DANIELS, 80
  O. F., 34
LEWIS
  Cynthia Ann (Brown), 82
  Helena (____), 112
  Irene R., 112
  John, 82
  Sylvanus, 112
LINCOLN
  Francis, 109
  Mary (____), 109
  Mary P. (Kingsley), 117
  Orrin, 109
  Orrin A., 117
LITTLE
  Laura L. *wed* HUTCHINZON, 119
LOCKWOOD
  ____ (____), 36
  David S., 109
  Edwin, 113

Elizabeth (____), 109, 113
Elizabeth *wed* CALDWELL, 84
Emma Elizabeth, 111
J., 36
Jerusha (____), 111
Melina, 109
Nancy *wed* GOSS, 82
Rosaltha A., 113
Samuel, 3
Timothy, 135
William, 111
LONDON
  Cheney (White), 160
  John, 160
LOOMER
  ____ (____), 31
  Anna, 126
  Anna (____), 40
  Anna (Hutchinson), 78
  Daniel, 78, 89
  Daniel's child, 94
  Daniel's dau, 89
  Daniel's son, 89
  John, 36
  John's child, 92, 93
  Lucy, 26, 27, 93
  Lucy (____), 27
LOOMIS
  ____ (____), 39
  Amy L. (Babcock), 122
  Anna (Hall), 79
  Charles, 75, 79
  Esther *wed* TRUDE, 122
  George H., 122
  Jacob, 20, 21
  Levi, 78
  Louisa (Lothrop), 78
  Lucy (Ford), 75
  Mary (____), 24, 27
  Mary T. *wed* HUTCHINSON, 83, 120
  Mary *wed* PEASE, 78
  Mrs. Anna (Horsford), 151
  Nelson, 39
  Rachel *wed* POLLY, 162

Samuel Jr, 151
LORD
    ____ (____), 110
    Anna Elizabeth (Hutchinson), 83
    Anne E. (Hutchinzon), 119
    Benjamin, 148
    Ebenezer, 148
    Elisha, 44, 45, 71, 72
    Elisha Manly, 71, 95
    George H., 119
    George Hinman, 83
    Mr., 50
    Noble E., 110
    Prudence, 125
    Sylvester George, 72
    Twin sons, 110
LOTHROP, LATHROP
    ____ (____), 10, 11
    Abagail, 53
    Abagail *wed* PITKIN, 77
    Anna, 52
    Anna *wed* GILBERT, 76
    Betty (Hubbard), 78
    E., 10
    Elijah, 3, 10, 11, 47, 48, 49, 50, 51, 52, 53, 54, 55, 56, 57, 59, 73, 90
    Elijah L., 67, 78
    Elijah Leonard, 56
    Elisabeth, 54
    Elisabeth (Rollo), 75
    Elizabeth Septame *wed* KELLOGG, 78
    Hannah, 49, 51
    Hannah *wed* WELLS, 76
    Laura, 89
    Laura Dreima, 59
    Laura Lenesa, 68
    Leonard E., 68, 69
    Leonard E.'s infant, 90
    Leonard Elijah, 67
    Loisa Octavia, 55
    Louisa *wed* LOOMIS, 78
    Lucynana, 57
    Lucynana *wed* LANGDON, 78
    Mary, 48
    Mary Elizabeth, 68
    Mary *wed* BROWN, 76
    Silence, 50
    Silence (____), 90
    Silence Laurinda, 69
    Silence *wed* KING, 76
    Simon, 163
    Solomon, 18, 19, 75
LOVELAND. *SEE ALSO* LOVEMAN
    Aaron, 59
    Anna (Malley), 74
    Edwin, 110, 113
    Emily (____), 110, 113
    Fayette, 110
    George, 60, 74
    Israel, 59
    Jemima *wed* CHAMPLIN, 75
    Jerusha (Loveland), 75
    Jerusha *wed* LOVELAND, 75
    Malachi, 59
    Pain, 59
    son, 113
    Thomas, 75
    William, 60
LOVEMAN. *SEE ALSO* LOVELAND
    Jerusha, 58
    Thomas, 58
LUCAS, LUKUS
    Electa M. *wed* POST, 81
    Samuel, 48, 49
    Sarah, 48
    Sibil, 49
LUKUS. *SEE* LUCAS
LUTHAM. *SEE ALSO* LATHAM
    William, 36
LUTHER
    ____ (____), 13
    Abigail, 20, 21
    Calvin, 64, 80
    Edmund, 89
    Ellis, 12, 13, 63, 64, 76, 79, 89, 90
    Ellis *alias* HORTON, 71

Polly B. (Hutchinson), 80
Sarah (Merrils), 79
Sibil, 63
Sibil (Post), 76
Sibil *wed* HORTON, 79
Sybel (Post), 12
Sybil (POST), 90
LYMAN
  David, 7
LYON
  Lydia (____), 35
M____
  Polly (____), 13
M'IVER
  Daniel, 11
MACK
  ____ (____), 43, 86, 88
  Aaron, 34, 52, 66, 72, 96
  Abagail, 49
  Abigail, 60
  Anna *wed* COVEL, 75
  Chester Hall, 67, 90
  daughter, 31
  David, 47, 75
  David E., 114
  David Hall, 72
  Deborah, 30, 68, 93, 95
  Ela A., 81
  Elisabeth (Rowley), 75
  Elisha, 47, 48, 49, 51, 52, 53, 55, 56, 57, 58, 86, 87
  Ely, 71
  Ely A., 72
  Esther (Cone), 81
  Esther *wed* ROW, 74
  Eunice, 53
  Eunice (Fish), 73
  Eunice *wed* INGHAM, 77
  Experience, 49
  Experience *wed* HUTCHINSON, 77
  George, 118
  Hannah, 56
  Hannah *wed* ELLIS, 78
  Harriet (Barber), 118
  Henry, 30, 31, 51, 65, 66, 67, 68, 77, 90, 96
  Henry's infant, 90
  Huldah, 50
  Jerusha Jane, 71
  Joel, 52
  John, 51, 53, 54, 56, 57, 58, 59, 60, 64, 73, 86, 88, 96
  John Fish, 54
  John Giles, 72
  John Henry, 96
  Josiah, 18, 19, 42, 43, 47, 48, 49, 50, 51, 52, 66, 75, 86, 89, 92, 94
  Josiah Augustus, 72
  Laura (Hutchinzon), 114
  Lois, 48, 57, 86, 87
  Luise, 148
  Lydia, 58, 66, 86
  Lydia (Gilbert), 77
  Lydia *wed* WILCOX, 75
  Mabel, 96
  Mabel (Ford), 34
  Mahetable (Hall), 77
  Martha, 65
  Martha *wed* SPENCER, 81
  Mary, 48
  Mary (____), 42, 89
  Mary (Talcott), 75
  Mary *wed* SMITH, 82
  Mary *wed* WILCOX, 76
  Mehitable (Hall), 96
  Melicent *wed* SCOTT, 78
  Mercy, 64, 88
  Millesent, 57
  Mindwell, 55, 87
  Molly, 52
  Oleander, 50, 52
  Orlandder, 148
  Phila, 68
  Prudence, 59
  Ralph, 17, 51, 64, 65, 66, 68, 69, 77, 91
  Ralph Gilbert, 68
  Sally, 44, 45

Sarah, 56, 58
Sarah *wed* PHELPS, 74
Sibil, 47
Sibil *wed* DAVIS, 75
Sibil *wed* HUTCHINSON, 76
son, 114
Susanna, 50
Warin, 53
Welthia, 65
William Champion, 69
MAINE, 3
   Bates College, 159
MAJER
   Mary, 86
MALLEY
   Anna *wed* LOVELAND, 74
MALONEY
   Mary I., 129
MAN. *SEE* MANN
MANCHESTER, 38, 40
MANLEY, MANLY
   Cloha *wed* PERKINS. *See*
   Cornelia *wed* JONES, 153
MANLY. *SEE* MANLEY
MANN, MAN
   ____ (____), 27, 32, 33
   A., 27
   A. K., 16
   Abigail *wed* BAXTER, 143
   Abijah, 22, 23, 32, 33
   Ab't, 17
   Andrew, 26, 39
   Charles C., 108
   Cyrus, 45, 108, 112
   Cyrus Edwin, 44
   daughter, 115
   David, 115
   Deborah *wed* PHELPS, 77
   EDMOND CYRUS, 44
   Elizabeth C. (____), 108
   Elizabeth E. (____), 112
   Enoch, 23
   family, 3
   Genette (____), 115
   Hannah (____), 26
   J., 28
   Joel, 28, 29
   John, 14, 15, 78
   John, Jr, 148
   Joseph, 10, 11, 29, 35, 37
   Juliet, 34
   Lydia (____), 19
   Lydia (Dutton), 78
   Lydia (Horton), 18
   Manley, 17
   Manlius, 16
   Marcy (____), 29
   Mary (____), 28
   Mary *wed* CALKINS, 73
   Nathaniel, 148
   Patience (____), 35
   Phebe (____), 28, 29
   R., 34
   Richard, 148
   Rodolphus, 18, 19
   Sarah, 16, 17
   son, 45
   William Worthington, 112
MANNING
   Calvin, 152
   Desiah (Rose), 152
   Phebe *wed* WATERS, 159
MARKS
   Content (Dunham), 77
   Joseph, 149
   Lucina, 55
   Lucinda Marvil, 86
   Mary (____), 55, 86
   Mary *wed* PETERS, 149
   Samuel, 77
MARTAIN
   Eleanor (Shepard), 76
   Joseph, 76
MARTINDALE
   ____ (____), 10, 11
   Hannah *wed* WELL, 79
   Hiram H., 39, 82, 127
   Martha M. (Webster), 82
   Sibyl (Shipman), 73
   Zadek, 73

Zadock, 10, 11
MARVIN
  Abigail *wed* KELLOGG, 151
  Anna *wed* DAY, 149
  Azubah (Case), 76
  Elihu, 20, 21, 76, 149, 150, 151, 152, 153
  Elisabeth *wed* DAY, 152
  Harvy, 70
MASON
  John, 5
MASSACHUSETTS, 10
  Barnstable, 157
  Boston, 3, 4, 94
  Cambridge, 19, 35
  Deerfield, 3
  Gloucester, 156
  Lee, 156
  Lenox, 16, 17, 32
  Ludlow, 118
  Marthas Vineyard, 154
  North Brookfield, 149
  Peru, 143
  Pittsfield, 145
  Plymouth, 123
  Salem, 159
  Springfield, 118
  Tidinham, 151
  Topsfield, 159
  Washington, 120
  Westfield, 143
  Wrentham, 147
MATION
  Abigail *wed* HOUGHTON, 147
MCCALL. *SEE* MCKALL
MCCULLOCK
  Hannah (Rollo), 76
  James, 76
MCKALL, MCCALL
  Caroline (Foote), 123
  David R., 123
  Elihu, 145
  H. (Danik), 145
  Lucy (Rockwell) *wed* POST, 156
  Lucy 2d (Rockwell) *wed* POST, 149
  Mary *wed* ALLEN, 149
  Mehitabel *wed* ALGER, 149
  Mehitible *wed* ALLYN, 149
MCKINNEY
  J. M., 83
  Phebe A. (Watrous), 83
MENTER
  Mary (Hunter) *wed* BAXTER, 147
  Mercy *wed* BAXTER, 143
MENTON
  Mercy *wed* BAXTER, 143
MERREL. *SEE* MERRILL
MERRIL. *SEE* MERRILL
MERRILL, MERREL[LS], MERRIL[S]
  ____ (____), 33
  Abigail, 39, 55, 127
  Anna, 57
  Asher, 51, 53, 54, 55, 56, 57, 58, 59, 61, 63, 73, 86
  Benjamin, 61, 88
  Daniel, 78
  Delight, 51, 54
  Delight (Sawyer), 73
  Elisabeth, 55
  Elizabeth *wed* SKINNER, 73
  Esther, 54, 61
  Esther (____), 86
  Ezekiel, 50
  family, 3
  Fowler, 9, 89
  Gad, 50, 52, 53, 54, 56, 57, 73
  Hannah, 54
  Hosea, 52
  Huldah (Ellis), 78
  John, 28, 29, 32, 33, 53, 54, 55, 57, 59, 61, 66, 74, 93
  Lydia, 53
  Mary, 66
  Mary (Skinner), 73
  Olive, 61

Oliver, 59
Ormanda, 57
R[e]uben, 53
Ruby, 57
Sarah, 53
Sarah (____), 32
Sarah (Culver), 74, 94
Sarah wed LUTHER, 79
Sibil, 56, 59, 86
Simeon, 58
MERRILS. SEE MERRILL
METHODIST SOCIETY, 4
MICHIGAN
　Kalamazoo,, 142
MIDDLETON
　Mary (Woodworth), 122
　Orlando, 122
MIHOT. SEE MINOTT
MILLER
　Alpha, 3
MINER
　Adeline (____), 109
　Joseph C., 109
　Ralph H., 109
　Sally Clarissa, 71
　Selden, 71
　Theoda wed ROGERS, 160
MINOTT, MIHOTE
　Mary (Davis), 121
　William, 121
MORE
　Elam, 80
　Joseph, 150
　Lydia (Wells), 80
　Mrs. Abigail (Root), 150
MORGAN
　Anna wed FINLEY, 78, 90
　C., 42
　Charles, 114
　Charles' child, 96
　daughter, 114
　Mary (____), 114
　Sliva wed BURDON, 78
　Susan (Carr), 42
　Swan E. wed CARR, 122

MORLEY
　Abner, 75
　Alice, 62
　Alice (____), 62
　Alice (Townsend), 75
MORRIS
　Hannah wed HORTON, 76
　Rhoda wed FINLEY, 78
MORRISON
　Harvy, 78
　Prudence (Dunham), 78
MORSE
　____ (____), 36
　Otis, 36
　Sarah wed JONES, 121
MOSHER. SEE ALSO MOSYER
　Stephen, 153
MOSYER. SEE ALSO MOSHER
MOSYER, MOSIER
　____, 153
　Margaret (Stone), 153
MUDGE, MUDG
　Ebenezer, 148
　Marcey, 148
　Mary, 148
　Micah, 148
MUNSON
　Jesse, 74
　Miriam (Rowley), 74
MURRY, MURREY
　Elizabeth wed PETERS, 149
NASH
　Anna E. (Post), 124
　James H., 124
NETTLETON
　Sabra wed FOX, 76
NEW HAMPSHIRE, 126
　Manchester, 82
　Oxford, 156
　Surrey, 160
NEW YORK, 4, 34, 35, 37, 39, 45, 142, 156
　Augusta, 117
　Austerlitz, 146
　Ballston, 18, 19, 35, 36

Brockford, 153
Cambridge, 91
Col. Co., 142
Columbus, 119
Del. Co, 148
Fairfield, 148
Franklin, 152, 153
Granville, 161
Horsick Falls, 160
Milton, 28, 29
Oswego Bay, 130
Sanborn, 147
South Hampton, 3
Southold, 145
Spencertown, 150
Stratford, 145
Yonkers, 159, 160
NEWCOMB
   Mrs. Mary (Post), 149
   Obidiah, 149
NEWELL
   Erastus, 72
   Erastus Henry, 72
NICHOLS, NICOLES
   Adeline A. (Strong), 82
   C., 1, 2
   Charles, 3, 71, 72, 81, 118, 119, 120, 121, 122, 123
   Hannah (Finley), 79
   Joseph C., 82
   Julia, 72, 95
   Julius, 41, 72
   Louisa (West) (Post), 81
   Orry, 79
   Ruth *wed* GROVER, 75
NILES
   Abigal {Beach), 149
   Anna (Skinner), 153
   Barabras, 153
   Daniel, 149
   David, 18, 19, 108, 118, 126
NOBLE
   Catherine *wed* INGHAM, 73
   David, 47, 48, 51, 54
   Enos, 54
   Hannah, 47
   James, 53
   John, 48, 53
   Mr., 51
   Rebekah, 51
   Ruth, 48
   Ruth *wed* DUNHAM, 145
   Tarzo *wed* BOOTH, 73
NORTHAM, NORTHOM, NORTHUM
   ____ (____), 96
   daughter, 114
   David, 35, 62
   David S., 107
   Dea., 96
   Elisabeth (White), 76
   Emily, 110
   Harriet A. (____), 110
   Harriet G. (____), 114
   John, 35, 62, 76
   John Butler, 107
   John H., 110
   John R., 114
   Jonathan, 35, 97
   Joseph, 22, 23
   Laura, 38
   Mrs Lois *wed* BOWLS, 152
NORTHOM. *SEE* NORTHAM
NORTHUM. *SEE* NORTHAM
NORTON
   ____ (____), 9, 11, 13, 22, 23, 38, 92
   Abby M. (Strickland), 84
   Almira, 69
   Almira *wed* BROWN, 82
   Anna, 66, 154
   Anne (Trapp), 154
   Benjamin, 61
   Betsey, 12, 13, 154
   Betsey H., 126
   Betsey H. (____), 39
   Betsey *wed* SWETLAND, 80
   Chester, 37
   Daniel I., 115
   daughter, 113

David, 20, 35, 64, 65, 66, 67, 68, 69, 77, 80, 92, 96, 97
David S., 113
Davis, 44, 154
Deborah, 94
Deborah (____), 20, 21
Deborah (Phelps), 77, 92
Depsey, 33
Depsy (Deborah), 32
Duane, 21
Ebenezer, 92
Elisabeth, 60, 65
Elizabeth (____), 154
Elizabeth (Woodward), 113
Elizabeth A. (Kingsley), 37
Emma (____), 115
F., 9, 10, 12
family, 3
Frances, 10, 24
Francis, 11, 12, 20, 21, 154
George Solomon, 84
Hannah Louisa, 69
Hepzibah (Coffin), 154
Ichabod Trumbull, 68
J. Francis, 38
Jemima, 154
Jemima wed ROOT, 16, 17
Jethro, 18, 19, 36, 64, 65, 77, 97
John, 60, 61, 154
John F., 126
John Flavel, 39
Joseph, 154
Louisa, 44, 130
Lova wed RIPLEY, 76
Lydia, 65
Lydia (Davis), 10, 12, 154
Mahitable (Ingham), 80, 96
Martha (Well), 80
Martha A. wed HARRIS, 121
Mary, 10, 11, 25, 64, 154
Mary (____), 154
Mary (Boyes), 154
Mary A. (____), 39
Mary D. wed WHITE, 117

Mary E., 24
Mary wed SKINNER, 80
Matilda (____), 109
Matilda (Webster), 82
Mr. Frances, 13
Nancy wed CHAPEL, 80
Nicholas, 154
Russell, 15
Samuel Smith, 67
Sibyl (Sumner), 77
Solomon, 18, 19, 22, 23, 66, 68, 82, 91, 92, 109
son, 109, 115
Susanna, 67
Susannah wed BURNHAM, 81
Sybil (____), 18, 19
Tabitha (Darman), 154
Tabitha (Dorman), 12
Thalia (Hayden), 154
Thalia (Owen) (Hayden), 24, 38
Thankful wed PERRY, 77
William, 39, 64
OLCOTT
Daniel, 152
Jerusha (Daniels), 152
Oliver, 152
Patience (Root), 133
Theodore (Gay), 152
William, 133
OTIS
Maria L. (West), 83
Maua L. (West), 123
S. Leander, 83
Samuel L., 123
OWEN
____ (____), 20, 21
David, 20, 21
Deborah (Holdrige), 74
Elijah, 74
family, 3
George, 150
Isaac, 85
John, 149
Jonah, 149

Josiah, 149
Noah, 9
Sibbell (Horsford), 150
Silas, 9, 20, 21
Talbot, 14
Talburt, 15
Thalia *wed* HAYDEN, 24, 38
PAGE
    Elizabeth (____), 34
    Jonathan, 38
    Joshua, 75
    Margery (Wells), 75
PAINE, PAYNE, PAIN
    ____ (____), 32, 33
    Heamon? T. (____), 114
    J., 32
    John S., 7
    Joseph, 33
    Sarah *wed* WRIGHT, 161
    son, 114
    Stephen, 112, 114, 121, 128
PALMER
    ____ (____), 32
    Abraham, 20, 21
    Anthony, 123
    Elliot, 81
    Emeline *wed* JONES, 120
    family, 3
    Florilla (Sumner), 81
    Joshua, 150
    Lucy, 41
    Martha (Bronzon), 143
    Marthar, 154
    Marthar (Brunson), 143
    Mary, 154
    Mr, 33
    Mrs. Sarah (Taylor), 150
    Samuel, 143, 154
PALMERTER. *SEE* PALMETER
PALMETER, PALMERTER
    Abagail *wed* BUCK, 78
    Phebe *wed* SKINNER, 78
PARISH
    Sarah *wed* WHEELER, 83, 119
PARK. *SEE* PARKS

PARKER
    John Wilks, 150
    Joseph, 7
    Lydia (Horton), 77
    Rebeccah {Stiles}, 150
    Thadeus, 77
PARKS, PARK
    Abijah, 110, 127
    Alfred F., 120
PARMELE
    Ira, 35
PAYNE. *SEE* PAINE
PEASE
    Abial, 78
    Barnabas, 9
    D., 36
    Desdemona (____), 36
    John, 36
    L., 36
    Lemual, 34
    Mary (Loomis), 78
    Oliver, 34
    Persis *wed* SUMNER, 73
PECKHAM
    ____ (____), 17
    Philo, 17
PEEKMAN
    Robe, 91
PERKINS
    ____ (____), 30, 31
    Amos, 9
    Ann M. (____), 108
    Cloha (Manly), 152
    Eliza (Boynton), 156
    James B., 108
    John, 30, 31
    Mary Eliza, 156
    Mr., 26, 27
    Ruth *wed* AYUEL, 139
    Sherlock W, 108
    Shubel, 152
    Timothy Dammick, 156
    William A., 156
PERRIN, PERREN
    Aaron, 64

Andrew, 57
Ann, 60
Ann (Cellogg), 75
Anna, 59
Anna *wed* SUMNER, 78
Asahel, 80
Asel, 65
Betsey (Hammond), 80
Betty, 51, 63
Charlotte, 53
Charlotte *wed* DART, 77
Elisabeth, 49
Elisabeth *wed* DANIELS, 77
Elizabeth (Williams), 73, 87
Ephriam, 47, 86
Hannah (Wright), 79
Hiram, 57
James, 154
Jeremiah, 54, 79
Jerusha, 61
Jerusha *wed* PHELPS, 74
Jerusha *wed* SUMNER, 10, 78
John, 11, 49, 90
Julius, 70
Lidia *wed* TUCK, 149
Lucy *wed* STEVENS, 78
Martha, 57
Mary, 56, 63
Mary (Talcott), 76
Moses, 56, 86
Permelia, 64
Sarah *wed* JAGGER, 74
Solomon, 60, 61, 62, 64, 65, 75
Thomas, 47, 49, 51, 53, 54, 56, 57, 59, 70, 73, 86, 87, 89, 154
William Porter, 57
Zacheriah, 63, 64, 76
PERRY
  Abby Jane (Haugton), 117
  David, 75
  Kezia (Root), 75
  Mary (Raymont), 150
  Mercy *wed* CARD, 81

Morello L., 117
Sarah, 38
Silas, 77, 150
Susan *wed* TOWNSEND, 124
Thankful (Norton), 77
PERSONS
  Juliet M. (Post), 81
  Nathan, 81
PETERS, PETER
  ____ (____), 12, 13, 34
  Abigail, 91
  Abigail (____), 18
  Absalom, 34, 35, 48
  Andrew, 49, 51
  Ann (Barnett), 74
  Annice (____), 93
  Annis *wed* HORTON, 12
  Benisle, 36
  Betsy R. (____), 115
  Caroline (____), 43, 130
  Caroline (Cone), 42
  Ceasar, 22
  Ceaser, 23
  Cesar, 23
  Clarinda (Ballstone), 35
  Clarissa *wed* WELLS, 77
  D., 36
  Daniel McEntire, 41
  Daniel Phelps, 65
  daughter, 114
  Edward, 115
  Elizabeth (____), 36, 89
  Elizabeth (Scaif), 37
  Emily (____), 114
  Hannah, 97
  Hannah (____), 36, 114
  Hannah (Trumbull), 77
  Harry, 114
  Henry, 12, 13, 164
  J., 9, 18
  J. P., 44
  J.S., 36
  Jane, 45
  Jane Scaif, 44
  Jephthan, 50

John, 9, 14, 15, 43, 47, 48, 49, 50, 51, 52, 54, 56, 74, 88, 89, 91, 149
John H., 19
John Hugh, 18
John Jr., 154
John S., 2, 7
Jonathan, 20, 21, 42, 92
Joseph, 45, 76
Joseph P., 37
Joseph Phelps, 52
Joseph's infant, 89
Leverett, 83, 114
Lydia, 64
Lydia (____), 9, 88
Lydia (Adams), 164
Lydia wed BALDWIN, 74
Lydis (Phelps), 77
Marcey, 154
Margit, 47
Mary, 50
Mary (Marks), 149
Mary wed JUDD, 74
Mercy wed BEBE, 76
Mrs Elisabeth (Murrey), 149
Mrs. Abigail, 19
Phoebe Sutton?, 9
Phoebe wed SUTTON, 9
Samuel, 3, 30, 31, 32, 50, 77, 93
Samuel A., 44
Sarah (Wells), 76
Sarah Poplia, 56
Sim (____), 22, 23
son, 115
William, 54, 64, 65, 77

PETON
   ____ (____), 45
   John, 45

PETTICE
   Temperance wed BROWN, 79

PHELPS
   ____ (____), 9, 10, 11, 12, 13, 24, 25, 27, 28, 29, 38, 40, 44, 45

Aaron, 10, 14, 15, 151
Aaron, Jr., 152
Abbey (Warner), 117
Abel, 28
Abiah wed TALLCOTT, 73
Abiatha wed POST, 28
Abigail, 155
Abigail (____), 32, 33
Abil, 29
Abitha, 155
Abitha wed POST, 74
Adeenah wed WATERS, 151
Albert, 36
Alexander, 8
Almira (____), 108
Amos, 37
Anna, 28, 29, 48, 62
Anna (____), 26, 27
Anna (Jones), 77
Anna wed BROWN, 76, 97
Anna wed HUNT, 79
Asabel, 74, 156
Asell, 155
Ashael, 13
Augustus, 108
Azubah, 47
Azubah wed CASE, 75
Bariah, 65
Barret, 60
Bathsheba, 48
Benjamin, 12, 13, 34, 44, 45
Buly, 87
Capt., 89
Capt.'s Negro child, 87
Charles C., 108
Christian wed DEWEY, 74
Cornelas, 155
Dan, 129
Daniel, 8, 38, 41, 52, 87
daughter, 112
David, 109, 112, 114, 119, 127
Debarough (____), 17
Deborah, 51, 54
Deborah (____), 16

Deborah (Mann), 77
Deborah *wed* NORTON, 77, 92
Dolly, 41
E., 17
Eleazer, 16, 32, 49, 76, 77
Elihu, 85, 150
Elijah, 155
Elisah, 155
Elizabeth (____), 34, 112, 114
Elizabeth (Beach), 150
Erastus, 34, 40
Esther, 56
Eunice (Gurley), 152
Eva Josephine, 114
Ezekiel, 40
family, 3
Frederic, 16, 17
Freny, 155
George, 117
Hannah, 9, 155
Hannah (____), 18
Hannah (____) (Post), 77
Hannah (Horton), 76
Hannah (Post), 77
Ichabod, 9, 10, 11, 20, 21, 47, 48, 51, 52, 54, 55, 56, 58, 59, 62, 74, 77, 87, 89, 92, 155
Ichabod Trumbull, 59, 87
Ichabod's child, 88
Irene *wed* TILLETSON, 158
Ireny, 155
J., 34, 36
Jerusha (Perrin), 74
John C., 40, 126
Jonah, 55, 56, 74
Joseph, 8, 9
Joshua, 8, 24, 25
Louisa (____), 130
Lucinda, 36, 54
Lucy, 56
Lucy A. *wed* WEBSTER, 123
Lydia, 55
Lydia *wed* PETERS, 77

Martha, 130
Martha (Trumbull), 74, 89
Martha *wed* TRUMBULL, 73, 85
Mary, 58
Mary Molly, 59
Mrs Seenah *wed* WATERS, 151
Mrs Zeruah *wed* COUDRE, 151
Mrs. Hannah, 19
Nathaniel, 4, 8, 48, 49, 51, 53, 54, 55, 87, 155
Noah, 52, 85, 155
Oliver, 39, 125
Ozias, 40, 128, 133
Patty, 42, 43
Peleg, 55, 85
Rachel, 51
Reuben, 10
Roger, 14, 15, 28, 29, 32, 39, 77
Roger L., 112
Roger S., 128
Roger's dau, 66
Roxelanie *wed* COLBURN, 76
Roxsa, 60
Roxsalona, 53
Royce, 8
Ruba, 65
Ruben, 11
Sally *wed* ATHERTON, 79
Sarah, 22, 23, 52, 56
Sarah (Mack), 74
Solomon, 9
Susan C. *wed* BACKUS, 37
Sylvanus, 16, 17, 26, 27
Thankful (Post), 151
Theron, 11
Therzy (Brown), 133
Timothy, 2
Timothy 3rd, 155
Ulrica E. *wed* SWAN, 81
Uzziel, 42, 125
William, 18, 19, 36

Zilpah *wed* TRUMBULL, 74
PIERCE
  Hannah (Case), 162
PINNEO
  Hannah *wed* DUNHAM, 73
PINNEY
  Abby L. (Strong), 82
  Carrie *wed* GRISWOLD, 83
  Isaac, 155
  Oliver, 155, 156
  Roswell G., 82
PIPER
  Josiah, 90
  Lucy (Daniels), 78
  Samuel, 78, 90
PITKIN
  Abigail (Lothrop), 77
  Mary, 65
  Paul, 65, 66, 77
  Rebekah, 66
POLLEY. *SEE* POLLY
POLLY, POLLEY
  Abigail, 48
  Ann, 50
  Ann *wed* COOX, 73
  Daniel, 48, 49, 50, 51, 53, 55, 86, 156, 162
  Hannah, 49, 53, 86, 156
  Lydia *wed* WATERS, 73
  Rachel (____), 156
  Rachel (Loomis), 162
  Thomas, 55
POMEROY, POMROY
  ____ (____), 12, 13, 24, 25
  Benjamin, 3, 13
  Elihu, 8
  Josiah, 20, 21
  Mr., 47, 49, 50, 54
  Ralph, 24, 25, 26, 27
  Rev. Dr., 12
POMPSON. *SEE* THOMPSON
POMROY. *SEE* POMEROY
PORN___
  Margaret *wed* JONES, 148
PORTER
  ____ (____), 10, 11, 19, 32, 40
  ____ *wed* BLISS, 43
  Abigail (Strong), 75
  Anna, 22, 23, 127
  Asahel, 32, 33
  Bela, 26, 27
  Charles, 36
  Daniel, 155
  daughter, 45
  David, 44, 45, 80
  David's child, 96
  Epaphroditus, 110, 127
  Esther *wed* D[UN?], 163
  Fanny, 107, 135
  Fanny (____), 35
  Frances *wed* HEWETT, 120
  Gaylord, 32, 33
  George W., 109
  Hannah, 155
  Hannah (____), 97
  Hannah (Gear), 80
  Increase, 10, 11, 32, 33, 34, 47
  J., 36
  Jasper, 118
  Jerusha (Sumner), 80
  John, 37
  John 2nd, 155
  John Jr., 155
  Jonah, 30
  Jonah 2nd, 31
  Josephine E., 107, 135
  Judah, 43
  Jude, 40
  Lidia *wed* TARBOX, 152
  Lovinda C.(____), 108
  Marion J. *wed* TREAT, 83
  Mary, 47, 155
  Mary C. (Bissell), 118
  Mary C. (Buell), 118
  Mary L., 44
  Mercy, 155
  Mrs Salla *wed* BISSELL, 151
  Nehemiah, 19, 75, 80

Patience *wed* ROOT, 163
Polly, 24, 25
Reuben, 20, 21
Royal, 107, 135
Sarah, 28, 29
Sarah (Kilburn), 73
Sarah A. (Denison), 117
Selden T., 117
Simeon, 73
Thomas, 155
William 2nd, 108, 110, 120, 127

POST
____ (____), 25, 29, 31, 35
A.K., 128
Aaron, 61
Abagail, 61, 63
Abel P., 83, 113, 115, 121
Abiatha (Phelps), 28
Abiel Sherman Geer?, 2
Abigail, 44, 45, 62, 86
Abigail (Abby), 80
Abitha, 59
Abitha (____), 93
Abitha (Phelps), 74
Abraham, 2
Adaline, 37
Albert Warner, 109
Alfred B., 40
Alfred K., 129
Almira (____), 111
Amos, 41
Anna, 35, 56, 86
Anna Cemantha, 2
Anna E. *wed* NASH, 124
Anna *wed* BENTON, 2
Arunah, 81, 96, 97
Asahel, 35, 94, 97
Asahel's child, 93
Augustus, 24
Bela, 42, 43
Benjamin, 58, 86
Betsey, 68
Betsey *wed* HOLCOM, 79
Bissel E., 108

Cap't E., 25
Capt., 89
Caroline Matilda Fox, 2
Charles, 45
Charlotte Root?, 2
child, 155
Clarissa, 57, 63
Clarissa (Brown), 81
Clarissa *wed* BROWN, 79
Comfort *wed* WRIGHT, 75
Daniel, 55
David, 20, 21, 35, 39, 47, 64, 65, 66, 68, 92, 97
David W., 32, 33, 94
David Warner, 64
Deborah, 70
Deborah (____)(Tarbox), 89
Deborah (Curtice), 86
Deborah *wed* WEBSTER, 74, 92
Destamena, 63
Dinah, 53
Dinah (Brown), 87, 142
Dinah *wed* CULVER, 77
Diodate, 45, 64
Dorothy, 51
Dorothy *wed* ABENS, 77
Ebenezer, 45
Eldad, 50, 53, 55, 56, 57, 156
Eleanor (____), 2
Eleazer, 44, 80
Electa M. (Lucas), 81
Elijah, 54, 66, 89
Elisabeth, 52, 59, 61
Elisabeth (Culver), 76
Eliza (____), 108, 114
Elizabeth, 87, 88
Elizabeth (Bissel[l]), 2, 73
Elizabeth Jr., 45
Elonor *wed* HUTCHINSON, 74
Ephriam, 60
Esther, 58, 60, 89
Esther *wed* WARD, 74
Ezekiel, 50, 57, 155

Ezekiel A., 68, 69, 70, 71, 72, 80, 81, 92, 93
Ezekiel A[u]gustus, 60
Ezekiel A's infant, 92
Ezekiel Lavius, 72
Ezekiel's infant, 92
family, 3
Flavius Augustus, 71
Frederic B., 115
George, 93
George Washington, 62
Gideon, 2, 54
Hannah, 16, 50, 59, 65
Hannah (____), 24, 91, 92
Hannah (Case), 156
Hannah (Geer), 24, 92
Hannah (Hosmer), 2
Hannah (Mrs.) *wed* PHELPS, 77
Hannah L. *wed* SHATTUCK, 80
Hannah Lencey, 68
Hannah *wed* BARBER, 140
Hannah *wed* FORD, 80
Harriet M. *wed* KEENEY, 82
Harriot Mariah, 71, 93
Harriot Marilla, 71
Henrietta M. *wed* BIDWELL, 82
Henrietta Manervy, 71
Henry, 59, 84
Ichabod, 21, 59, 68, 92, 109
Ichabod W., 20
infant son, 128
Ira, 134
Israel, 53
J., 34
James, 9, 75, 89
James' infant, 88
Jazaniah, 2, 52, 55, 56, 73, 86
Jedediah, 22, 23, 47, 48, 50, 51, 59, 60, 63, 65, 66, 86, 89, 92, 97
Jedediah G., 69
Jeremiah, 2, 61

Jeremiah Hammond?, 2
Jerusha (Daniels), 81
Joel, 20, 21, 32, 36, 55, 57, 58, 60, 61, 63, 74, 87, 88, 89, 92, 93, 94, 149, 154, 155, 156, 162
Joel's child, 87
Joel's infant, 86
John, 30, 31, 51, 52, 53, 54, 76, 85, 86, 96, 97
John H., 71, 81, 93, 108
John Henry, 66, 94
Jordan, 56, 57, 59, 60, 62, 63, 64, 89
Joseph, 16, 24, 25, 68, 91, 92, 95
Joseph Otis, 55, 81
Joshua, 64, 67
Julia D., 126
Julia M. *wed* PERSONS, 81
Katherine, 52, 85
Katherine (____), 86
Levi, 55, 96
Levina (____), 109
Louisa (West) *wed* NICHOLS, 81
Lucy, 55
Lucy (____), 94
Lucy (Rockwell) (McKall), 156
Lucy (Rollo), 79
Lucy 2nd (Rockwell) (McKall), 149
Lydia, 54, 59
Lydia (____), 114
Lydia *wed* GILBERT, 58, 73, 87
Martha (____), 66
Martha (Warner), 39
Mary, 51, 55
Mary (Chase), 2
Mary (Jordan), 2
Mary (Prat), 76
Mary (Thompson), 86

Mary Ann *wed* BUELL, 82, 113
Mehetable (____), 89
Melissa (Huxford) (Root), 84
Melisunt, 64
Mindwell, 54, 60, 87
Molly, 56
Molly (____), 30
MOLLY *wed* HUTCHINSON, 28, 93
Mrs. Mary *wed* NEWCOMB, 149
Norman P., 114
Norton, 114
Patience (____), 34, 97
Peter, 51, 53, 54, 55, 56, 58, 59, 60, 61, 62, 86, 87
Peter's child, 88
Phebe, 52
Phebe *wed* BISSEL, 26
Phebe *wed* TRUMBULL, 73, 85
Phineas, 35
Phineas B., 40
Polly, 16, 17, 91
Polly C? *wed* HUTCHINSON, 81
Polly Caroline?, 2
Rachel, 55
Russell, 56, 114
Ruth, 59
Sally (____), 30
Sally (Sumner), 81, 93
Sally Sumner, 71
Samuel, 60, 70, 79
Samuel Edwin, 2
Sarah, 55
Sarah (Bushnell), 74, 88, 154, 155, 162
Sarah A. (____), 115
Sarah A. (Rollo), 83, 113, 121
Sarah S. *wed* GILBERT, 83
Sarah *wed* GILBERT, 119
Sarah *wed* ROSE, 154
Sena (Brockway), 80
Sibil, 48, 57
Solomon, 67
son, 114
Sophia, 66
Stephen, 2, 58, 87
Sybil *wed* LUTHER, 12, 76, 90
Thankful (Wells), 75
Thankfull *wed* PHELPS, 151
Thomas, 9, 18, 19, 28, 29, 59, 60, 61, 74, 76, 87, 88, 91, 93, 142, 155
Weltha *wed* WARNER, 80
Welthy Lauretta, 94
William Alfred, 44
POWERS
    ____ (____), 10, 11
    Abigail (Barber), 142
    Benjamin, 79
    Eliza (Amos), 79
    Harry, 95
    Lawrence, 142
    Martin, 10, 11
PRAT. *SEE* PRATT
PRATT, PRAT
    David, 54
    Huldah, 50
    James, 50, 51, 54
    Mary *wed* POST, 76
PRENTICE, PRENTISS
    Andrew, 82, 113, 121
    Calvin A., 84
    Calvin Andrew, 111
    Clarissa V. (____), 111
    Clarissa V. (Hutchinson), 82
    Rosa D. (Strickland), 84
    Sarah H. *wed* BURT, 84
PRENTISS. *SEE* PRENTICE
PUFFER
    ____ (____), 9
    Eleazer, 35
RACE IDENTIFIED, 2, 11, 24, 25, 29, 31, 33, 42, 43, 45, 50, 54, 55, 58, 59, 60, 69, 72, 75, 78, 86, 87, 89, 90, 91, 92, 93, 94, 95, 96, 107, 114, 118, 121,

122, 125, 130, 146, 150, 151, 153, 157, 164
RAMSDALE
  William, 41
RANDAL. *SEE* RANDALL
RANDALL, RANDAL
  Abby A., 126
  Abby A. (____), 40, 108
  Abby S., 108, 126
  Erastus, 40
  Erastus R., 108
  Sarah J. *wed* GILLETT, 116
  Sarah M., 108
RATHBONE. *SEE* RATHBUN
RATHBUN, RATHBONE
  Angeline (____), 114
  Anthony, 38
  Charles C., 113
  George, 38
  Harriet *wed* WHITE, 135, 161
  Huldah Ann *wed* LATHAM, 117
  Mary Jane, 113
  Orin, 45
  Orrin, 44
  Spencer, 40, 128
RAWLIN
  Larance, 76
  Thankful (Hutchinson), 76
RAYMOND, RAYMONT
  Mary *wed* PERRY, 150
  Mrs Lucy *wed* CULLUM, 149
  Sibel *wed* ARCHER, 149
RAYMONT. *SEE* RAYMOND
REED[E]
  ____ (____), 18, 19, 30, 31
  Daniel, 18, 19, 22, 23, 30, 31, 35
  daughter, 29
  Eben, 29
  Ebenezer's dau, 28
  Henry, 80
  Laura (Sumner), 80
RHODE ISLAND, 122, 130
  Scituate, 120

RICHARD. *SEE* RICHARDS
RICHARDS, RICHARD
  ____, 22
  Charles, 94
  Grace, 96
RICHISON
  Martain, 159
RIDER
  Amy (Bill), 133
  Zelotes, 133, 134
RIGHT. *SEE* WRIGHT
RILEY
  Hannah (Youngs), 74
  Isaac, 74
RIPLEY
  Lova (Norton), 76
  Peter, 76
RISLEY, WRISLEY
  ____ (____), 37
  Florenda *wed* WEST, 81
  Florinda *wed* FINLEY, 79
  Hannah (____), 86
  Job, 37
  Mary P., 128
ROAD[E]
  Horace, 16
  Horris, 17
ROBINSON
  Benjamin, 156
  Peter, 74
  Sarah (Buck), 74
ROCKWELL
  Lucy 2nd *wed* MCKALL, 149
  Lucy *wed* MCKALL, 156
ROGER. *SEE* ROGERS
ROGERS, ROGER
  ____ (____), 12, 13, 19
  Ammi, 4
  Evan, 4, 12, 13
  Josiah, 40
  Mr., 13
  Nathaniel, 160
  Samuel, 39, 125
  Theoda (Miner), 160
ROLLO

Abagail, 48
Apollos, 61, 79
Augustus, 66, 81
Barbarry (Allen), 78
Betsey (Wass), 79
Ebenezer, 164
Elisabeth, 89
Elisabeth *wed* LOTHROP, 75
Eunice *wed* HALL, 164
Hannah, 50
Hannah *wed* MCCULLOCK, 76
John, 48, 49, 50, 51, 58, 68, 78, 86
John Hall, 59
John N., 88
John Noble, 62
Joseph, 65, 78
Joseph Allen, 65
Judith, 51
Lucinda, 70
Lucy, 61
Lucy (Hall), 75, 89
Lucy Ann, 70
Lucy *wed* POST, 79
Martha (Horton), 81
Mary, 61, 65
Mary (Wells), 76
Mary *wed* JUDD, 75
Mercy, 63
Mercy *wed* ELLIS, 79, 92
Patience, 48
Philomelia (Trumbull), 78
Rachel *wed* DAVIS, 74
Ralph R., 70, 71, 92
Ralph Rodolphus, 62, 70
Samuel, 47
Samuel Augustus, 71
Sarah, 95
Sarah A. *wed* GOSLEE, 83
Sarah A. *wed* POST, 83, 113, 121
Sibil Emeline, 70
Susannah (Usher), 164
Walter, 49, 61, 62, 91
Weltor, 76

William, 58, 59, 61, 62, 63, 65, 66, 68, 75, 86, 89, 90
William Egbert, 71
William Henry, 70, 92
Zacheriah, 94
Zecheriah's child, 89
Zerubebel, 47, 48

ROOT
____ (____), 12, 13, 32, 33, 34, 41
Abial, 24, 25
Abigail *wed* TALCOTT, 91
Abijah, 150
Anna (Filer), 146
Asahel, 47
Benjamin, 12, 13, 53, 61, 63, 65, 90
Betsey (Jackson), 81
Caleb, 12, 13, 30, 31, 163
Chancey, 38
Charity (Jones), 150
Charlotte, 2
Chauncey L., 81
Chauncey L.'s child, 96
Cynthia M. (Sumner), 81
Dan, 146
Daniel, 48, 49, 51, 53, 59, 61, 85, 88
Daniel's child, 87
Deborah (Buck), 74
Deborah (Sumner), 80
Ebenezer, 74
Edward, 59, 78
Eleanor *wed* HILLS, 163
Elijah, 61
Elisabeth, 61
Elisha, 80
Elizabeth, 96
Emeline L. *wed* WELLS, 83
Emily M. *wed* CHITTENDEN, 122
Esther (____), 129
Ezekiel, 51
Florilla S. *wed* COLLINS, 83
Hannah (____), 15

Hattie (Church), 83
Ira, 34, 66, 134
Jacob, 47, 49
Jemima (Norton), 16, 17
Jerusha, 68
Jerusha A. *wed* SMITH, 120
Joel, 97
John, 39, 49
Jonah, 79
Jonathan, 150
Joshua, 32, 33, 41, 48, 61, 65, 66, 68, 81, 89, 95
Kezia *wed* PERRY, 75
Levina (Gillet), 150
Louisa D. *wed* HUTCHINSON, 83
Lucy, 49
Lucy *wed* BISHOP, 79
Lydia *wed* WATERS., 73
Mary, 62
Mehitable *wed* JAGGER, 74, 86
Melissa (Huxford) *wed* POST, 84
Mindwell, 61
Mrs Abigail *wed* MORE, 150
Naomi, 49
Naomi *wed* INGRAHAM, 76
Olive, 24, 25
Patience (Porter), 163
Patience *wed* OLCOTT, 133
Polley wed STRICKLAND, 152
Polly *wed* GILBERT, 79
Rachel, 58
Rachel *wed* BILL, 75
Rhoda, 65, 89
Rhoda (Finley), 134
Rhoda *wed* BABCOCK, 82
Sally (Root), 79
Sally *wed* ROOT, 79
Samuel, 83
Sarah, 88, 125
Sarah (____), 39
Sarah J. *wed* CARPENTER, 83

Solomon, 42, 58, 59, 61, 62, 63
Thankful (Shattuck), 78
ROSE
  Desiah *wed* MANNING, 152
  Fred, 154
  Hannah *wed* STARK, 163
  Josiah, 7, 88
  Sarah (Post), 154
ROSWELL, ROSELL, ROSWEL
  ____ (____), 23
  Mahetable (Allen), 77
  Nehemiah, 77
  Nehemiah's child, 89
ROUVIERE
  Hylday (Howard), 133
  Lewis, 133
ROW
  Elisabeth, 57
  Elisabeth (Bill), 75
  Esther (Mack), 74
  James, 74
  John, 48, 49, 57, 75, 156
  Maana, 49
  Martha, 48
  Mary (Williams), 156
ROWLEE. *SEE* ROWLEY
ROWLEY, ROWLE[E]
  Abijah, 20, 21, 63, 73, 76
  E. Patrick, 116
  Elisabeth, 63
  Elisabeth (Culver), 76
  Elisabeth *wed* MACK, 75
  Elizabeth (Fuller), 157
  Eunice (Cooper), 76
  Hannah (____), 20, 21, 92
  Hannah (Curtice), 73
  Martha, 14
  Mary (____), 116
  Mary (Cone), 34
  Miriam *wed* MUNSON, 74
  Moses, 157
  Samuel, 86
  son, 116
  Thankful *wed* HUBBARD, 75

Thomas, 76
Walter, 15
William, 10, 11
RUDE
  Betsey, 156
  Horace, 156
  Storan, 156
  Sukey (____), 156
RUSS
  Charity *wed* GOTT, 17, 162
RUSSEL. *SEE* RUSSELL
RUSSELL, RUSSEL
  ____ (____), 14, 15
  Esther (Dunham), 75
  Jacob, 66, 75
  John, 14, 15
  Levi, 12, 13
  Obediance, 66
  Polly, 15
  Robert, 32, 33
RYDER
  Georgia (Talcott), 83
  Henry C., 83
RYLE
  Hulda (____), 156
  Jonth, 156
SACHEM
  Uncas, 5
SALLET. *SEE ALSO* LAWTETTE
  Sally *wed* BROWN, 151
SAMPSON
  Peter, 146
SAUNDERS
  child, 97
  Julia A., 37
SAVERY. *SEE* SAVORY
SAVORY, SAVERY
  John, 14
  Joseph, 26, 27
  Solomon, 22, 23
SAWTELLE. *SEE ALSO* SALLET
  Mary E. *wed* SMITH, 122
SAWYER, SAYER
  ____ (____), 9, 90
  Anne, 139

Benjamin, 58, 75
Deek, 33
Delight *wed* MERRILS, 73
Edward, 85, 156
Elisabeth *wed* ELLIS, 74
family, 3
Isaac, 156
Jacob, 156
John, 9, 89, 157
Mariann, 58
Mary *wed* ELLIS, 73
Moses, 157
Prudence *wed* BROWN, 75
Sarah (Dewey), 75
Stephen, 139
Susannah (____), 139
SAXTON, SEXTON
  Anna (Horton), 18
  Anna (Houghton), 19
SAYER. *SEE* SAWYER
SCAIF
  Elizabeth, 37
SCOTT
  Melicent (Mack), 78
  Samuel, 78
SCRIPTURE
  Dwight, 83
  Harriet (West), 83
SEELEY
  Mabel (Horton), 79
  Nehemiah, 79
SELDEN
  Sylvester, 3, 36, 134
SEXTON. *SEE* SAXTON
SHADOCK. *SEE* SHATTUCK
SHALER
  ____ (____), 86
  Hannah (____), 139
SHATTUCK, SHADOCK
  Gilbert, 80
  Hannah L. (Post), 80
  Josiah, 80
  Pethena (Wells), 80
  Thankful *wed* ROOT, 78
SHELDON

H. Waters, 160
SHELDON
   H. Waters, 159
SHEPARD, SHEPHERD
   child, 95
   Eleanor *wed* MARTAIN, 76
   Elliner, 49
   George C., 4
   Israel, 50
   James, 134
   Mary, 51
   Rachel (Hutchinson), 73
   Sally *wed* Sprague, 80
   William, 49, 50, 51, 73
SHEPERSON
   Nathaniel, 157
SHEPHERD. *SEE* SHEPARD
SHIFFORS
   Nathaniel, 139
   Nathaniel J, 139
   Rachel, 139
SHIPMAN
   family, 3
   Martha, 34, 52
   Samuel, 7, 52
   Sarah, 10, 11, 52
   Sibil *wed* MARTINDALE, 73
   Temperance *wed* HORTON, 73
   William, 2
SHIRTLIFF
   Abigail (Webster), 81
   Jonathan, 81
SHORT
   Dorathy *wed* WRIGHT, 152
SILLS. *SEE ALSO* STILES
   Abigill, 157
   Nathan, 157
SIMONS, SIMONDS
   Luta Ann, 70
   Samuel, 7, 39, 70
SIMS
   ____ (____), 12, 13
   Edward, 160
   Mary (White), 160
SKINNER
   ____ (____), 13, 24, 25, 34
   Addi, 63
   Anna (White), 151
   Anna *wed* NILES, 153
   Benjamin, 4
   David, 4, 12, 13, 36
   Ebenezer, 54, 59, 61, 63, 74, 88
   Elisabeth, 57
   Elizabeth (Merril), 73
   Elizabeth *wed* BEACH, 143
   Elizur, 56
   Esther, 58
   Eunice, 54
   Eunice (Culver), 74
   Ezekiel, 55, 164
   Isaac, 34
   Israel, 50
   Jacob, 78
   John, 50, 52, 53, 54, 56, 57, 58, 59, 73
   John's infant, 87
   Joseph, 24, 25, 163
   Josiah, 55
   Mary (Norton), 80
   Mary *wed* MERRIL, 73
   Oliver, 152
   Phebe, 61
   Phebe (Palmeter), 78
   Salla (Brown), 152
   Salmon, 53
   Samuel, 45, 80
   Sarah (Wiatt), 164
   Stephen, 26, 27
   Timothy, 54
   Waitstil, 61
   William., 151
SMITH
   ____ (____), 42, 43
   Dea[co]n, 43
   Hannah (Wells), 80
   Jerusha (____), 130
   Jerusha A. (Root), 120
   June (Cuson), 123
   Lura (Jones), 152

Lyman, 122
Mary (Mack), 82
Mary E. (Sawtelle), 122
Nathan, 42
Obadiah K., 80
Peter S., 120
Rhoda, 42
Rhoda (____), 130
Samuel H., 123
Spencer, 82
Thomas, 30, 31
Zadock, 152
SNOW
  Aaron, 119
  Ebenezer, 153
  Lucinda (Gott), 153
SPARROW
  Abigail (Strong), 133
  James, 133
SPENCER
  Levi, 81
  Martha (Mack), 81
SPRAGUE
  Augusta (Dickinson), 83
  Benjamin, 36
  Henry, 83
  John, 80
  Julia (Birge), 36
  Sally (Shepherd), 80
STALLWORTHE
  Mary *wed* WATERS, 159
STANTON, STAUNTON
  Albert L., 109, 112
  Charles S., 112, 128
  James, 109
  Lavina (____), 112
  Lurania (____), 109
STAPLES
  ____ (____), 42
  Emily *wed* WEIR, 118
  Laura L. *wed* GEER, 119
  Mrs. ____ (____), 131
  Sarah *wed* STRONG, 82
STARK
  Dick, 163

  Hannah (Rose), 163
STARR
  Alphonso B., 107
  Betsey (____), 108
  E.R., 147
  James M., 107
STAUNTON. *SEE* STANTON
STEEL
  John, 50
STEVENS
  Lucy (Perrin), 78
  Mary, 58
  Mary (Wayers), 74
  Thomas, 67, 78
  Timothy, 58, 74
  William Dart, 67
STEWART, STUARD
  James, 157
  John, 157
  Thomas, 157
STILES
  Dr. ____, 7
  Rebeccah *wed* PARKER, 150
  Sarah *wed* CARVER, 150
STONE
  Margaret *wed* MOSYER, 153
STRICKLAND
  Abby M. *wed* NORTON, 84
  Alfred R., 113, 115
  Carrie Martha, 115
  Clara (West), 83
  Clarence D., 83
  daughter, 111
  Elisha, 152
  Florence (Bolles), 84
  Hettie Elisabeth, 113
  Ida B. *wed* HUTCHINSON, 84
  Jonathan, 126
  Julius J., 84
  Martha E. (____), 113, 115
  Matilda (____), 111
  Melissa (____), 108
  Polley (Root), 152
  Rosa D. *wed* PRENTICE, 84

Thompson, 108, 109, 111, 119, 127
STRONG
 ___ (___), 14, 15, 33, 43
A., 24
Abby L. *wed* PINNEY, 82
Abby Louisa, 71
Abigail *wed* PORTER, 75
Abigail *wed* SPARROW, 133
Adeline A. *wed* NICHOLS, 82
Adeline Amelia, 71
Adonijah, 62
C. Jane *wed* RESTON, 119
Caroline A. *wed* LATHAM, 81
Caroline Adelia, 71
Chauncey, 42, 130
child, 109
Clarissa (Bissell), 80
Cyrus, 44
David, 30, 31, 80
Ebenezer, 152
Edwin, 42, 43
Edwin W., 82, 115
Eleazer, 14, 15, 24, 25, 32, 33, 79
Eleazer B., 45, 71, 72, 94
Eleazer B.'s infant, 91
Eleazer E., 82
Elijah, 80, 81
Emely, 71
Florenda, 71
Florenda *wed* BLISS, 82
Franklin H., 112
George, 44
Harriet N. *wed* HYDE, 82
Harriot Newell, 71
Henry, 24, 25, 62
Henry Cushman, 72
Humphrey H., 109, 112
Humphrey Hutchinson, 71
Jerusha (___), 109
Jerusha *wed* ADAMS, 82
Jesse, 52
John, 77, 163
Joseph H., 109

Judson, 109
Lu___ (___), 81
Lucy (Finley), 80
Lucy (Warner), 82
Lydia (Sumner), 77
Lyman, 3
Mary (___), 109
Mary A. *wed* ELY, 81
Mary Ann, 71
Mary E. (___), 112
Mrs., 43
Norman O, 91
Olive, 52
Phineas, 8
Polly (Day), 152
Sarah (___), 42, 115, 130
Sarah (Staples), 82
son, 115
Thankful (Brown), 163
William Henry, 71, 96
Zenas, 7
Zilpha (___), 32
Zilpha (Hutchinson), 79, 94
STUARD. *SEE* STEWART
SUMMERS. *SEE ALSO* SUMNER
SUMMERS, SUMMER
 ___ (___), 30, 31
Elizabeth (___), 15
James, 152
Phena (Thomas), 152
Ruben, 15
Thomas, 30, 31
SUMNER. *SEE ALSO* SUMMERS
 ___ (___), 11
Abigail, 56, 60, 87
Anna, 51
Anna (Perrin), 78
Benjamin, 52, 53, 54, 55
Benjamin S., 113
Benjamin T., 108, 115
Benjamin Thomas, 69
Betsey, 64
Betsey *wed* WEST, 79
Charles B., 113
Clament, 51

Cynthia M. *wed* ROOT, 81
Cynthia Mariah, 68
daughter, 115
David Hubard, 54
Deborah, 65
Deborah *wed* ROOT, 80
Ebenezer, 73
Elisabeth, 49, 51
Elisabeth *wed* COOK, 76
Elisabeth *wed* TAYLOR, 74
Elizabeth (____), 14, 91
Florilla, 69
Florilla *wed* PALMER, 81
George Oliver, 68
Hannah, 49
Hannah *wed* WARNER, 75
Harvey, 20, 21, 92
Henry, 35, 69, 78, 97
Henry P., 10, 11, 67, 68, 91
Henry Peterson, 59
Henry Tudor, 68
Hiram, 68
Jemima (____), 34
Jemima (Tarbox), 77, 96
Jemima *wed* CARRIER, 79
Jerusha, 67
Jerusha (Perrin), 10, 78
Jerusha *wed* PORTER, 80
John Henry, 55
John's infant, 97
Laura, 67
Laura *wed* REED, 80
Lydia, 51
Lydia *wed* STRONG, 77
Mary, 52, 57, 61, 87
Mary A. *wed* WOODBRIDGE, 82
Mary Ann, 70, 92
Mary E (Buell), 108
Mary E. (____), 113
Mary F. (____), 115
Mary M. *wed* DOAN, 82
Matilda, 68, 91
Mr., 55

Nancy L. *wed* KEENY, 83, 118
Persis (Pease), 73
Prudence, 52
Rebeker (Downer), 74
Reuben, 7, 14, 16, 17, 20, 21, 37, 49, 51, 52, 54, 55, 56, 57, 59, 60, 61, 67, 68, 70, 78, 87, 91, 92
Sally, 67, 71
SALLY *wed* POST, 81, 93
Sibil, 55
Sibil *wed* NORTON, 77
Thomas, 74
W., 34
William, 34, 52, 64, 65, 66, 67, 68, 69, 77, 96, 97
William A[u]gustus, 66
William Benjamin, 53
William Henry, 70
William Orsimus, 69
SUTLIFF
  Abiah, 79
  Clarissa (Webster), 79
SUTTON
  David, 7, 14, 21, 91, 157
  family, 3
  John, 32, 33, 157
  Mary (____), 39
  Phoebe (Peters)?, 9
  Seth, 157
SWAN
  daughter, 108
  John, 39, 81, 108, 126
  Nancy (____), 108
  stillborn, 126
  Ulrica E. (Phelps), 81
  Ulrica Elenora (____), 39
SWEETLAND, SWETLAND
  ____ (____), 17
  Ann (Bond), 73
  Azariah, 16, 17, 26, 27
  Benjamin, 73
  family, 3
  Harriet, 28, 29

Jonathan, 157
Joseph, 161
Lydia *wed* BROWN, 74, 143
Mary (Babcock) *wed*
 WOODWARD, 161
Noah, 157
Peter, 73
Phebe (Wilcox), 73
Sarah *wed* ARCHER, 164
SWETLAND. *SEE* SWEETLAND
TAINTOR
 John, 147
 Sarah (Horsford), 147
TALCOTT. *SEE ALSO* TOLCOTT[E]
TALCOTT, TALLCOT[T]
 ____ (____), 13, 17, 19
 Abagail, 58
 Abiah (____), 159
 Abiah (____) *wed* DURHAM, 159
 Abiah (Phelps), 73
 Abigail (____), 16
 Abigail (Root), 91
 Abigail *wed* HUNTINGTON, 78
 Anna, 52
 Anna *wed* BUCK, 77
 Anne, 158
 Benjamin, 57, 92
 Bennet, 60, 88
 Catherine, 126
 Daniel, 51, 64, 77
 Elizabeth, 88
 Ezra, 59, 88
 Gad, 12, 16, 17, 57, 58, 59, 60, 61, 63, 64, 89, 90, 91, 95
 Georgia *wed* RYDER, 83
 Grace, 12, 13, 60, 90
 Hannah, 63, 89
 Hannah (____), 12, 90
 Harriet Hester, 72
 Harriet Horton, 72
 Harriot (Warner), 28, 93
 Henry Wait Warner, 72
 Hester (____), 94

James, 113
John, 48, 49, 50, 51, 64, 73, 75, 86, 158, 159
Lucy, 49
Lucy *wed* CHAPMAN, 75
Lydia, 64
Lydia (Ellis), 64, 77
Mary, 50, 58
Mary (____), 18, 91
Mary (Carter), 57, 58, 59, 60, 62, 63
Mary *wed* MACK, 75
Mary *wed* PERRIN, 76
Mary *wed* WARNER, 78
Mosely, 61
Rosa (Talcott), 84
Rosa *wed* TALCOTT, 84
Sally *wed* HUTCHINSON, 26, 79, 93
Samuel, 28, 64, 72, 76, 84, 93, 94
Sarah, 62
Susannah, 94
Thomas Blish, 69
Wait, 59, 69
Waitstill, 9
Widow ____ (____), 52
William, 16, 17, 18, 19, 57, 58, 59, 60, 62, 63, 69, 88, 91
William Hubbard, 69
TALLCOT. *SEE* TALCOTT
TALLCOTT. *SEE* TALCOTT
TARBOX. *SEE ALSO* FARBOX
 ____ (____), 12, 13, 18, 19, 24, 25
 Aaron, 164
 Aaron Donelson, 164
 Benjamin, 88
 David, 16, 17
 Deborah (____) *wed* POST, 89
 Deborah *wed* BROWN, 38, 76
 Elish, 19
 Elisha, 18, 152
 family, 3

223

Godfree, 31
Godfrey, 24, 25, 30
Jemima *wed* SUMNER, 77, 96
Jonathan, 164
Lydia (____), 164
Lydia (Porter), 152
Samuel, 158
Solomon, 12, 13, 164
TAYLOR
    ____ (____), 22, 23
Benjamin, 18
Ben'y, 19
Daniel, 77
David, 18, 19, 75
Desire, 36
Elisabeth (Sumner), 74
Elisabeth (Wells), 77
Elizabeth (Lee), 84
Esther (Lee), 82
Eunice *wed* BINGHAM, 84
family, 159
Henry, 82
John, 22, 23, 35, 77
Joseph, 74
Lawrence, 159
Mary *wed*? FULLER, 146
Nancy *wed* JONES, 152
Polly (Wonks), 153
Prudence *wed* GATES, 152
Rebecca, 41
Robert, 153
Rosehannah (Gilbert), 75
Ruhamah (Ellis), 77
Salla *wed* ASHCRAFT, 153
Sarah *wed* ASHCRAFT, 153
Sarah *wed* PALMER, 150
William, 84
TAYON. *SEE ALSO* TRYON
Rupell, 13
TEFFT, TIFT, TIFFE
Hannah A. *wed* JONES, 120
Samuel, 44
TENANT
Avery, 38
Delendia, 127

TERRAQUEOUS BULL, 119
THOMAS
    ____ *wed* ARNOLD, 24
Eunice, 57
Henery, 57
John, 14, 15, 57, 74, 91
Lavina, 94
Lovinia (Brown), 74
Lovinne, 57
Lyman, 72
Phena *wed* SUMMERS, 152
Sarah, 2, 72
THOMPSON, THOMSON, THOMPZON
    ____ (____), 96
Ann *wed* FOOT, 74
daughter, 110, 115
Elias, 115
Emily (____), 115
Emma (____), 110
Ephriam H., 109
Fanny (Bill), 82
Israel, 78
James H., 82
Jard L., 115
John, 159
Lothrop, 110
Mary (____), 109
Mary *wed* POST, 86
Royal A, 110, 118
Royal C., 126
Royal R., 108
Samuel, 110, 127
Sarah (____), 115
Sarah (Foot), 78
Sarah J.(____), 110
son, 109, 115
THOMPZON. *SEE* THOMPSON
THORNTON
Mary, 53
Medad, 53
TICKNOR, TICHNOR
Abalena *wed* HIGGINS, 97
David W., 82
Elizabeth *wed* BROWN, 83

Ellen *wed* JOHNSON, 83
Hannah M. (Gear), 82
TIERNER
  Bartholomew, 150
TIFFE. *SEE* TEFFT
TILDEN
  Ann, 158
  Elizabeth (Brown), 77
  Joseph, 77
  Mercey *wed* BILL, 142
TILLOTSON, TILOTSON,
  TILLETSON
  ____ (____), 86
  Abraham, 158, 159
  Abraham Junr., 159
  Abram, 158
  Benjamin, 53
  Content (____), 158
  Cybil, 159
  Cybil (____), 158
  Darckis, 157
  Darkis, 157
  David, 78, 159
  Elenor (____), 24, 25, 159
  Elezur, 158
  Elisabeth, 56, 159
  Elizabeth (____), 158
  Elizabeth (Brooker), 73
  Elizer, 65, 66
  Elizer Olcot, 65
  family, 138
  Freny, 157
  Irene (Phelps), 158
  Isaac Junior, 157, 158
  Jonathan, 158, 159
  Jonathan Junr, 158
  Joshua, 53, 55, 56, 58, 73,
    157, 158
  Lazir, 157
  Margery, 159
  Martha (____), 87, 158, 159
  Mary, 53
  Mindwell, 58
  Morris, 8, 158, 159
  Rachel, 159

Rebecca (Chamberlin), 159
Sarah, 55, 158, 159
Sarah (____), 159
Sarah (Wells), 78
Sarah *wed* WRIGHT, 158
Sary, 158
Sary (____), 158
Sibil, 158
Sibil (____), 158, 159
Turner, 66
Zeruiah, 158
Zerujah, 158
TILOTSON. *SEE* TILLOTSON
TINNEY
  Henry, 123
  Mary Ann (Barber), 123
TISDALE
  Almira P. (Johnson), 120
  Almire P. (____), 130
  Betsy *wed* FOLEMAN, 153
  Charles H., 120
TISHER
  C.R., 123
TITSOM
  Dar's, 4
TOLCOTT[E]. *SEE ALSO*
  TALCOTT[E]
  ____ (____), 29
  Samuel, 29
TOON
  Chloe (Townsend), 75
  John, 75
TOPLIFF
  Amassa A., 121
  Mary A. (Bascom), 121
TOWNSEND, TOWNZEN
  Alfred, 89
  Alice *wed* MORLEY, 75
  Amasa, 73
  Azubah *wed* WHITE, 76
  Chloe *wed* TOON, 75
  David, 22, 23
  Henry, 40
  James H., 123, 124
  Jonathan, 64, 89, 90, 95

Jonathan's infant, 88
Justin, 64
Lucinda (____), 40
Lucy Ann (Franklin), 123
Marten, 73
Mary (Basset), 77
Nathaniel, 77
Phebe (Ingham), 73
Philomelia, 90
Rhoda (Ingham), 73
Susan (Perry), 124
TOWNZEN. *SEE* TOWNSEND
TRACY
   Eliza *wed* HALL, 83
   Harlow, 84
   Lizzie (Dunham), 84
TRAPP
   Anne *wed* NORTON, 154
TREAT
   ____ (____), 36
   Joseph, 83
   Marion J. (Porter), 83
   Rev. Mr., 36
TROWBRIDGE
   Daniel, 110
   Eliza (____), 110
   John F., 110
TRUDE
   Esther (Loomis), 122
   Thomas, 122
TRUMBULL, TRUMBUL
   ____ (____), 9, 33
   Asaph, 28, 29, 53, 54, 55, 56, 57, 58, 59, 61, 62, 63, 64, 65, 74, 86, 93
   Azubah, 56
   Azubah *wed* HALL, 34, 78
   Benjamin, 9, 65, 73, 85, 90
   Benoni, 73, 74, 85, 86
   Betsey (Elizabeth) *wed* BROWN, 79
   Betsey *wed* BROWN, 94, 143
   Capt., 89
   Clarissa (____), 113
   David, 58, 66, 78
   David W., 19
   David Whiting, 18, 72
   Elisabeth, 62
   Hannah, 53
   Hannah *wed* PETERS, 77
   Jonathan, 16, 61, 72, 92
   Jonathan's infant, 91
   Laura, 113
   Laura *wed* Bissell, 81
   Marget (Warner), 74
   Martha, 64
   Martha (Phelps), 73, 85
   Martha *wed* PHELPS, 74, 89
   Martha *wed* WELLS, 133
   Mary, 54
   Mary Minerva, 72
   Mary *wed* WELLS, 77
   Patta, 66
   Patty, 89
   Phebe (Post), 73, 85
   Philomelia, 61
   Philomelia *wed* ROLLO, 78
   Sally *wed* WARNER, 79
   Sarah, 57, 59, 86
   Thankful (Wells), 78
   Thankful *alias* BALDWIN, 18
   Whiting, 91, 92
   William H., 113
   Zilpah, 55
   Zilpah (Phelps), 74
   Zilpah *wed* WELLS, 77
   Zilpha (____), 32
TRYON. *SEE ALSO* TAYON
   George, 71, 93
   George's infant, 93
   Mary Ann, 71
   William, 93
TUCK
   Lidia (Perrin), 149
   Richard, 23, 149
TURNER
   ____ (____), 36
   Catherine (Adams), 80
   Champion S., 82
   George W., 36, 80

Matilda C. (Fox), 82
TUTTLE
  Austin, 37
TWINING
  Rachel (Jones), 81
  Thomas, 81
TYLER, TYLOR
  Lydia, 163
  Mr., 68
  Royal, 3
USHER
  Susannah *wed* ROLLO, 164
UTAH
  Ogden, 145
VALLET. *SEE ALSO* LAWTETTE
  Sally *wed* BROWN, 151
VERMONT, 67, 133
  Bennington, 160
  Bradford, 162
  Halifax, 160
  Oxford, 148
  Rutland, 147
  South Fairlee, 160
  Strafford, 148
VIBBARDS
  Lydia Clarissa (HORTON), 40
WADSWORTH
  Elisha, 57, 58
  Joseph Wells, 57
  Mary *wed* HALL, 73
  Thankful, 58
WALDEN
  Wiley W., 130
WALDER
  Emma E. (____), 111
  son, 111
WALDO
  Enoch G., 112, 128
  Hannah (____), 131
WALES
  Enoch G., 108
  Jemma E. (____), 108
WALTERS. *SEE ALSO* WATERS
  Mary, 160
  Oliver, 160

WARD
  Esther (Post), 74
  Jedediah, 74
  Sally (____) *wed* GILBERT, 40
WARLAND
  Mary F, 45
  Mr., 4
  William, 45, 122, 123
WARNER
  Abbey *wed* PHELPS, 117
  Abigail (Buell), 81
  Charles H., 130
  Daniel, 75
  Elijah, 81
  Hannah (Sumner), 75
  Harriot *wed* TALCOTT, 28, 93
  Hosea C., 118
  Ichabod, 24, 25, 96
  Ichabod M., 78
  John., 85
  Kirtland, 79
  Lavina P. *wed* FULLER, 118
  Lucy *wed* STRONG, 82
  Lydia Ann (____), 113
  Marget *wed* TRUMBULL, 74
  Martha *wed* POST., 39
  Mary (Talcott), 78
  Mary *wed* HUTCHINSON, 80
  Masse, 28
  Norman P., 113
  Olive M. (Hutchinzon), 83, 122
  Philadelphia (Beach), 118
  Philatheda (____), 129
  Philena (____), 41
  Sally (Trumbull), 79
  Warren, 80
  Weltha (Post), 80
  Will J., 1
  William T., 83, 122
WARREN
  Cyrus, 3
  Esther (Cone), 79
  James, 79
  MRS. Charity, 19

WARTERS. *See* WATERS
WASHBURN
   Mrs Mary *wed* GILLETT, 151
WASHINGTON
   George, 153
   Welthy (Chanberlin), 153
WASHINGTON, D.C., 4
WASS
   Anna *wed* GRISWOLD, 78
   Betsey *wed* ROLLO, 79
   John, 12, 90
   Polly, 12, 90
WATERS
   Adeenah (Phelps), 151
WATERS, WARTERS
   Abner, 48, 49, 50, 52, 53, 55, 73
   Adam, 160
   Benjamin, 53
   Elisha, 160
   Emily (____), 113
   Gideon, 73, 93
   Hiram, 160
   Huldah (Jones), 152
   James, 159
   John, 77
   Joseph Junr., 152
   Lydia, 48
   Lydia (Polley), 73
   Lydia (Root), 73
   Mary, 160
   Mary (____), 160
   Mary (Stalworthe), 159
   Mindwell (Jones), 77
   Miriam, 49
   Mrs Seenah (Phelps), 151
   Olive, 52
   Oliver, 55, 160
   Phebe (Manning), 159
   Phoebe (Beebee) (Judd), 160
   Richard, 159
   Samuel Sr, 159
   Sophia, 160
   Theda,, 160
   Worthy, 160
   Zenus, 151
WATROUS
   Abby (Dingly), 121
   Abby G. (____), 116
   Abby J. (____), 114
   Abby J. (Dingly), 120
   daughter, 116
   Emily, 113
   Emily (____), 114
   Gideon, 28, 29
   Henry, 114, 116, 121
   Ichabod, 81
   Jonathan, 36
   Josiah's infant, 96
   Julia (____), 113
   Julia (Dingley), 119
   Julia E. (Dingley), 83
   Julia Elizabeth, 113
   Levarate, 114
   Leverete T., 113
   Mrs., 96
   Phebe (Freman), 81
   Phebe A. *wed* MCKINNEY, 83
   Simeon F., 83, 119
   Simion F., 113
   son, 114
   William A., 120
WATSON
   Harriet *wed* BENJAMIN, 82
WAY
   ____ (____), 26, 27, 93
   Anna (Gridley), 83
   Charles D., 83
   Clara E. *wed* HANMER, 83
   Clarissa (____), 34
   D. S., 19, 22
   Daniel, 19, 33, 40, 82, 91, 127
   Daniel S., 32, 91
   Daniel S.'s infant, 92
   David, 23
   Elizabeth J. (____), 111
   Elizabeth Jerusha (Welles), 82
   Emma *wed* BECKWITH, 80

Harriet B. (Hutchinson), 82
James A., 83
John H.W., 41, 128
John M., 41, 82, 111
Kate (Chesebro), 83
Maria, 22
Mariah, 23
Mr., 92
son, 111
Thomas, 24, 25, 26, 27, 93
WAYERS
  Mary *wed* STEVENS, 74
WEBSTER
  ____ (____), 30, 31
  Abigail *wed* SHIRTLIFF, 81
  Amelia R. *wed* BRAY, 82
  Augustus, 67
  Betsey, 94
  Bridget, 163
  Carlos H., 123
  Celia Almira, 71
  Clara, 62
  Clarrissa *wed* SUTLIFF, 79
  David, 163
  Deborah, 55
  Deborah (____), 20
  Deborah (Post), 74, 92
  Dorothy, 69
  Dudley, 71
  Elijah, 20, 24, 25, 55, 57, 58, 60, 61, 62, 67, 74, 87, 92
  Elijah Lyman, 67
  Elisabeth (Wilcox), 74
  Ezekiel, 57, 60, 69, 70, 71, 72, 87, 96, 113, 129
  Ezekiel Ela, 96
  Ezekiel Ely, 69
  Joel, 58, 61, 70, 87
  Joel Carlos, 72
  John L., 82
  John Luman, 69
  Jonathan, 74
  Joseph, 80
  Laura, 69
  Laura *wed* WOOD, 82
  Lucy A. (Phelps), 123
  Martha M. *wed* MARTINDALE, 82
  Martha Mariah, 70
  Mary Luesia, 70
  Mary M. (Chapel), 82
  Matilda *wed* NORTON, 82
  Mrs. Anna, 26, 27
  Mrs. Deborah, 21
  Rebekah (Brown), 74
  Rebekah *wed* JONES, 77
  Sally (Gray), 80
  Sarah, 67
  Simeon, 74
  Thomas, 30, 31, 40, 52, 125
  William Chapin, 70
WEIR, WIER
  Alfred F., 128
  Emily (____), 113, 116
  Emily (Staples), 118
  son, 113, 116
  William H., 113
  William W., 116, 118
WELL. *SEE* WELLES
WELLES, WELL[S], WILLS
  ____ (____), 86, 91, 92
  Abiaih (Dunham), 78
  Abigail, 63
  Alfred, 62
  Almira, 24, 25, 92
  Andrew, 45, 133
  Aner, 67
  Anna, 55
  Annar, 57
  Asher, 52
  Austin, 51
  Azzan, 58
  Bateman, 57, 58, 59, 60, 61, 62, 63, 64, 65
  Benjamin Carter, 61
  Capt., 87, 90
  Clarinda *wed* HORTON, 45
  Clarissa (Peters), 77
  Daniel, 48, 61, 64, 65, 76
  Daniel Lothrop, 61

David Trumbull, 66
Don Lewis, 62
Edmond, 19, 58
Edmond Henery, 58
Edmund, 48, 50, 51, 75, 85
Elihu, 60, 62, 63, 75
Elihu Chester, 60
Elijah, 10, 11
Elisabeth, 47
Elisabeth *wed* TAYLOR, 77
Elizebeth Jerusha *wed* WAY, 82
Emeline L. (Root), 83
F.B., 45
family, 3
Frederick, 81
Gardiner, 64
Gaylord, 7
George, 64, 94
George Alfred, 95
George E., 83
Gustavus, 26, 27
Hannah, 47, 65, 66
Hannah (Hutchinson), 75
Hannah (Lothrop), 76
Hannah (Martindale), 79
Hannah *wed* GRANNIS, 75
Hannah *wed* SMITH, 80
Harman, 13
Harmon, 12
Harriot *wed* BRADLEY, 80
Henry, 53, 85
Henry H., 79
Henry Howel, 60
Howel, 59, 87
Isabella, 62
J.H., 38
James, 62, 80, 96
Jane *wed* COOLEY, 83
Jerusha (____), 38
Joel, 54
John, 57, 59, 60, 62, 64
John B., 18, 19, 91
John Bill, 57
John Bill's infant, 90

John H., 87, 94
Joseph, 47, 48, 49, 51, 52, 53, 55, 56, 58, 78
Laura, 64
Leonard, 64
Levina, 66
Lizander, 65
Luana, 63
Lucy, 45
Lydia *wed* MORE, 80
Margery, 48
Margery *wed* PAGE, 75
Maria (Coleman), 81
Martha (Wells), 133
Martha *wed* NORTON, 80
Mary, 24, 25, 61, 63, 92
Mary (____), 19, 87, 90
Mary (Trumbull), 77
Mary *wed* ROLLO, 76
Nabby *wed* GILBERT, 79
Nancy (Corkins), 80
Pethena *wed* SHATTUCK, 80
Phathena, 67
Phebe, 60
Polly *wed* GEAR, 79
Pruda, 66
Prudence *wed* CARRIER, 76
Randolph, 66
Reuben, 12, 13, 77, 92
Rufus C., 33
Russel, 63, 64, 65, 66, 67, 76
Russel Carter, 32
Salle, 65
Sarah, 50, 58
Sarah (Carter), 76
Sarah *wed* PETERS, 76
Sarah *wed* TILLOTSON, 78
Semerimis, 51
Shaler, 52
Shipman, 65, 66, 67, 77
Sila (Wells), 79
Sila *wed* WELLS, 79
Sile, 65
Silve, 54
Thankful, 59

Thankful *wed* POST, 75
Thankful *wed* TRUMBULL, 78
Thomas, 32, 77, 91, 94
Timothy, 49
Trumbull, 79
Welthia (Goodrich), 75
Whiting, 65
Zilpah (Trumbull), 77
Zilpha A., 92
WELLS. *SEE* WILLS, *SEE* WELLES
WEST
   Betsey (Sumner), 79
   Betsey *wed* CARPENTER, 82
   Clara *wed* STRICKLAND, 83
   Florinda (Wrisley), 81
   Francis, 81
   Harriet *wed* SCRIPTURE, 83
   Joshua, 62
   Levi, 26, 27
   Louisa *wed* POST, 81
   Maria L. *wed* OTIS, 83, 123
   Mr., 68
   Nancy (Horton), 79
   Reuben, 79
   Roswell, 79
   Sarah, 62
WHEATON
   ____ (____), 116
   father, 116
   son, 116
WHEELER
   Sarah (Parish), 83, 119
   Sherwood, 83, 119
WHITCOMB
   Clara Cordelia, 113
   Ebn. M., 110
   Harriet (____), 114
   Harriet M. (____), 110, 113
   Jonathan, 110, 114
   Jonathan C., 113
   son, 114
WHITE
   ____ (____), 24, 25, 34, 35, 40, 41, 44
   Aaron, 24, 25

Adela, 135, 161
Adonijah, 7, 76
Alexander, 76
Amanda, 135, 161
Anna *wed* SKINNER, 151
Azrebah (Townsend), 76
Betsey (Archer), 133
Cheney *wed* LONDON, 160
Daniel, 34
daughter, 160
Ebenezer, 160
Edward James, 135, 161
Elisabeth *wed* NORTHUM, 76
Elizabeth Frances, 72
Emma, 110, 135, 161
Eunice *wed* BROWN, 84
family, 3
Fred Kellogg, 135, 161, 162
Frederic, 35
Frederick, 97
George L., 112, 128
Hannah (Kingsbury), 76
Harlan Rathbone, 135, 161
Harriet (____), 135, 161
Harriet (Rathbone), 161
Henry, 44, 74
Isabella Saloma, 135, 164
Jabez L., 38
James, 14, 15, 44, 72, 80, 107, 110, 160
James A., 112, 114, 128, 135, 161
James Alexander, 135, 161, 162
James' child, 107
James Sr., 160
Jerusha (____), 110, 114, 135, 161, 162
Jerusha (Kellogg), 135
John, 133
John Bliss, 135, 161
Joseph, 24, 32, 33, 40
Joseph W., 112, 128
Joseph Waldo, 41
Joseph, Jr, 25

Laura A. *wed* WILKIE, 122
Laura Ann [____], 112
Lucina (Horton), 80
Mary, 135, 162
Mary (Norton), 117
Mary A., 44
Mary *wed* SIMS, 160
Mrs. Charles, 135, 162
Obadiah, 12, 13
Orrin Bushnell, 135, 164
Orrin C., 7
Polly, 41
Rachel (____), 160
Salome (Hibbard), 24
Samuel, 160
Sarah, 24, 25
Sarah (Dewey), 74
Sidney, 135, 161
son, 114
Waldo, 35
William, 41, 160
William Allen, 161
William W., 117
WHITFIELD
  Mr., 5
WHITTLESEY
  ____ (____), 41
WIATT
  Sarah *wed* SKINNER, 164
WICKHAM WICKUM
  Elisebeth (Buell), 79
WICKHAM, WICKUM
  Hezekiah, 79
WICKUM. *SEE* WICKHAM]
WIER. *SEE* WEIR
WILCOX, WILLCOX
  ____ (____), 39, 42, 43
  Abel, 54, 74
  Abel's child, 85
  Asa, 49
  Azubah, 62
  Azubah *wed* DAVIS, 79
  Betsey *wed* DAVIS, 79
  child, 107
  Clarissa Mariah, 70
  Dorcas, 125
  Ebenezer, 60, 85
  Eleazer, 76
  Elihu, 64
  Elisabeth, 61
  Elisabeth *wed* WEBSTER, 74
  Elizabeth (____), 85
  Emeline Cornelia, 72
  Ephriam, 42, 43
  Ezra, 62, 90
  Frances H. (____), 107
  George, 107
  George Manton, 72
  George Oliver, 71, 94
  Gustavus Hammond, 70
  Jane (Gillette), 121
  Jehiel, 58, 59, 60, 61, 62, 63, 64, 75, 90, 95
  Jesse H., 121
  Joel, 2, 43, 44, 109, 118
  John, 47
  Joseph, 151
  Lucy, 48
  Lucy (____), 44
  Lurana Olmstead, 70
  Lydia, 30, 31, 58, 93
  Lydia (Mack), 75
  Martha, 52
  Martha *wed* HALL, 73
  Mary, 59
  Mary (Mack), 76
  Mary *wed* BIDWELL, 81
  Mrs. Sebbel (Wright), 151
  O., 72
  Obadiah, 47, 48, 49, 50, 52, 54, 160
  Oliver, 63, 70, 71, 72, 94
  Phebe, 54
  Phebe *wed* SWETLAND, 73
  Rachel (____), 129
  Sarah, 50
  Steven, 160
  Susanna, 54
  Susanna (Hall), 74
WILKA

____ (____), 42
Parson, 42
WILKIE
　Caroline (____), 129
　Laura A. (White), 122
　W., 120
　Walter, 117, 118, 120, 121, 122
WILLCOX. *SEE* WILCOX
　Lucy Ann (____), 131
WILLEY
　____ (____), 10, 11
　Asa, 10, 11
WILLIAMS
　Edmond, 160
　Elizabeth *wed* PERRIN, 73, 87
　George, 81
　James, 160
　Jerusha (Cone), 81
　Mary, 159
　Mary *wed* ROW, 156
　Nathaniel, 159
WILLIAMS CITY, 161
WILLS. *SEE* WELLS
WILSON
　____ (____), 95, 96
　Philis (____), 89
　Sampson, 89, 90
　William, 96
WITTER
　Eben, 82
　Mehetable (Jewett), 82
WONKS
　Polly *wed* TAYLOR, 153
WOOD
　Laura (Webster), 82
　Lucuis, 82
　Persis (Buck), 77
　Spencer, 77
　Spencer's infant, 89
WOODBRIDGE
　Christopher A., 82
　Mary A. (Sumner), 82
　Nathaniel, 30
　Nathaniel L., 31

WOODWARD
　Elijah, 7
　Elijah A., 112
　F. B., 117
　G. Bird, 112
　Henry, 161
　James, 117, 119
　Mary (____), 112
　Mary (Babcock) (Swetland), 161
WOODWORTH
　Mary *wed* MIDDLETON, 122
WRIGHT, RIGHT
　____ (____), 24, 25
　Aaron, 160
　Benoni, 152
　Comfort (Post), 75
　David, 76
　Dorathy (Short), 152
　Dudley, 80
　Ebenezer, 75
　Elihu, 40, 44
　Elisabeth *wed* CURTICE, 151
　Elisha, 163, 164
　Eliza (Ambros), 80
　Elizabeth (____), 160
　Elizabeth *wed* BROWN, 119
　Enos, 158
　Ezekiel, 49, 88
　Hannah, 30
　Hannah *wed* PERRIN, 79
　Isaiah, 161
　Jane A. *wed* BROWN, 118
　Jeremiah, 47
　Jerusha (Dunham), 75
　Jude, 12, 13, 47, 49, 90
　Judith *wed* CURTICE, 74
　Laura, 127
　Laura (____), 40
　Leveret, 37
　Mrs Silbel *wed* WILLCOX, 151
　Mrs.Hannah, 31
　Patience (Bill), 76
　S., 30

Samuel, 24, 25, 31
Sarah (Payne), 161
Sarah (Tilletson), 158
Sebbel *wed* WILLCOX, 151
Simeon, 135
Simeon's child, 87
Simeon's infant, 87
William, 75
WRISLEY. *SEE* RISLEY
YEAMON
   Hannah *wed* ADAMS, 73
YOUNGS
   ____ (____), 89
   Anna, 56
   Burnham Fitch, 63
   Constantia, 58
   Constantia *wed* CRANE, 162
   Eli, 47
   Eliphalet, 47, 48, 50, 51, 53, 55, 56, 57, 58, 60, 61, 62, 63, 74, 88, 89, 162
   Eliphalet' infant, 88
   Elisabeth (Curtice), 73
   Ephriam, 73, 85, 162
   Hannah *wed* RILEY, 74
   Joseph, 162
   Mabel, 62
   Martha, 55
   Martha (Burnham), 74, 88
   Mary, 56
   Mrs., 9
   Philoathia, 57
   Sarah, 48
   Susannah *wed* BISSEL, 75
   Theodosia, 50, 53
   Tryphena, 51
   William Clark, 61

www.ingramcontent.com/pod-product-compliance
Lightning Source LLC
Chambersburg PA
CBHW050138170426
43197CB00011B/1875